A LIFE

A LIFE

Gabriel Josipovici

London Magazine Editions
in association with the
European Jewish Publication Society

First published in Great Britain 2001
by London Magazine Editions
30 Thurloe Place, London sw7 2HQ
in association with the
European Jewish Publication Society, EJPS,
PO Box 19948, London N3 3ZJ
Website: www.ejps.org.uk

Set in Monotype Ehrhardt by
Rowland Phototypesetting Ltd
Printed in Great Britain by
St Edmundsbury Press Ltd
both of Bury St Edmunds, Suffolk

A CIP catalogue record for this book
is available from the British Library

The European Jewish Publication Society is a
registered charity which gives grants to assist
in the publication and distribution of books
relevant to Jewish literature, history, religion,
philosophy, politics and culture.

CONTENTS

Even now, eighteen months after her death, I still occasionally find myself putting two cups and saucers on the little black metal tea-trolley she bought from Habitat with the thirty pounds she received from the first and only public reading of her poetry she ever did. She was so nervous her voice had difficulty emerging from her throat. As I watched her struggle I remembered the time she had won the Florio Prize for her first translation and was invited to the Italian Institute for the presentation. 'You'll just have to say a few words,' the elegantly dressed lady from the Society of Authors told her. 'I hope you don't mind.' They stood her up against a wall and not a word came out of her. I could see her struggling to speak, appalled by the whole occasion; she who had got us through the war in France, who had got us out of Egypt and into England, who had nursed our epileptic dog, not leaving his side for two whole years – she found herself unable to utter the few words that would no doubt have come effortlessly from the lips of the Society of Authors lady and the dozens of other well-dressed, loud-talking people attending the award ceremony. 'Sacha Rabinovitch says she is delighted to have won the Florio Prize,' the elegant lady said without turning a hair, 'and would like to thank the jury and everyone associated with the occasion.'

Then they let her go.

The poetry reading, many years later, was at least an improvement on that. True, when she spoke her voice hardly carried beyond the first row, but as the room grew hushed and those further back – I was in the last row – craned forward, I realised that these were poems meant to be read aloud. On the page it was easy to overlook them, to let the eye skim across them far too quickly and so miss the remarkable combination of lightness and depth, simplicity of metre and diction capturing great complexity of feeling and thought. I felt that then and I felt it again even more strongly the next time I heard them read aloud, by more self-confident and experienced readers this time, at the memorial service we held for her in the Quiet Room of the Meeting House at the University, where she had so often sat, participating in our annual Bible and Literature days, though there too she hardly ever opened her mouth, content to sit and listen and ponder the implications of what was being said. And that day I felt too how, despite my conscious attempts to encourage her, aware as I was of her lack of self-confidence, of how difficult it had been for her to change from writing in French to writing in English midway through her life, I had always underrated them. I felt proud then that she should have written so well, and sorrowed that I had not been able, in spite of my efforts, to get more of them published, and sorrowed even more that I had not – I knew – been able to keep from her the impression that I felt they were not terribly good. Staying with the poet Jon Stallworthy shortly after the memorial I said this to him and he tried to comfort me by saying: 'Would it not have been worse if, hearing them, you had suddenly realised they were not very good?' He was right, of course, but that does not assuage the guilt. I can only surmise that children always feel reluctant to give full credit to their parents; that one can never evaluate correctly the work of those one sees every day; and that two writers in one family inevitably makes for awkwardness ('Naturally,' said Mahler, one of the composers Sacha least

2

liked, to his young bride, 'now we are married you will stop composing.'). But it still pains me that I could not find it in myself to respond more spontaneously to the poems she wrote so regularly and went on writing to the very end – till her heart attack and fall down the stairs finally knocked the stuffing out of her, as she and her sister, brought up by an English nanny and using such old-fashioned expressions quite unselfconsciously in a world that had all but forgotten them, might well have put it.

I had followed the ambulance and brought her notebook and some of her favourite books – Dante, Wallace Stevens, Muriel Spark – for her to have by her in hospital, but – and this should have warned me that she was not recovering as I was being led to understand she was – they remained unopened, and she did not add a single word to the poem she had been working on at the time. Even the *Independent* crossword, which she would do every day no matter how tired she was, remained untouched day after day.

In the months that have passed since her death I have never doubted that I would have to write about her; I have only doubted my ability to do so. The pitfalls have been quite clear to me: when I was so full of her, in the days and weeks after her death, I knew that if I began to write about her I would be in danger of descending into a black hole from which I might never be able to escape. I knew equally well, however, that if I left it too late I would be in danger of losing her for ever. Of course there was always the possibility that that wouldn't happen, that letting her go was in fact the only way for her to return to me as she was and not as I imagined her. But I cannot take the risk. Besides, I want to write about her now, as a way of bringing her close to me, of talking to her again, every day, as I used to do.

I do not want to write a memoir. If I am to write about her it will have to be about her, not about me and my grief. The very otherness of the rituals of mourning is what gives them their meaning. I have no rituals, only my writing, so my writing will have to be my ritual, my way of spending every day in her presence, but *at work*. Of course that sense of escaping from one's immediate feelings and impressions and trying to see the world as it is and not as I imagine it, has always been my reason for writing and what I have striven for in my fiction. But in this case it is even more important that this is what I do, that I tell her life as hers, not mine. Only by doing this will it be possible for me to understand our relationship and so help me understand what I am and how I can live without her. Yet of course it cannot be totally achieved; this will always be *my* account of her life. Nevertheless, my aim will be to tell *her* life, not my memories of her or my feelings about her.

Aharon Appelfeld, her dear friend and mine, ended his little contribution to the memorial by saying: 'Sacha's story should be told one day in all its length and with all its details. It will not be a sentimental story with a happy end but a story of struggle and determination, and therefore a very Jewish story. She was a woman not of this world, so thin and delicate, so full of soul and spirit, and so she will remain with her friends for ever: *tihye nafshah tsrurah betsror hahayim*; May her soul be bound up in the bundle of life.' This story will indeed be a very Jewish story. But it will also be a story of the twentieth century. She was born, after all, ten years after it began, before the outbreak of the First World War, which most historians now see as marking the start of the century proper, and she died four years before it ended, six years after the Berlin Wall came down, an event which she, like many of those who had experienced the Second World War, felt had finally brought that war to an end. She was born at the edge of Western civilisation, in an Egypt which had for a century been looking Westward yet still remained indubitably a part of the Middle East, that multi-racial Eastern Mediterranean world which came into being with the death of Alexander the Great and whose last major representative was an Alexandrian Greek, Constantin Cavafy. She was descended on her mother's side from those who had helped Egypt in its quest to belong to the nations of Europe: her mother's grandfather had come to Egypt from Ferrara as a young doctor in 1838; her uncles had fought in the Italian army in the First World War; her mother's mother belonged to a clan which traced its line in Egypt back to the eleventh century and beyond; her father had come to Egypt, also as a doctor, from the most Mediterranean of all the Russian cities, the Black Sea port of Odessa. She herself spent a part of her youth in Mussolini's Italy, ten crucial years in France between 1935 and 1945, and eleven in Egypt from 1945 to 1956 as that country finally threw off the shackles of foreign occupation and emerged as an Arab nation; and the last third of her life was spent in an England which was making the painful transition from being the hub of an empire to becoming a part of a new Europe. Sadly, she died in the last days of the Thatcherite Tory government she so deeply loathed – 'She reminds me of Hitler,' she said, when Thatcher first came on the scene. 'Surely not,' I said in my confused liberal way. 'It's something about her eyes and voice. A total conviction that she is right and a total contempt for those who would stand in her way.' I still didn't agree with her, but, curiously, I heard the same comparison from the lips of an Austrian Jewish lady in Oxford a few months after her death, so that she must have understood something that I, without her experience, was incapable of grasping.

Though Sacha, dying, as she had lived, in the right way, was able to call me to her in hospital, tell me she was dying, and speak a few last words, she was too weak and tired for more and I now wish we had managed to talk about all the important things one keeps putting off because to speak of them is to acknowledge that death is near. She kept no diaries, wrote no memoirs. In later life people, learning of her exotic origins and adventurous life, would urge her to write about them, but she wouldn't: 'I was too unhappy. Besides, to write one's memoirs is to cease to look forward. It's a form of nostalgia and self-indulgence.'

She was right, of course. I couldn't agree more. Yet I could have done with some memoirs now. They would have helped me fill the gaps in her life and perhaps helped me to see how she viewed her own existence. But she was the least sentimental of people and writing one's memoirs was, to her mind, a way of filling the past with a meaning it never had and of feeling sorry for oneself, and she was not going to be a party to that. Instead, she wrote poems. One of the last, which I found written out neatly in her notebook at the end of thirty pages of drafts and corrections, when I brought it home from the hospital, gives a glimpse of how the past survived for her as she grew older – not as memory in the ordinary sense of the term, but as a kind of Proustian invasion of the entire self by something unexpectedly seen or heard, an invasion which reactivated that which had long since been forgotten. In this case the immediate cause was a walk we took in the gardens of the Bishop's Palace in Fulham a year or so before she died: a flower and a word:

Wisteria

suddenly runs riot
over London Town,
drips from porches, festoons facades,
rests grey elbows
on balconies
whence clusters cascade,
and in the Bishop's Garden
off the Fulham Road

straddles – giant
lavender caterpillar –
some fifty yards
of gently curving trellis.
Sour-sweet, the scent pervades.

Long long ago
in my native land
I lived in a bungalow
adorned with wisteria.
Briefly in summer
I would wake
to the blessed coolness
of a perfumed dawn,
open my eyes
on those fantastic hangings.
It was my grandmother's favourite flower.
She called it
glycine.

Her poems then, and the dozens of photos she carried in an old envelope through the war and our constant moves from flat to flat in Egypt and our first years in England, till the day when a publisher invited me to write a brief autobiographical piece and include a dozen photos, and we used the occasion to transfer them from the old envelope where they were getting bent and torn into the brand-new albums I went out and bought at Boots.

I am thankful now we did that, for it gave me a chance to learn the circumstances in which they were taken and who were the unknown people who appeared in many of them. Unfortunately we didn't write this down on the backs of the photos and now I find many of them baffling, cannot, try as I will, recall what she said about them. But the photos of her as a child with her sister and mother – there are none of her alone – are not only beautiful, as are so many photos of the period, but evocative: they call out for commentary. They too, though, are frustratingly selective: there are none of her in her early teens when she was so ill and unhappy with her grandparents; very few of her as a young woman; very few of her in Egypt after the war. But they, like the poems, will have to do. Appelfeld's injunction to write her life in full and in every detail cannot be carried out. I know very little about her father's family of Odessa tea-merchants, for example, and there is no-one left from that side of the family to help. And what did she think about her self-effacing grandmother, with whom she lived from the death of her mother when she was ten to the day she got married, at twenty-four? What did she think of my father when she married him? And when things began to go wrong between them in France? Not that she refused to speak about these things, but that they never seemed important to me and so I never pressed her about them. But now I would like to know.

Because we lived together for most of my life she wrote me very few letters; most of those she did write, when I was away at Oxford or on holiday, were brief and perfunctory: she distrusted letters almost as much as she did the phone, feeling I think that one could only really speak to a person when one was face to face with them. I wish I had kept the letter she wrote to me when I was away teaching at a summer school in Dijon in 1969 and our dog Bimbo died in her arms. She knew how much he meant to me and she made an effort to describe in detail exactly what had happened. Or even the few other letters which said no more than that she was well and hoped I was having a good time. I might have been able to glean something from them now. But they are gone, lost. I know she wrote to her sister when my cousin Monica died in her sixty-fourth year, less than three months before Sacha herself, because I read my aunt's response: 'What strange lives you say we have both had, Sacha dear, and I just want you to know that despite all our quarrels you are, after Anna and Monica, the person I have loved most in the world.' But it took a death to make her put into the words of a letter what she felt. In the normal course of things I think she sensed that there was something too easy about writing letters, too irresponsible. It was out of respect for the truth, for life itself and its complexity, that she was so reticent, not out of any dryness of spirit. That reticence, like her hatred of humbug and self-pity, was the essence of her, though what people found baffling at first was that it went with a warmth, a generosity, a laugh, that were certainly not English, but were not quite Italian or Russian or Levantine either, but were uniquely hers. Since her death, though she has often entered my dreams, I have been unable to hear her laugh. Perhaps if I am faithful to the ins and outs of her life it will return.

I   EGYPT

I imagine him standing at a tall window, staring out at the grey skies of the Ile de France, or sitting with his brother on a bench in the garden at Neuilly. What is going through his mind? Thoughts of his wife and two little girls in far-away Egypt? Of his own childhood in an Odessa so distant as to belong to another time, another world? Of student days in Berlin? Of the horrors of the war in Asia? Or is his mind as blank as his face, across which flit the shadows of the clouds?

I cannot imagine madness. I know that reality is always different from all our imaginings and that what we take for empathy is often only sentimentality and self-deception. Yet something drives me to try to imagine, to understand.

I study the family photographs and see:

– an elegantly dressed couple, exuding an air of happiness, material ease and innocence (they are so young, though the eyes, hers in particular, also convey that Jewish wariness we have all inherited, no matter how light our spirits). He sits on the arm of a sofa, his top hat in his left hand, which rests on his left knee, while his right arm is around her waist, drawing her towards him; she stands, drawn towards him yet retaining her distance, in her right hand a bunch of flowers, pointing downwards, her long white dress forming a pool of light as it seems to flow about her feet: my grandparents on their wedding day:

– a man at the wheel of a car whose shining metallic bonnet belies the carriage behind, which seems to belong more to the age of the horse than to that of the machine: my grandfather in one of the first cars to be seen in Helwan;

– a man with a small black beard and one gleaming eye staring out at the world (the other shadowed by his wide-brimmed, black-ribboned hat), sitting with a black dog on a sort of camp-stool between his knees, facing him but twisting its head round towards the camera: my grandfather in his mad Parisian years.

As always, it is difficult to separate the people in the photographs from the aura of the period, from all the other photographs of the time I have seen, in books, in exhibitions, in the family albums of others. The costumes, the props, the lighting, the poses, all serve to ensure the triumph of the horizontal over the vertical, of period over genealogy and family history.

His father, a Jewish tea-merchant in Odessa, that most vibrant and cosmopolitan of Russia's cities ('the Russian Florence' was how it was sometimes known, but in fact it had more in common with the bustling port cities of the Mediterranean, Alexandria, Naples or Marseilles, a city which encouraged enterprise and where you were a merchant first and a Jew, a Moslem or a Greek or Russian Orthodox second) – his father had had in later life to be confined to his house, according to one tradition as the result of insanity brought on by drinking too much tea (but is that likely?); according to another because of a nervous ailment (a term much used at the time and which could mean many things, from outright lunacy to mild compulsive disorders). A man of immense size and strength, he was said once to have been walking through the back streets of the town when, looking up, he saw a baby hurtling through the air towards him. Instinctively holding out his arms, he caught the child and waited there with it in his arms till the distraught mother rushed out of the house and clasped his knees in thanks, sobbing with relief.

There were three sons, handsome, intelligent, and almost as big as their father, much more Russian than Jewish in appearance. Two of them decided to become doctors and went abroad to pursue their medical studies, one to Paris, the other, my grandfather, to Berlin. In later life they would frequently argue over the relative merits of the two cities as centres of medical excellence.

Returning from Berlin at the end of his studies, he enlisted as a medical orderly in the Russo-Japanese war. Wounded, he was invalided home.

Was it in the Far East that he caught the syphilis which would almost certainly destroy his life? Or as a student in Berlin? (Again, one family tradition has it that it was not syphilis at all but that famous 'nervous ailment' inherited from his father. But only suspected syphilis could account for the conditions soon to be imposed on him by his future father-in-law.)

Making a rapid recovery he was soon off once again, having decided to see the world before settling down. In the course of his travels he visited Egypt and was enchanted by the little town of Helwan, some ten miles south of Cairo, whose sulphur springs, he always maintained, made it one of the healthiest spots in the world. Today Helwan is a mass of crumbling high-rise blocks under a perpetual cloud of pollution emitted by the cement factories which have grown up all round it; it is here that a substantial part of Cairo's enormous work-force is housed, here that the bread-riots of the eighties often started. But at the time, in 1906, it was a resort, a place of *villégiature* for wealthy Cairenes, and here the young doctor from Odessa decided to settle and open a practice. Shortly after his arrival he attended a ball and danced for most of the night with the beautiful daughter of an Italian Jewish lawyer who lived in the town. The next morning she woke up with a bad attack of 'flu'. The new Russian doctor was called, and soon the young couple were engaged. However, the prospective father-in-law insisted on a year's moratorium, presumably to make sure there was no sign of the young doctor's illness recurring.

The year passed without mishap. The Wasserman syphilis test, to which he readily submitted, proved negative. The young couple, obsessed with all things English, ordered their wedding furniture from Maples in London, and when, the following year, their first child was born, they hired an English governess to look after her. He converted to Islam, changed his name from Alexis to Ali, his practice blossomed, and he was much loved by the local population as he gave his services free to those who could not afford to pay.

(1989. My aunt, that first child, now eighty, meets an old Egyptian lady who, on hearing who she is, tells her: 'My mother was one of your father's patients in Helwan before the First War. Ali and his wife were said to be so beautiful, my mother told me, that when they made love the angels in heaven wept with joy.')

The baby, named Vera but known throughout her life as Chickie, was taken in triumph to visit his family in Odessa. The English governess and the mother's maid of course went too. Might she teach her charge to say her prayers at night when she grew a bit older? asked the Governess. 'There is only one God,' Alexis/Ali replied, 'we are all free to worship Him in our own way.'

In 1910 a second child, Alexandra or Sacha was born. But this time there was no trip to the city on the Black Sea. The young doctor, who had always been a bit eccentric, liable to do the unexpected, was beginning to arouse genuine concern. Once, after an argument with a fellow doctor, he pulled out a pistol and held it to his head. On the boat, returning from a trip to France, he assaulted a stevedore. Other incidents followed. Alarmed, the young wife wrote to her brother-in-law, asking him to come and take his brother back to his clinic in Paris and there try to treat him. Her father, always a man of strong principles, disapproved, feeling that a wife must take responsibility for everything her husband does and that the fact that the wife in question was his beloved eldest daughter made no difference. The brother-in-law too was highly critical of her attitude, and would in fact never speak to her again. She, however, was adamant: her children must be protected at all costs. So he came and took Ali back to Paris with him.

In the summer of 1914, as war was breaking out over Europe, his wife and two little girls came to Paris to visit him. Certified now, and confined to his brother's care, he was nevertheless able to have lunch with them and even accompanied them back to their hotel. It was the last time they would ever see him.

Late in her life, living now in England and writing in English,
Sacha wrote a poem about him:

My Father

He came from a far country,
Handsome and dark and tall,
His pockets full of roubles,
the best man of them all.

He came from a cold country
To the desert and the sun,
Settled and had two daughters,
I was the younger one.

He was gone before I knew him,
He was gone out of his mind,
Then off to die in Paris.
In the home he left behind

One room was never opened:
'That is your father's room.'
His coats hung in the cupboard
In naphthalene and gloom.

One question was not answered.
When asked how father died:
'He had some kind of fever . . .'
Mother and nurses lied.

But: 'Your father was a madman,
Your father who is dead,
Your father was a lunatic,'
Our little playmates said.

There are more photographs of her in the album than of almost anyone else:

    – as a pretty baby;

    – as a liberated young woman of the turn of the century, in a checked blouse, skirt and tie, sitting on the edge of a wicker chair with a tree in bloom behind her and a very small bunch of flowers in her left hand;

    – on a verandah, in a long skirt and frilly blouse, with a small

hat on her luxuriant hair and a closed parasol across her lap;

– standing sideways on to the camera, turning her oval Rossi face straight towards it, her hair elegantly piled on top of her head, in a splendid white lace dress;

– as a young mother holding her first child up before the camera;

– as a young widow in black, standing between her two daughters, looking down at them as they face the camera, the elder rather ingratiatingly, the younger suspiciously;

– in the garden by a high wall over which climbs a thick flowering creeper, holding her eldest daughter by the hand, swathed in a long dress which brings out the graceful shape of her body and gives her the appearance of gliding rather than walking;

– standing with the children in the garden, dressed in white, a white parasol in her hand, the left clasped over the joined hands of her two children, who look out at us with their two quite distinct expressions;

– in a decolletée black dress with a long necklace, bare arms and shoulders, looking away from the camera;

– and many, many more.

She was a beautiful woman and she clearly knew it. Only in the wedding photograph does that hint of anxiety briefly surface. No wonder it is through a photograph that Sacha chose to recall her:

A Body in the Sun

Because she was a body in the sun
and someone liked the figure that she cut,
youthful, white-clad with parasol,
she stands outlined in sepia on the print,
grandmother to my then unthought-of son.
A daughter on each side clasping her one
free hand scowls at the stranger and the sun
whose ardours thus combined to trap,
purloining from the past, this scrap
of time white-clad with parasol.

Hers is perhaps the life which evokes the most pathos in a family which had more than its share of sorrows over five generations, for life, one feels, overwhelmed her without giving her any time to react, and death took her away before she had a chance to show if suffering would make or break her. Her grandfather, Elie Rossi, was fond of quoting Vauvenargues, the eighteenth century French moralist: 'Si le bonheur m'avait élevé dans ses bras, il m'aurait étouffé, et je n'aurais pas eu la force d'étouffer le malheur' – Had happiness raised me in his arms he would have stifled me and I would not have had the strength to stifle misfortune. His granddaughter, one feels, had neither the strength nor the time to stifle misfortune.

The favourite and beautiful eldest child of Dr. Rossi's son Théophile, brought up if not in luxury then at least in great comfort, married at twenty-two to a striking and handsome Russian doctor, within a few short years she would be struck a double blow and die at thirty-five.

First there was the tragedy of Alexis. The trip to Paris in the summer of 1914 must have made it clear that he would never recover; by 1915 he was dead. But she was young, handsome and not lacking in suitors. As was the way in those days she left the task of bringing up her children to the governess and maids. She

would take them out to tea, pose for photographs with them, come up to kiss them in bed, and then be off for the evening with one or other of her admirers. By her lights she was a good mother, and indeed they loved her dearly; but, whether consciously or unconsciously, she must have felt that she still had much to look forward to.

Egypt was filling up with Australian and New Zealand soldiers, waiting to be shipped off to the war in Europe, and with them came journalists, war correspondents, administrators, and back-up staff. Amongst them was a young Australian called Philip Schuler, a war correspondent for *The Anzac*, 'who typed his cables in a room next to ours at the Hotel,' my aunt wrote to me when I asked her, after Sacha's death, for information about those years, 'and was killed at Ypres. He loved our mother and she loved him.'

Nelly had moved with her two children from Helwan to a Cairo hotel out of fear that in any attack Helwan would be the first to be overrun. ' "What strange lives we've both had", wrote Sacha in the last real letter she sent me,' Chickie goes on, in the darting, impressionistic style in which her letters about their childhood, which poured out of her in the months after Sacha's death, are couched, 'and I suppose we did, in a sense. It seems as though all through our lives, from very early on, we "heard the rustle of Azrael's wing" as the Arabs say. When Philip Schuler died it wasn't death, *our* death, we felt, but Death's hollow mould, the stamp it leaves on those it has bereaved. We were sleeping, as we often did when she was not out "gadding" with her smart friends (princes and prime ministers and suchlike) with our mother. And very late at night there was a ring at the door and Netta went to answer it and came back very excited to say that there were two officers wanting to see our mother "and one looked rather like Philip", she told us when our mother had gone out to see them. After a time we heard them leaving and our mother came back to us. "They came," she said, "to say that Philip is mortally wounded – and now you must go to sleep." She was crying – I knew that mortal wounds were wounds you died of – but then he was not *dead*. But he was. She told us the next morning and showed us the silver cigarette case she had given him, all dented and twisted by the shrapnel, and the photograph of his grave at Ypres where so many had died in the great battle there. And she asked Sacha if she could see where he was now, for Sacha, since she was very small, had a gift of second sight – it seemed to counteract the practical, sardonic, commonsense side of her – she was the one who always *saw* the ghosts and fairies, I just followed, fascinated, and embroidered on her data. But this time it failed her, she made up some quite irrelevant answer and mummy gave up trying.'

But she did not entirely give up. She erected a tablet to his memory in the cemetery at Helwan and sought comfort with an Anglican missionary, Sister Margaret Clare, whom Sacha remembered always dressed in a habit and with a huge silver crucifix dangling between her knees. One day their mother called the two little girls into the living room of the Helwan house to which they had returned. Sister Margaret Clare was there with her. 'Sister Margaret is going to tell you a story,' she said. When Sister Margaret finished her story she paused and then asked the two little girls: 'So, which would you rather be, the good people who followed Jesus or the bad people who killed him?' 'What possible answer could one give to such a question,' Sacha said to me when she told me the story, 'when one is only seven or eight? I felt that there was something wrong somewhere, but it was a long time before I could put my finger on it.'

So the children were baptised, much to the horror of their grandparents, and each given a small leather-bound Bible. I still have Sacha's copy, inscribed 'Alexandra Rabinovitch, from her Godmother, Sister Margaret Clare.' She carried it with her throughout the war and it was only when her eyes started to fail that she asked me to buy her a larger one so that she could go on reading the stories of Abraham and Jacob and Moses and David and Jesus, with whose every twist and turn she was deeply familiar – she would try to send herself to sleep in later life when her insomnia was bad by reciting the names of all twelve sons of Jacob.

'The second event which must have marked us even more deeply than the death of Philip Schuler,' Chickie wrote in another letter, 'was my mother's remarriage to Max Debbane. First we were angry with her for disobeying our wishes – we both – and Nanny too – strongly disapproved of Max. We called him "Mr. Scented" and made up a nasty little song with a refrain which

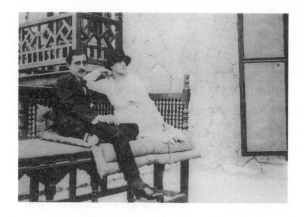

went "He's a silly scented Syrian". Besides this, the change this marriage entailed was radical – it not only meant leaving the Helwan house which we loved, it meant not sleeping with Mummy except on the rare occasions when Max was away at his farm in Mansourah – and everything was different. In Helwan we had been not so much a real "family" (first of all there was no man "at our head"), as a strangely disparate yet very close conglomerate. The "head" of the family was of course my mother, who came from "la bonne bourgeoisie juive', but, unlike many Jewish families in Egypt, one that had very well adapted itself to its Egyptian entourage – there were ministers in the family and several wives were Dames d'Honneur at the court. The Cattaouis had been in Egypt for ages, spoke and lived like well-off Egyptians and were thoroughly integrated into Egyptian society. On my grandfather's side his father had been physician to the Khedive and was "Rossi Pasha". My mother, like most Egyptian ladies, had a strangely ambivalent attitude towards her "staff". Nanny was not considered a servant and had a special intermediate position, eating at table with us, unless Mummy had guests and dined in the "Downstairs" (there were no stairs) dining-room. Then Nanny and Netta dined with us in the playroom.

'Europeans often say that Egyptians treat their servants badly,' she goes on. 'This is not exactly true – the lady of the house may at one moment be bawling her head off at an errant maid or suffragui, calling them names and even resorting to blows – and half an hour later she will be gaily chatting with her victim, gossiping in the friendliest way while the servant does not seem to resent past treatment at all. On the other hand she extends a sort of feudal protection over all those in her service, guards the virtue of the girls, provides dowries when they marry, is responsible (to a certain degree) for the debts incurred by the menfolk whom she "bails out" of prison when they get jailed for striking someone in a brawl. My mother was this sort of lady of the house, and while Netta, who had only served in one family before us and had not had time to get accustomed to the "mores" suffered badly at first, Ahmed the cook, who had been in the family for thirty years, never turned a hair, however bad the storm.

'Of all of us five,' Chickie goes on in this extraordinary letter which is in effect a little essay on a vanished world, 'Netta was I think the most vivid and vital personality. She came to us at eighteen from her Yugoslav village of Biglia, where she lived with her step-father and step-sister at a little farm called Obers. Her mother had died, she had one brother, and it was to pay his expenses at University that she had gone into service as a ladies' maid. She left us at twenty-eight to get married, but came back with her first baby, Ricardo, as dame de compagnie, when, because of Sacha's bad chest, we spent a year and a half in Bressanone. So we five and Ahmed the cook and Popsy the dog and Otta the cat lived very happily there in the Gabalaya house (the name means grotto and there was a wonderful grotto in the garden) in Helwan, though Mummy had periods of terrible money worries. Yet we had all the presents and toys we could absorb, numberless dolls and dolls' furniture, pen-knives and carpentry sets and fretwork sets, Beatrix Potter books and stuffed animals. There was

nothing we wanted we didn't have (except ponies – these the Prime Minister promised to give us but Mummy cynically warned us that men seldom keep such promises and sure enough he didn't keep his). So, when we moved into the beautiful, mysterious house in Moharrem Bey in Alexandria where Mummy was to spend the last few years of her life and give birth to our baby sister Charlotte, we weren't prepared to like it much, but we couldn't help falling under its spell.'

One day in the 1970's Sacha turned, after glancing at the rest of the paper, to the colour supplement of one of the Sunday papers and drew in her breath sharply: 'Good Heavens! It's the Ambron house!'

Inside was an article on Lawrence Durrell and the cover showed the house he had lived in for a time in Alexandria. Twenty five years earlier that was the house to which the tight-knit little family had moved when Nelly Rabinovitch married Max Debbane. Sacha wrote a poem about it, though whether it was before or after she saw it reproduced on the cover of that colour supplement I can't recall:

A New Home

On the night we moved in
all the lights failed.
Under her breath,
in her own tongue,
our Italian maid
was prophesying death
as she brought candles
and more candles
for the countless rooms
through which we were led
– the unfamiliar spaces
expanded and contracted
with the flickering flame.

'This is your new home,'
our mother said with tenderness and pride,
her arms about our shoulders
and her new husband at her side.

Here she lived two years
and here, in her prime, she died.

In 1920, at the age of thirty-five, Nelly Debbane, née Rossi, died of typhoid, in the epidemic which swept the country and nearly carried off her second daughter as well. There are no letters from her, and those who had known her are nearly all dead. So she lives on in the letters of her eldest daughter, in the poems of her second daughter, and in the many photographs that have come down to me, in some ways a typical product of the haute bourgeoisie, European and Middle Eastern, of the end of the nineteenth century into which she was born, in other ways the victim of the blows – war, disease – which that period dealt out impartially to rich and poor alike. With her death Sacha's childhood effectively ended.

How can one understand an Edwardian childhood without having experienced it oneself? In a sense it is easy, since it is the world of the best-loved children's books – *Alice in Wonderland* and *Through the Looking-Glass*, *The Wind in the Willows* and *The Secret Garden*, both the world in which these books were written and that which, through various prisms, they describe and bring to life. This world, as Penelope Lively's marvellous memoir, *Oleander, Jacaranda*, makes clear, lingered on in Egypt until the thirties, long after it had disappeared in England itself. And for Egypt there exist at least two books that recapture in almost miraculous fashion that world of strict separation between the realm of the parents and that of the children, that world of nannies and maidservants, gardeners and gardeners' boys, cooks, suffraguis and undersuffraguis: Penelope Lively's own book and Priscilla Napier's classic, *A Late Beginner*, whose time-span exactly co-incides with the childhoods of Chickie and Sacha.

Of course there are differences between even the most Euro-peanised native families and the English: for one thing, there was no 'back home', no mother country, however alien, for those whose families were, if not Egyptian, at least a part of the fabric of Egypt. And for the Jewish families, no matter how assimilated or how Anglicised, there was the further sense that though this was the only country they could call their own they did not exactly belong to it.

Nevertheless, when she read the memoirs of Napier and Lively late in her life, Sacha felt at once that they described, to a large extent, just the sort of childhood she herself had known in the years before her mother's death.

'Dearest Gabriel,' Chickie wrote to me when, after Sacha's own death, I felt the need to know everything I could about her, 'you asked me for memories of Sacha as a child, but they are so many and so disparate that I don't even know how and where to begin, so I'll start with her physical appearance. You will be surprised – in view of her later thinness – to learn that she was a very

plump little girl. Indeed, her other, nursery nickname was "Fatty", though until she was twelve or thirteen she was usually known as Totty. We were Chickie and Totty, which our little English friends translated into "Bicky and Chocky". There are two stories about Sacha's "puppy fatness". In one she is tenderly stroking her round abdomen and murmuring: "Fat tummy dear". In the other she is absentmindedly punching bracelets of fat on her arm and wondering what's inside: "P'raps it's cotton wool". In photos she is mostly looking with uncompromising, smileless resolution *away* from the "little bird" supposed to pop out of the camera. I was always the one with the ingratiating grin.

'In Helwan we would be taken to Hotel Gardens to meet the other Nannies – especially Nurse Robson, the Nanny of all Nannies and our Nanny's shining exemplar of what a Nanny should be, so that we hero-worshipped her too, though she was red-faced and rather vulgar. But she knew all about children, and our Nanny (Miss Ward to the others, and probably ranking next to Miss Robson in importance) was visibly flattered when Miss Robson once said enviously: "What bonny legs your girls have." Miss Robson – and Teddy Bears and, later on, all English people – was like Edgar Allen Poe's ghouls, "neither man nor woman" but some sort of angelic sexlessness.

'Later on, when our Mother married Max and we lived in the Ambron House in Alexandria, we were to meet all these other nannies and their broods of children, who turned out to be mostly relatives, Cattaouis, Menasches, Tubys, etc., with a smattering of little Greeks and much fewer English children, who were the ones we snobbishly preferred. We went to the park at first and then later, with a select few who were related to us, to "Aunty Gabriel's Garden". I remember less about Sacha because she was in a way more gregarious than I was and played with the many little boys I disliked, whereas I singled out a rather pretty but dimwitted little girl as a special protegée and played with her, though Nanny said disparagingly that she talked "through her nose like a Jew" – which of course she was.

'Nanny, who came to us when she must have been seventy already, was a wonderful person. She was what was then called "a decayed gentlewoman". She had come from a good and quite comfortably off family. Her father kept a carriage and pair and she knew everything about horses and would explain to us about strawberry roans, bays and chestnuts, pie-balds, skewbalds and dappled greys (though she never told me about Palomenos and I shall always remember the thrill of seeing a marvellous golden horse one morning early on the dunes at Berque-Plage). She had held other sorts of jobs before becoming a children's nanny. One she often talked about was in Tenerife at a hotel run by a Spaniard she called Don Azoo – it took me a long time to realise he must have been Don Jesu with the Spanish pronunciation of the J. What the job was exactly I never knew, but it couldn't have been menial – I know she sat beside Don Jesu at Table d'Hôte because of a story she told us about how once while eating some rather rich food he turned to her and said: 'I find this rather heavy on the stomach, don't you, Miss Ward?' and she answered: 'English people have no stomachs.' 'Oh?' he said, 'and what then *do* they have?' 'They have *chests*,' she said proudly. We, being children, were allowed a little more latitude. We had Tummies and BTMs and Behinds, and once in a while we were allowed to hear the word "stomach", as in the story of the little boy who went to a party and had chocolate cake and seed cake and plum cake and then went home and had stoma cake.'

Sacha remembered Miss Ward always quoting from the Bible and Shakespeare and Dr. Johnson: 'We never knew which was which, and we thought Dr. Johnson was an old friend of the family. When we spat out a bit of potato because it was too hot to swallow she would say: "Quite right, a fool would have swallowed it, as Dr. Johnson said."'

'We probably loved her more than Mummy,' Sacha said to me. 'Certainly her death, the year after Mummy's, was the final shattering blow.'

They were eleven and twelve and couldn't even brush their own hair: 'Nanny had always done it for us.'

'I was naturally jealous of Sacha,' Chickie went on, 'so our relationship was a bit ambiguous. I was jealous first because she was the "totty one" (hence her nickname) and so got all the attention a new baby gets – and later because with her particular brand of

rather caustic poker-faced humour she was a great pet with visitors, had them laughing and fussing over her, and as they were
mostly young officers whom we both hero-worshipped (I was more
given to that than she was though) and the people interested in
me were the thoughtful, dreamy kind of elderly ladies who were
less fun than the officers, though we liked them well enough, it
was hard to bear. I was wildly envious, so our relationship had
its ups and downs, at one moment I had the upper hand, the next
she was in the ascendant – I remember being aware of that at a
very early age. When we hated each other we would fight and
pummell each other furiously, but our worst form of revenge was
to get hold of the other and forcibly administer "wet kisses",
which were what our least-loved aunts gave us when they came
to visit. And as an inner form of revenge known only to myself
I despised Sacha – she tended to "grizzle", as Nanny called it,
which I considered sissy-ish; also I thought her way of dressing
her dolls and toy animals was "slovenly" (and anyway I didn't
like dolls, only toy animals, of which I had seven who slept in
my bed, two of them I still slept with when I was fifteen, and
one, "ragged puppy", I continued to cherish in a drawer until

well after I was married and he fell to pieces). But in spite of my jealousy it was a love-hate relationship and hatred as much as love somehow made it very close. We were always "us", somehow – at least that is how it seems to me looking back. And our mother's death drew us together even more I think, because later when we were living at our grandparents' house I did consciously realise how dear Sacha was to me, especially after she became very ill there.'

Sacha on Chickie: 'Even then she was totally obsessive about all living creatures. When we went to bed under our mosquito nets she would hold her arm outside the net for what seemed to me like hours, insisting that "mosquitos must have their dinner too".'

And there were Englishmen other than officers who befriended the little fatherless girls. Sacha remembered an English astronomer, Langton Gregory, who would take them on the back of his motorbike up to the Observatory in the Mokattam Hills, above Helwan. Once inside the room with all the seismographs and other instruments he would put his finger to his lips: 'Shshshsh. You must walk very very softly in here or you'll set all the instruments going.' When his term in Egypt came to an end he returned to England but went on writing to them, telling them of his marriage and sending them a photo of his new-born son.

In 1975 Richard Gregory, whose books on impossible objects and other aspects of perception had long fascinated Sacha, came to lecture at the University of Sussex, and we went along to hear him. 'I'm sure he's my Mr. Gregory's son,' Sacha whispered to me as soon as he came on to the platform. 'He looks just like him.' 'Go and ask him after the lecture,' I said. But she was too shy.

In 1992, at a New Year's party in Lewes, Sacha was guided to a seat on a sofa next to a very old man who was introduced to her as Professor McRea, the distinguished astronomer. He appeared to be fast asleep, but eventually stirred and, turning to her, asked her what she did. She told him she was a translator. He relapsed into silence and Sacha, not knowing what to say, told him the story of Mr. Gregory and the instrument room in the Helwan Observatory. 'What I've always wanted to know,' she said, 'is, was he having us on or does one really have to walk on tiptoe?' 'Of course, of course, the old man said,' suddenly animated. 'He was telling you the strict truth. Those instruments are very delicate. But . . . you knew Langton Gregory? All those years ago? How extraordinary. He was a dear friend of mine and a long-time colleague.' He stared at her. 'Well I never! So you knew Langton Gregory in Egypt seventy-five years ago? Well I never!'

It was one of the many loops in time and space that seemed to characterise Sacha's life.

'There is another episode from those early years which I have to
tell you about,' wrote Chickie in another of those essay-length
letters she wrote to me after Sacha's death, as I pressed her to
tell me all she could remember about their childhood. 'It probably
made more of an impression on me than on Sacha, because she
was very young at the time, not more than three and a half. That
was the time we spent at the Cottage des Dunes in Berque-Plage
in Normandy.' (But it had made an impression on Sacha, she
often talked to me about Berque-Plage and the donkey-rides on
the beach – the nearest she had got to the England her Nanny
had talked to her about and she had read about in books till we
stepped ashore at Folkestone in September 1956.) 'We were there
because I had a "glandular swelling" on my neck that had to be
punctured by Dr. Calvet who ran the sanatorium there for TB
patients. I suppose I was suspected of having TB myself. I was
also seen by a "nerve doctor" who said I must not learn to read
till I was seven years old, and also added – so I was told – "gare
au mysticisme" (this was because our father was already mad
and hospitalised in his brother, Oncle Serge's, clinic in Neuilly-
sur-Seine). Cottage des Dunes, with its cosy cottage beginning
and eery-sounding 'doom' ending, was a weird sad place. First
there was the 'sighing wind' that went round the house at night
rattling shutters and soughing through key-holes – and the dunes

themselves, silvery, soiled sands with grey rushes shivering on them and a grey crawling sea on the other side of which Nanny said that on clear days you could see the Dover cliffs. One night we were wakened by an explosion in the house and voices and people running about and a feeling of something terrible having happened – and it was in fact rather terrible, for a young man (who perhaps had been told he was incurable) had committed suicide. Who can have told us? But we *were* told.

'But there was also the beach, which was beautiful, with incredibly lovely shells and a lady called Mrs Harding with a lovely voice who sang "Annie Laurie" (which still, when I hear it sung, gives me that yearning feeling in the pit of my stomach of which Wilhelm Reich speaks somewhere in *The Orgone*) and who had a son I liked – red-haired and freckled. Karl made a sort of sand-castle wall and said it was an "Orora-Bora-Ailiss", and that solemn, ominous, beautiful name seems like the name of that chapter of our lives, though what he really meant was an Aurora Borealis, which it didn't look like at all. At that time I was haunted by a recurrent dream of a marsh that kept metamorphosing into all sorts of different things – it was called The Sissy Sack – also a "numinous" name.

'And then by August 1914 the war broke out. Mummy was in

Paris when it happened and told us that a strange sudden darkness fell over Paris so that the shops put their lights on in full daylight. We began to prepare to leave but there were no ships going to Egypt. Belgian refugees began to fill the little hospital. One night I woke and thought there was a storm. The light was on in our room. Nanny was packing. There was a far away booming sound like thunder. Next morning when she gave us our breakfast Nanny said: "What you heard last night wasn't thunder, it was the guns at Calais."

'I had just turned five so Sacha must have been three and a half – perhaps this does not concern her at all – it must have left its mark on her though even if she didn't quite understand. We took the night train to Paris because the Germans were getting so near – I saw the dawn break and the sun looked like a wheel of fire rolling over the gorse bushes on the hills beside the railroad. Then we were in Paris with searchlights scouring the sky for enemy planes. We were taken to see our father and there was a kind matron called Mlle Bazin. My father rushed downstairs to meet us and lifted Mummy right up in his arms. Then I sat on his knee and he gave me a plaster-of-Paris lamb with all the Allied flags stuck in it – the Union Jack, the French Bleu-Blanc-Rouge, and the Russian flag too – and I think the Belgian. I had to tell him a white lie – that I hadn't been operated on for my gland – because for some reason he was against the operation. They said it would make him ill and miserable to know the truth, so though it was a lie it was "white".

'And then we were on board ship sailing to Egypt at last. At Naples I think it was we saw a German ship on fire burning with high flames and I was anxious about the sailors but was told they were all saved (not likely). Netta was with us on board and they tried to prevent her landing with us because she was an Austrian subject, a Yugoslav, and therefore an enemy alien, but Mummy guaranteed her and she was let through. So we all went, Mummy,

Nanny, Netta and us, to the Continental Hotel, where we spent the early months of the war and where we met the man Mummy was to fall so deeply in love with, Philip Schuler.'

On her deathbed Nelly had made Max promise that he would look after her children no matter what happened. He was deeply in love with her (and remained so: on remarrying, a few years later, he startled his new bride by insisting, on their wedding night, on plastering the walls of his room with photos of Nelly, a moving tribute to the enduring power of love but hardly the most tactful thing to do), and was determined, in his grief, to carry out her wishes to the letter. But the grandparents were naturally horrified: here were their two granddaughters, aged ten and eleven, in the hands of a man who was completely unrelated to them, whom they had never liked, and who was, moreover, a Syrian Christian and not a Jew. The grandfather, Théophile Rossi, demanded to have custody of the children; Max, mindful of his promise, refused.

There were other interested parties. Sister Margaret Clare, the Anglican missionary, was no more enamoured of Syrian Christians than were the Jewish grandparents. She pressed for a legal guardian to be appointed, a Mr. Vinogradoff, the Russian Vice-Consul – though, in effect, after the Revolution he no longer had any diplomatic status but went on looking after the interests of White Russians in Egypt, of whom of course Alexis Rabinovitch had been one. Sister Margaret persuaded him and Max to let the little girls spend a few weeks at the Vinogradoffs' house in Maadi, then a newly-developing town just south of Cairo. What was expected to happen to them once they'd been extricated from Max's clutches was unclear: there were rumours of an attempt to smuggle them out to Russia, to England. Most probably Sister Margaret wanted to get them away from Max while she tried to decide what to do next. Miss Ward had just died and Netta had left to go back to her village to get married. So Chickie and Sacha were packed off to Mr. Vinogradoff's dingy house in Maadi, where he lived, according to Chickie, with his beautiful, sad looking wife and their odious little boy, Niki.

The grandparents had invited them to spend a few days with them in their spacious flat in Cairo, but the Vice-Consul, his suspicions aroused, refused. One day, however, when he was away and the grandparents were supposed to come and visit, there was a phone call to say that Théophile had broken his leg and couldn't move, so would the girls go there to lunch instead. Mrs Vinogradoff, suspecting nothing, agreed. Once he had the children safely under his roof Théophile, who had nothing wrong with him at all, ordered the doors to be locked, and so began the state of siege that was to last for three months and would end with the grandparents acquiring custody of the children.

Chickie rather enjoyed it. She got on well with her grandfather and was delighted with the presents brought by the steady stream of relatives and friends of the family to the poor little orphans. She had, moreover, been horrified by Max's despair in the wake of Nelly's death: 'I was the one entrusted to wean him away from the ether to which he had resorted after Mummy's death by surreptitiously removing the bottle from under his bed. Once he caught me at it and shook his head sadly: "Chérie, tu crois vraiment que je ne peux pas m'en acheter une autre?" I had also overheard the maid, Virginia, Netta's replacement, saying to our other maid, Bertha, that every morning when she brought in the breakfast-tray she was sure she would find him lying dead on the black velvet divan.' But Sacha hated the huge dusty flat in Haret Zogheb in the heart of Cairo, still lit, in the kitchen and bathroom regions, by greenish hissing gas-jets. And while Chickie made up to the grandfather, he and Sacha entered into a battle of wills almost as soon as they arrived and which was to last until she left fourteen years later to get married. She hated the way he bullied his wife, his children and especially the servants. His loud voice terrified her. At lunch on the first day, as they sat down at the vast elaborately laid table, he turned to her and said: 'Mind you don't upset your glass of water.' Promptly, to her horror, she knocked her glass over. After that she refused to drink at meals, and when the servant came round with the water, put her hand over her glass. The habit stayed with her all her life.

The trusted bawab or doorkeeper was given strict instructions to let no unauthorised person into the house, and so well did he

carry out his instructions that he threw down the stairs the husbands of several of the friends of Théophile's youngest daughter, Germaine, known as Pussy, who was only nine years older than Chickie and still living at home, when they came in search of their wives. Occasionally a young Italian lawyer, Edoardo Malatesta, would take the little girls out for a moonlight drive in his car. 'He became my first great love and a cause of friction between the two of us,' Chickie wrote, 'for Sacha had a soft spot for him as well.'

The excitement of the siege was just beginning to wear off when Pussy announced that they were all going to Italy on holiday – no doubt partly to let both Max and Sister Margaret cool off. Soon they were crowded into a compartment of the Cairo to Alexandria train, specially reserved and guarded by a liveried dragoman from the Italian Embassy, and on their way to catch the Venice boat. It was on that trip that they first saw the little Alto Adige town of Bressanone, which would play such an important role in Sacha's life, and, of course, Venice itself. On later trips Sacha would see the Acropolis, deserted then, and which left such an impression on her of perfect beauty and simplicity that she was determined to see it one day with me. On a Swann's Tour, fifty years later, we toiled up the hill in an unending stream of tourists, got to the top to see the temple enclosed by barbed wire, but still managed to feel that pang which indicates: perfection.

In November 1921 they returned to the gloomy flat in Haret Zogheb. The dispute between the grandparents and Max and the Russian Residency was over. For the rest of their childhood and adolescence the two little girls would live 'chez les grandparents'.

Leaving childhood meant, among other things, leaving the English language in which they had grown up, the English books and the quotations from the Bible, Shakespeare and Dr. Johnson. It meant entering the French and Italian world of the Rossis and the Cattaouis. They would no longer be the small warm unit of Mother, Nanny, Netta and the children, but a part of the enormous web of aunts, uncles, cousins, grandparents, great-uncles and great-aunts which, at its furthest reaches, comprised the entire upper stratum of Egyptian Jewry. Sacha spent her life escaping from this, first by immersing herself in European literature from Plato (starting with the *Symposium* in Shelley's translation) to Proust, then by marrying a man with French connections who wished to go and study in France, and later by settling with me in England. Nonetheless, she was involved with them from her tenth year on and they cannot but have affected her life.

Théophile Bienvenu Rossi, Avvocato Rossi as he was universally known (rumour had it that a letter had once arrived for him, addressed simply to: 'Avvocato Rossi, presso al cavallo' – i.e. next to the equestrian statue – 'Cairo'), was the fifth of ten children born to Dr. Elia Rossi, prolific author, specialist on the bubonic plague, and, in his last years, personal doctor to the Khedive. Sacha wrote a poem about this remote figure who died twenty years before she was born, as well as about her Russian father's

parents, whom she never knew either, and although she says there
that 'no spark of recognition flares' up in her for any of them,
she meditates on the fact that 'their conflicting blood-streams
blend and flow in mine' and that certain distinctive physical fea-
tures have been passed on down this genetic stream:

Ancestors

Tight-lipped, his portrait overawed my childhood.
Throughout my youth the pressing question: Would
he perhaps not wholly have approved?
inhibited, each time I spoke or moved.
He'd left Ferrara, a stern young man of twenty-one,
to make his fortune in the Middle East. This done
– thanks to a hard-earned medical degree
and letters from his erstwhile friend, mentor and referee,
the local Rabbi, to some eminent Jews
(one of whose heiresses the immigrant eventually would choose
as bride) – he settled down and raised five daughters
and five sons beside the Nile's life-giving waters.
Facing his portrait hung that of his bride, ladylike, slim

– she always addressed him by his patronym –
on whose unruffled brow the same bird flies
that spreads his inkline wings over my own son's eyes.
At least that Judeo-Italian lot was civilised.
Not so my Russian cousins, those epitomised
by the tea-merchant who mailed his excrement to friends in a
    sealed packet
and died too forcibly confined in a strait-jacket.
Is it his lady's dutch-doll face (on a proud neck
gold chains so weighty and so numerous bedeck)
glows from this miniature I have? No spark
of recognition flares either for these, my dark
forebears, or for the staid and steady line,
even though their conflicting blood-streams blend and flow in
    mine.

The obituary of Elia Rossi in *L'Univers Israélite* for 1 February
1892, signed J. Sanua, presumably James Sanua, an Alexandrian
Jew, better known by his pen-name of Shaikh Abu Naddara, a
journalist and playwright of considerable reputation at the time,
reads as follows (though my translation cannot do justice to the
flowery eloquence of the original French): 'The Egyptian Institute
and forty-five European Academies have just lost one of their
most illustrious members, who, for fifty years, has not ceased to
enrich the sciences and the arts with his remarkable works. Dr.
Elie Rossi-Bey was born in 1816 in Ferrara (Italy), where he
studied medicine. At the age of twenty-eight [*sic*] he came to
Egypt, where he allied himself with one of the most honourable
families of Cairo. He is the first Israelite to have obtained the title
of Bey in the East, and the only one to have been allowed to visit
the sacred cities of Islam, Mecca and Medina. Mehmet-Ali the
Great, founder of the present dynasty, his sons Saïd and Halim,
and his grandsons Abbas and Ismaïl, all testified to the esteem

and affection in which they held the deceased, and entrusted to him the most important scientific missions. But it is not only the viceroys of Egypt who honoured with their great bounty the eminent doctor; the wise, the enlightened and lovable poet Victor-Emmanuel, the king *galantuomo*, appreciated his merits and conferred upon him the highest honours of Italy. During his long medical career he never deserted his post, even when the plague was infecting the country. He has always treated with equal solicitude rich and poor alike, without distinction of race or creed; the Eternal One, blessed be he, has granted him the joy of seeing his daughters and sons allied to the great families of the country, such as the Cattaouis, and Chaloms, the Greens, the Viterbos, the Mosseris, etc. etc., all occupying pre-eminent positions. May God spread the treasure of His consolations over the noble family of Elie Rossi-Bey and welcome amongst the elect in the sky the pure soul of this illustrious man! Therein will he still pray for the greatness and the glory of Israel and for the happiness of its people!'

Well, obituaries are obituaries, but the biography his erstwhile mentor, Moses Leone Finzi of Ferrara, wrote, and which was published in Rovigo in 1856 as *Biografia Elia Rossi*, confirms and elaborates on what is written here. The eldest son of a family fallen on hard times, and a brilliant scholar, his father approached Leone Finzi with the suggestion that he take charge of the boy's studies. Responding to the warmth, intelligence and moral fervour of the boy, Finzi accepted. In 1838 Mohamed Ali, trying to press his country into becoming a modern state, set up a series of recruitment centres throughout Europe to attract the brightest professionals to Egypt. Many of these were of course Jews, debarred, by the *numerus clausus* laws then prevailing in so many countries, from finding careers in their native lands. Elie Rossi went to Bologna and signed up. After adventures which read more like Greek romances than accounts of modern travel, including shipwreck off the coast of Sicily, he reached Egypt and was posted to the Yemen as a doctor to the army there. In the course of his long life he published ten books, among them an important volume on the plague, which may have been used by Proust's father when he came to write *his* authoritative book on the subject (and which was in its turn used by Camus for his novel, *La Peste*). Other anecdotes, both in the biography and in the typewritten memoirs of one of his grandchildren, recount how, infected with the plague himself, he cut the buboes from his own flesh with a pocket knife; and how once, riding alone in the desert, his camel stumbled and he fell and broke his leg; having passed out with the pain, he came to to find himself surrounded by a group of fierce-looking bedouin, armed to the teeth; fearing his last hour had come, he said the *shema* under his breath, whereupon the leader of the bedouins rushed up to him, embraced him, and said: 'My brother!'

The names he gave his children tell us much about the strange world of Enlightenment liberalism which comes so powerfully through the pages of Moses Finzi's biography and which was such a feature of European Jewry from the time of Napoleon to the rise of Hitler: Grazia, Regina, Joseph, Ida, Théophile Bienvenu, Isaac Fortuné, Victor Emmanuel, Napoleon Abraham, Gemma,

Ines Roma. The names of their spouses tell the same story of the easy commerce between traditional Jewish and modern European secular traditions: Moise Cattaoui, Rachel Cattaoui, Emilie Tilche, Alfred Chalom, Moise Soria. As for his own bride, Bamba Hakkak, not much seems to be known about her. How Sacha knew that she addressed him by his patronym and what happened to that portrait are mysteries. I would dearly like to have seen it and the tell-tale eyebrows, which do not seem to have been passed on to any other member of the family I have seen, and which, till I read the poem carefully, I had always presumed belonged to those less reputable Russian ancestors.

A veritable patriarch, then, and a man of his time. When poor Napoleone fell in love with a (non-Jewish) Italian ballerina he would not countenance the match, though whether for snobbish or religious reasons is unclear. In this he was abetted by his second son, Théophile, who seems to have inherited both his moral uprightness and his intransigence. Napoleone, however, married his ballerina, was cut off, had nine children, and they all lived in Milan, according to their grandchildren, at once desperately poor and blissfully happy.

Not so the children of Théophile: Nelly, the eldest, converted after the death of her first husband, married a Syrian and died of typhoid at the age of thirty-five; Charles, after running through the family fortune, also married a goy, though a very wealthy one; René too died young; Guido never really fulfilled himself; and Théophile made the life of his youngest daughter, Pussy, a kind of hell with the strictness of his upbringing. He was, in effect, a tyrant, 'a bit,' Chickie writes, 'like Elizabeth Barrett Browning's father, and he had taken an irrational dislike to Sacha and was particularly mean to her, mostly I think because she was brave enough to show her indignation openly at his awful way of treating the servants. Everyone treated the servants pretty badly, but Grandfather was a very violent man and I remember him knocking one meek little souffragui's tarbouche off his head . . . To me, *au contraire*, he had taken a great liking, so that when the family wanted to wangle something out of him I was their emissary. I actually rather liked and in a way respected him. He was a scholarly old gentleman and knew Latin and Greek as well as he knew Italian and, politically, his views were in the right place, only he failed to practice what he preached, for he was a liberal like

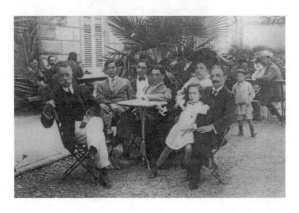

Carducci and Herr Settembrini in *The Magic Mountain*. But he was bookish and sensitive too. Once we were both reading in the sitting room and I was reading Francis Thompson's "Assumpta Maria". A word, often repeated in the poem, struck me by its strange solemn sound, and I realised it was Greek and asked him what "thanatos" meant. He looked up over his spectacles from what he was reading and said very quietly and gravely: 'Ça veut dire La Mort, chérie", and I felt then though I couldn't explain it as though a sort of understanding had been established between us and that the same things meant the same to us both, moved and awed us in the same way – I really and deeply liked him, which didn't prevent me from taking advantage of his *point faible* for me to obtain favours for myself and for others.'

By marrying Rachel, the daughter of Joseph Cattaoui, Théophile

(like his sister Ida, who married Joseph's half-brother, Moise Cattaoui) forged links with the foremost Egyptian Jewish family, which traced its descent back to the Middle Ages and which, by the late nineteenth century, had produced from within its ranks many of the leaders of the Jewish community in Egypt and had a finger in every financial pie. But Rachel, like her mother-in-law, was totally submissive and totally dependent on her husband. It was he, not she, who did the household accounts; he, not she, who decided how the children should be brought up. Once, when he had not been able to travel to Italy with them on their annual holiday and when the hotel in Pisa they had booked into proved to be inexplicably closed, she sat down on one of the seventeen suitcases with which the family regularly travelled and said to Pussy: 'Envoie un telegramme a Papa'. It was only with difficulty that she could be persuaded that there were other hotels in Pisa and that they did not need to ask his permission to book into one of them.

She spent her days playing patience and smoking up to a hundred cigarettes. On only one day of the week was her gentle nature not to be taken for granted, and that was bound up with why the little girls were there in the first place. When her mother died of typhoid Sacha was herself struck down by the disease and the doctors did not hold out much hope for her. Her grandmother vowed that if she came through she would give up smoking for one day a week for the rest of her life, and she stuck to this vow till the day of her death, in 1947, seventeen traumatic years after her husband (she and Pussy were carried over the Alpine passes to safety from Italy to Switzerland in 1943 by the smugglers who

at the time specialised in such exploits, but never really recovered from the shock of that terrible journey). But on the day in question the entire household held its breath and wished she had never made the vow.

And so, for the two little girls, the years with the grandparents began, which would only end when each of them got married.

Saul Bellow has written of how his recovery from a serious illness at the age of ten brought with it the sense of 'a duty that comes with survival', a feeling 'that I'd better make it worth the while of whoever has authorised this'. I don't know if Sacha felt the same way. I don't think she did. The typhoid fever from which she recovered only to learn that her mother was dead inaugurated a period of wretchedness punctuated by other, often very serious illnesses – scarlet fever, pleurisy, pneumonia, bronchitis – which lasted all through her adolescence and affected her lungs for ever. I think that in those years she simply wanted to die, that the sorrow at her mother's death and the misery of living with her grandparents made her feel that the sooner her life came to an end the better. 'Whenever Sacha is ill she simply turns her face to the wall and gives up,' Chickie wrote to me when I informed her that Sacha had fallen down the stairs, that there was something wrong with her heart, that she was in hospital and not making any effort at recovery. 'She was thinking of my childhood illnesses,' Sacha said when I showed her the letter. 'I was so miserable then I used to hope when I went to sleep that I wouldn't wake up.'

But from each illness she recovered and life at the grandparents carried on as before. Because of the constant quarantines imposed on the two little girls they had very little regular schooling: a total of four terms at the *lycée* in six years. As a result of these four terms, though, Sacha could still recite chunks of Racine and Corneille six decades later, as well as the sillier portions of the fables of La Fontaine and the more lachrymose poems of the French Romantics and Symbolists:

Je vois mon profond soir vaguement s'étoiler.
Voici l'heure ou je vais, aussi moi, m'en aller.

And:

O toi qui sais aimer, reponds, amant d'Elvire,
Comprends-tu que l'on parte et qu'on se dise adieu?

Sully Prudhomme's poem, 'Le Vase brisé' was a special favourite: 'N'y touchez pas – il est brisé!' she would often cry out if I bent to pick up the shattered pieces of a cup or saucer accidentally dropped.

By themselves and with the succession of weak and compliant tutors their grandfather supplied them with the girls read everything they could lay hands on: Lang's Red, Blue, Golden and other books, *Treasure Island*, *Dr. Jekyll and Mr. Hyde*, *Puck of Pook's Hill*, *The Jungle Book*, Daudet, Maupassant, *La Princesse de Clèves*, *Manon Lescaut*, the Billy Bunter stories. But as they grew up their tastes began to diverge. 'I was up to my neck in esotericism to counteract the silly "governessy" feel of Theosophy,' Chickie wrote in another of her massive letters, 'so I was reading the Christian Platonists of Alexandria and the myth of Isis and Osiris (by Plutarch?), and a big Gnostic book called *Pistis Sophia* that I pretended to love though je ne pouvais pas en comprendre un seul mot, because it made me feel important I suppose – so I carried that huge cumbersome volume all around everywhere with me. But I finally landed up with Jacob Boehme and at least he really did have some sort of meaning on a queer totally noumenal level.' Sacha, more methodical, more down-to-earth, read her way through *The Odyssey* and Dante and Dostoevsky and Baudelaire and Rimbaud and – a passion of her aunt Pussy, whose two main interests, however, were men and cream cakes – the early Surrealists.

There was another sign of the growing differences between the two girls. Chickie has always claimed she is tone deaf and has no interest in music. Sacha, however, found that music appealed to her and that she had an aptitude for the piano. She was encouraged by her teacher, Jenö Takács, who had been a pupil of Bartók: 'The fact that I was in love with him spurred me on of course.' So much so that one year she insisted on sitting for her exams even though she had a raging temperature and immediately afterwards had to be put to bed where she struggled for several weeks with one of her recurring bouts of pneumonia.

(1996. My colleague, Gerry Webster, with whom Sacha and I sometimes used to go to concerts, comes to see me after her death to offer his condolences. He is a Bartók fanatic. I show him a photo in the album which Sacha always referred to as 'the Bartók photograph'. It is a group portrait of a large gathering on the occasion of a visit Bartók made to Egypt, but now Sacha is dead I don't know which is Bartók. Gerry scans the photo but can't find him either – or rather, there are several people who could be him. I tell him about Takács and he says: But how extraordinary! I have a book of Bartók photographs which includes some of him with a J. Takács. A few days later he sends me copies of the photos – taken, according to the captions, on the occasion of the Congress of Arabian Music in 1932. One shows Bartók and Takács (a tall, gaunt, handsome man with a *beret basque*) and an elongated, stooping figure in a panama hat – the musicologist E. M. von Hornbostel; another shows Bartók with Gertrud and Paul Hindemith (but Sacha never said anything about Hindemith visiting) and Jenö Takács (his full name is given here), in the same beret, posing in front of the Sakhara pyramid. How sad, I think, that Sacha never saw them. And that I never knew, while she was alive, what the Jenö Takács she had so often talked about looked like.)

She quickly realised, though, that she would never be able to make any real progress at the piano. Her paralysing shyness made it impossible for her to perform in public. Her big hands with their extraordinary wide span between the thumb and the index finger (which I have inherited), her ability to work hard, and her innate love of and feeling for music, would no doubt have made her, if not a first-class performer, at least a performer of distinction. But at seventeen she stopped playing and, since the man she married was as unmusical as her sister, in effect gave up all interest in music till we came to England and she began to listen to the Third Programme and go to concerts.

Strangely, the first piece of music I can remember going to with her was Bartók's Fourth Quartet. My father's much younger cousin, who befriended us when we first came to England, had got tickets for a reading of Eliot's *Four Quartets* in the Apollo Room of the Festival Hall. Between *East Coker* and *The Dry Salvages* the Allegri Quartet played the Bartók, an inspired bit of planning since Eliot is on record as having had the Bartók quartets in mind while writing his own. My cousin and I were seized with a fit of the giggles during the pizzicato movement (I suppose I had the excuse that I was sixteen and had never heard anything like this before, but it was a poor excuse). '*Listen!*' Sacha whispered fiercely. 'Just *listen!*' Later she became passionately fond of Stockhausen's extraordinary sonata for two pianos and ring modulation, *Mantra*, and urged me to listen to it. 'I don't like Stockhausen,' I said airily, 'all that short-wave radio and Indian mysticism.' 'Just listen to it,' Sacha said, and played me the record. I listened and was converted to Stockhausen.

Every year, if it did not coincide with one of Sacha's illnesses, there was the trip to Italy to escape the debilitating heat of the Egyptian summer. They would take not a passenger ship but a trading vessel which plied the Eastern Mediterranean, stopping to load and unload at Haifa, Athens and a few other ports on its way to its destination of Venice. There were very few cabins on deck, reserved for passengers. Much more fun, the girls agreed, though Pussy would have preferred a cruise ship with dancing in the evenings and handsome strangers proposing on the moonlit deck. In Venice they would stop off at the Danieli for a few days to 'get acclimatised' before taking the train north to the little walled town of Bressanone in the Italian Tyrol that their grandfather prided himself on having 'discovered'.

Bressanone lies just off the Brenner road that links Italy to Austria. Though only 500 metres up, it is surrounded by mountains which rise to 3000 metres, but lies in so broad a valley that its environs are rich in apple and pear orchards. From the town the little hill villages of S.Andrea, Cleran, Millan, Tiles and Varna can be clearly seen. It has grown in the confluence of two rivers, the narrow rushing Rienz, which comes straight down from the mountains to the East, and the broader, calmer Isarco, which flows down from the Austrian Alps to meet the Adige at Bolzano. Wherever one is in the town there is the sound of rushing water. Since the Middle Ages it has been the seat of a Bishop, and was once presided over by none other than Nicholas of Cusa, the great late medieval negative theologian. The main church has been sadly 'barochised', but the cloisters contain an extraordinary series of late-Gothic frescos. In any town down in the heart of Italy this would be touted as a major masterpiece, but – no doubt because the style is so un-Italian – the guidebooks pass it over with hardly a mention. This is perhaps fortunate, for Bressanone remains even today unspoilt by mass tourism, though it is a popular holiday resort for those Italians and Austrians more interested in walking than in lying about on beaches.

When I first came to Bressanone with Sacha in 1973, after the

death of our epileptic dog Pilic, she found it unchanged from the town she remembered from her youth. There were a few signs of light industry further down the valley, but a walled town cannot of course be spoilt by new building. The rivers still ran as they had always done, the apples still bloomed, and we found rooms in a hotel giving on to the Isarco, the Goldener Adler, where Montaigne had once stayed, run by two sisters who had lived there all their lives and who, Sacha soon found, knew or had known many of the people she had been acquainted with in the twenties. Fink, the pastry shop where the two girls and their young aunt had been in the habit of stopping for a cream cake between breakfast and lunch – 'How we ate in those days!' – was still there, run by the same family. One striking difference was that now German was taught in school alongside Italian, whereas in the heyday of Mussolini a vain and gigantic effort had been made to turn these independent mountain people into true Italians, leading of course to the mushrooming of hedge-schools and barely-concealed antagonism to all things Italian. Today, if you ask one of the shopkeepers if they are Italian – and the sign at the border, a mere fifty miles away, proudly proclaims: 'Benvenuto in Italia' – they answer simply: 'No, sono di qui' – no, I'm from here.

One person who no longer visits is Alberto Moravia. Sacha and Chickie struck up a friendship with the sick, tormented, brilliant Jewish boy – his real name was Alberto Pincherle before he turned himself into an *echt* Italian writer – who had been, like Sacha, sent to the mountains to recuperate. That was when she was seventeen and she and Chickie and Pussy and the grandmother spent a whole winter in Bressanone to help her get over her pneumonia. He had read everything: Homer, Virgil, Thucydides, Tacitus, Dante, Shakespeare, the Elizabethan dramatists, Leopardi, Dostoevsky, Proust. Sacha did not altogether like him but he fascinated her by his brilliance and his ambition. She had never met anyone like him in placid, easy-going Egypt.

Chickie and Pussy preferred the officers stationed in the barracks just outside the town – Pussy would eventually marry an Italian officer, the nephew of one of the heroes of Trentino resistance to the Austrians in the First World War. Sacha too preferred the less intense, gentler Italian boys who took her out dancing and skating on the town's ice-rink: 'When you toppled over and your head hit the ice the sound was extraordinary – such echoes, such reverberations!' But there were usually two young men at hand, one on either side of her, holding her arms, making sure she didn't fall.

And one can see why. She was turning into a beauty. A photo in the album shows her, boyish with her hair cut short, sitting at

a café table with a handsome young man beside her. 'But it was strange,' she told me, 'whenever I really got on with one of them he invariably turned out to be Jewish. I don't know how to explain it – Italians and Jews are after all identical in appearance and often in name in Italy – but it happened too often to be just a coincidence.'

The fact that the little girls had been baptized by Sister Margaret seems to have been allowed to fade into tactful obscurity. The grandmother fasted on Yom Kippur, but otherwise the family were as assimilated, as little concerned with Jewish practice, as any of their counterparts in Berlin or Paris. Théophile might have resented his brother marrying an Italian, or his daughter marrying a Syrian, but his Judaism was mainly ethical and blended with a kind of Victorian uprightness underpinned by a vague Enlightenment optimism. He expected all his family to uphold these values, but he was unfortunately so strict and so little aware of the feelings of others that all his children and many of his grandchildren turned out to be weak and self-indulgent once they were free of his influence. And in the end only his eldest daughter in her first marriage married a Jew, and of Nelly's three children only Sacha did.

She had been reading the Bible and had begun to work out why she had felt so uneasy about the story Sister Margaret had told them all those years before in the drawing-room in Helwan. Now she began to discover that Jewishness had little to do with practice but was so deeply ingrained – in her at any rate – that it would colour her views and mark her response to the world for the rest of her life: 'Of course living in France in the thirties and during the war helped. There's nothing like a strong whiff of anti-semitism to awaken the Jew in you. And you don't get much more anti-semitic than the French petite bourgeoisie. Mind you, the rich Jews on the *Côte d'Azur* didn't help matters by ostentatiously eating and dressing well when everyone else was struggling to find any food and clothes at all.'

As well as Bressanone there were prolonged stays at the lake of Carezza, some twenty miles east of Bolzano and about two thousand metres up. From the hotel – the only hotel – it was possible to walk up into the Rosengarten, the extraordinary Dolomitic chain that rises above the lake like grey lace. There, legend has it, the Sleeping Beauty lies imprisoned till her knight will come to kiss her awake and rescue her. Chickie and Pussy were not very fond of mountain walking, so Sacha would ask the hotel to make up a *cestino* and go out walking all day, sometimes with other young people from the hotel, sometimes on her own – 'But

there were always other walkers one could join if one felt like it.'
In the evenings and week-ends there were dances, and it was at
one of these that she met the first real love of her life. They
danced all night and he told her his family came from Trieste.
The next day when they met it seemed he had been making
enquiries about her because he said: 'I gather you're from Egypt,
and I believe our families are distantly related.'

He was a music student in Milan and his name was Giorgio
Nathan Rogers. He came from an old Triestine Jewish family with
English connections. Much later, when Richard Rogers became
famous overnight as the architect of the Pompidou Centre and
biographical sketches of him began to appear in the papers, Sacha
was very excited: 'He's Giorgio's nephew! And his parents Dada
and Nino, of whom I was so fond, are still alive!' 'Why not get
in touch with them?' I suggested, for one learned they were living

close by, in Wimbledon. But, typically, she never got round to it. As always, I suspect, her low estimation of herself made her feel that no-one would want to see her, and her pride made her feel that they would think she was trying to cash in on an ancient link now that their son was famous. It never struck her that perhaps they would be as pleased and moved to see her as she would have been to see them.

I never found out exactly what happened between her and Giorgio. There is no doubt that it was a serious affair, one of only two or three in her life. He was to sit his music exams in Milan and promised to meet her off the boat in Venice the following year when she and her family came back to Europe. But he failed to turn up. He sent her a toy donkey by way of apology, but she took this as adding insult to injury and never replied, though he continued to shower her with letters and apologies. I tried to write about it in the novel I devoted to memory and the Dolomites, *In a Hotel Garden*, but I was never quite sure what she thought of it or whether she approved of my using what had been such an important and painful episode in her life for my own selfish writerly ends. And she never talked to me about Giorgio again.

It's one of those circular photos, flattened at the base, which seem to have passed out of fashion. In the bottom row: five little children, three boys in sailor suits, two girls in long dresses and white gloves. Behind them, four young women in white, holding bouquets. They are standing in a garden and on the right, behind the tallest of the young women, two men in morning suits can just be made out. It is a photo of the bridesmaids at the wedding of Denise de Menasce and Alfred Mawas. Sacha is on the left,

her dark hair cut fairly short and parted on the side, swept back from her face to reveal a broad brow. The other three young ladies are either smiling dutifully at the camera or looking glum, but she is enclosed in a world of her own. Despite the smile hovering over her lips the predominant effect is one of sweet sadness, there, in the midst of the festivities, with that pretty necklace and cradling her elaborate bouquet. The year is 1930.

She had grown up in the extended circle of the Egyptian Jewish upper bourgeoisie. Many of the young men and women she had so briefly been to school with, and then mingled with at parties and dances, were related to her, since her grandfather was one of ten and her grandmother one of nine children. Now they were starting to get married. Pussy married her officer in that same year, and the following year, at twenty-two, Chickie got married to the only Catholic in their group, Albert Baiocchi. Her mysticism had found an outlet in a fervent Catholicism, so fervent that for a while, after she met Albert, she contemplated becoming a nun. She went to see her father confessor to ask his advice. 'You are made for this world,' that perceptive man told her; 'get married to your Albert and forget about nunneries.' She took his advice but her violent need for some kind of external discipline, combined with her total inability to submit to any, have been at war within her ever since, and there was even, in the seventies, a belated and quickly aborted attempt actually to enter a nunnery. More recently, in an old people's home in Cairo, she led a revolt of the inmates, feeling that they were being unfairly treated, and was naturally asked to leave.

Sacha's relation to discipline seems to have been much more straightforward: she would discipline herself. Life was clearly not about getting what you wanted; the important thing was to get through it with dignity.

But what was life about then? Theosophy was much in the air at the time. Chickie referred to it when she said that it was in reaction to its 'governessy' feel that she turned to the ancient mystics. Joe and Nadine Suarez, who had come to take the place almost of surrogate parents to the two girls, were completely under its spell. Joe, or Carlo Suares, as he signed his books, was an architect, painter and writer. In the course of his long life he produced books on colour theory, theosophy and cabala, as well as a great many unreadable novels, and had some influence on Henry Miller and Lawrence Durrell, who came to know him in Alexandria. Miller chose his book on Krishnamurti as one of the ten best books of all time. Sacha and Chickie were very fond of him, responding to his childlike enthusiasm and warmth, his innocence and kindness, without taking too much stock of his theories. Like most people though they found his wife Nadine – a fierce, overbearing woman who worshipped her husband and condoned his many infidelities with partners of both sexes – a rather uncomfortable person to be with, though there was no denying her fondness for them. Her brother, Joseph Tilche, the young Joe, as I called him to distinguish him from his brother-in-law, was another avuncular figure, more staid, more reliable, and throughout his life a good friend to both Chickie and Sacha.

The two Joes and Nadine would go off to theosophical jamborees in Holland with Lady Lutyens and the circle of worshippers of Krishnamurti, but to this, as to Chickie's new-found Catholicism, Sacha remained indifferent. I have copies of *Five Dialogues of Plato* and the *Nicomachian Ethics* of Aristotle in the Everyman editions, which she bought and read at the time. Many passages are carefully underlined, particularly in the *Ethics*: 'The Chief Good we feel instinctively must be something which is our own, and not easily to be taken from us.' 'For to constitute Happiness, there must be, as we have said, complete virtue and a complete life.' 'But the Virtues we get by first performing single acts of working, which, again, is the case of other things, as the arts for instance; for what we have to make when we have learned how, these we learn how to make by making: men come to be builders, for instance, by building; harp-players, by playing on the harp: exactly so, by doing just actions we come to be just; by doing the actions of self-mastery we come to be prefected in self-mastery; and by doing brave actions brave.' She obviously responds too to Aristotle's refusal of grand gestures, his steely realism: 'As for those who say that he who is being tortured on the wheel, or falls into great misfortunes is happy provided only he be good, they talk nonsense, whether they mean to do so or not. On the other hand, because fortune is needed as an addition, some hold good fortune to be identical with Happiness: which it is not, for even this in excess is a hindrance.' And: 'Some say that they who are blessed and independent have no need of Friends, for they already have all that is good. On the other hand it looks absurd, while we are assigning to the Happy man all other good things, not to give him Friends, which are, after all, thought to be the greatest of external goods.'

One can see her here using her reading to try to understand herself and especially to put some distance between herself and the easy-going, self-indulgent world she saw all round her. In a curious way she seems to have inherited some of the Victorian puritanism of her grandfather, but Aristotelianised, so to speak, more responsive to the paradoxes and contradictions life throws up. As a result she seems to have been able to come to terms with her nature, which was at once passionate and ascetic, which asked little of the world and expected even less, yet which responded to whatever the world had to offer with an openness which was to be one of her most striking attributes even in old age.

It was not all so serious. She attended gym classes with the other young women of her circle: 'Our teacher would show us how to hold our hands high up above our heads and walk slowly round the gym in a line while she called out at intervals: "Longue longue mince mince", and the motley collection of short plump Jewish girls strove in vain to grow tall and slim.'

There were films. Sacha spoke all her life of the extraordinary effect on her of a silent version of Poe's 'Fall of the House of Usher' and of the *sound* produced in the viewer by the sight of the great bell as it swung rhythmically from one side of the screen to the other.

She went to parties. She read. She went to concerts.

And then she met Jean.

She had known his cousin Stella first, a striking red-head who had been at school with her. Jean had been educated in France and then at the Cairo *lycée*. His father, Albert Josipovici (whose own father had come to Egypt from Jassy in Moldavia via Constantinople), was a famous author. At the age of twenty-two, with his brother-in-law, Albert Adès, he had published *Goha le simple*, a novel set in a romantically medieval Cairo which took Paris by storm in 1919 and was even short-listed for the Prix Goncourt the year Proust won it with *A l'Ombre des jeunes filles en fleur*. Jean had not had a happy childhood. Born in 1914, his parents had left him with grandparents in Egypt and spent the war years in France. He never forgave them for this, nor did he forgive his much younger sister Jaqueline for seemingly later managing to gain their mother's love as he had never been able to do. Handsome, vain, opinionated, brooking no dissent from his views, even at twenty, he was also an excellent tennis-player and, most important from Sacha's point of view, someone who, unlike most of the young men she had met, seemed to know clearly what he wanted to do with his life.

Unfortunately he was essentially interested only in himself and lacked any sense of humour. When I asked Chickie after Sacha's death what she and Albert had thought of him at the time she said: 'Nothing. We laughed at him a good deal, and this did not endear us to Sacha.'

Sacha, on the other hand, responded to his undoubted charm and fell for his seriousness. In her seventies, when we learned that he had become a faith healer in Calabria and was surrounded by a group of ardent, mostly female disciples, she was unsurprised: 'He always felt he had a message. And he was so persuaded of it himself that he had little trouble persuading others.'

Like his contemporary at the *lycée*, Edmond Jabès – who, in that same year of 1935 was to marry a distant cousin of Sacha's, Arlette Cohen, the granddaughter of Moise Cattaoui – and like his own father, Jean was determined to be a French writer. He would take the first step towards this by returning to France to pursue his studies. Though he was only twenty and Sacha twenty-four, he proposed and she accepted.

I have a photo of them at their engagement party: her party dress does not suit her, but she seems happy for the first time since her childhood. There is no sign of Chickie and Albert, who by now had two daughters, Monica, born in 1932 and Anna, born a year later.

Before the couple could get married there was an obstacle to be overcome. A busybody cousin had remembered that they had

been baptized as children, and before a Jewish wedding could go ahead she would have to be cleansed of this blemish. She was sent to the old synagogue, in the heart of Cairo, where she was met by a stern woman who drew her in roughly and frogmarched her through dark damp corridors till they came to a small room with a single small barred window, in the middle of which was an evil-smelling pool. An old man was chanting outside the window. 'Take off your clothes,' the woman ordered. 'All of them?' asked Sacha. 'Yes.' 'Please turn round then,' Sacha said, not used to being looked at naked by strangers. 'Take them all off and get into the pool, then call me,' the woman said. The water was icy and the sides of the pool were slippery and slimy. Gingerly Sacha lowered herself in and called out. The woman re-entered, knelt by the side of the pool and, before Sacha realised what she was up to, had placed her hand on her head and pushed her under. She came up spluttering. 'Finished,' the woman said. 'Get dressed now.' The old man had not ceased his chanting.

Going home through the streets of old Cairo, her hair soaking,

Sacha caught cold. The wedding almost had to be cancelled, but she recovered in time.

Jean had made his plans. They would go off to Aix-en-Provence and enroll at the University, where he would work on his doctorate under the distinguished philosopher, Jean Segond. Sacha would provide the money by which they would live, would keep house for him and type his manuscripts.

For her, I suppose, there was the sense that a new life was starting. She was married to the man she loved, she was moving to a new country, and she could put the sorrows of her early life behind her and perhaps, at twenty-four, find again the happiness she had known in her earliest years.

II FRANCE

When Sacha and Jean landed in France in the autumn of 1935 they found themselves on a continent in which the clock of history had suddenly begun to tick a little faster. In Germany Hitler had come to power in 1933 and had almost immediately set about testing the will of the countries which had imposed on Germany the disastrous Treaty of Versailles. In France politicians and industrialists were beginning to wake up to the fact that economically the country was falling behind her main rivals and that the Third Republic might be based on less secure democratic foundations then they had hitherto assumed. The catalyst here was the so-called Stavisky affair. In January 1934 Alexandre Stavisky, an East European Jewish financier, was found guilty of massive fraud and his fall seemed likely to drag down some of the leading French political figures as well. His mysterious death shortly after only fuelled speculation. The extreme right used the affair as an excuse to mount a campaign in which the usual themes of xenophobia, anti-semitism and anti-parliamentarism were all prominent. A series of increasingly violent demonstrations followed, culminating, on 6 February, in the attempt by a large gathering of right-wing groups in Paris to break through a police cordon protecting the approach to the Chamber of Deputies and a struggle ensued in which fifteen people were killed and two thousand injured. The Prime Minister, Daladier, resigned, thus creating a dangerous precedent of politicians giving way to street pressure.

Meanwhile, the parties of the left and centre-left, the Communists, the Socialists and the Radicals, were almost as much at loggerheads with each other as they were with the Right. But now, in the face of German re-armament and the growing threat of Fascism across Europe, Moscow gave orders to the Communists to make their peace with the others. Thus the Front Populaire was created, an uneasy alliance of three parties with very different aims and traditions but a common enemy. More demonstrations followed, and more pitched street battles, with the right warning of a threat of a Communist take-over and the left of an incipient Fascist coup. Leon Blum, the Socialist leader, was vilified in the Right-wing press: 'This naturalised German Jew, or son of such a person, who says to the French, publicly, in the Chamber, that he loathes them, is not to be treated like a normal human being. He is a monster . . ., a man to be shot, but in the back.'

Throughout 1934, 1935 and 1936 violent clashes took place in all the major French cities between Right-wing militants and supporters of the Front Populaire, the former chanting the Marseillaise, the latter the Internationale. Blum was attacked in the street and wounded. But in the elections of May 1936 the Popular Front at last got into power as a result of the disciplined way in which its diverse constituents rallied at the second ballot behind the candidate of the left most likely to win. It was the Front's finest hour. Blum, elected Prime Minister as head of the party with the largest parliamentary grouping, was of course dependent on the votes of all three parties within his coalition, yet each of these had its own vision of the future and its own sense of how the present European crisis should be dealt with. The workers, believing that at long last their hopes were about to be fulfilled, began a series of massive strikes to show their muscle; any concessions Blum made to them, though, angered and frightened the

Radicals. The defeated Right, meanwhile, never accepted what had just happened, the more moderate sections holding it as an axiom that it was the natural party of government, the more extreme seeing in the results only a confirmation of their belief in the folly of parliamentary democracy. Indeed, Vichy has been described by some historians as merely the belated revenge of the Right for its 1936 defeat.

Meanwhile, Hitler had reclaimed the Rhineland and Mussolini invaded Abyssinia, and it was clear that the democracies did not have the will to act in concert to prevent or reverse such blatant violations of international treaties. The Spanish Civil War broke out and the Blum government found itself under pressure from its left wing to go to the aid of the Republicans to counter the help Hitler and Mussolini were giving Franco. It is doubtful if any politician would have been able to deal with such a situation, especially in view of the way in which even quite respectable figures of the Right, such as Marshall Pétain, the 'hero of Verdun', were making it clear they thought France was becoming a tool of Moscow and that in this moment of crisis what was wanted was a true-born Frenchman at the helm and not a Jew, let alone a socialist Jew. Blum resigned in 1937 and by 1938 the Popular Front was in ruins. By then Hitler had taken over Austria and was hungrily eyeing Czechoslovakia, Franco was triumphing in Spain and England had shown little stomach for a fight. By the end of the year not even the most optimistic democrat could doubt that if Munich signalled peace in our time, that time would be very short indeed.

Into this maelstrom of international crisis, political ineffectuality, strikes and bloody street fighting stepped two young students from Egypt, bound for the philosophy faculty of the University of Aix-Marseilles. Jean was to work for his doctorate under Segond, the author of such diverse works as *La Guerre mondiale et la vie spirituelle* and *Logique du pari*, on what then passed for a philosophical topic, an exploration of the psychological potential of man; Sacha enrolled to do a master's diploma on the only slightly more modest topic of a Freudian view of Nietzsche.

The town of Aix-en-Provence, where they found a dark but relatively comfortable flat, has not changed much in the intervening years. The Cours Mirabeau (known as the Cours, pronounced Course) still dominates, with its imposing rows of massive plane trees and innumerable open-air cafés: while above the town, visible from every street, rises Cézanne's great mountain, the Mont Saint Victoire, with its abrupt and unmistakable silhouette.

They acquired a dog, Tossi, a shaggy mongrel whom they took with them everywhere, and a car, a Citroën *décapotable*. Sacha plunged into her new life as wife, house-keeper and student. She had never cooked in her life, so she got hold of some cookery books and followed their instructions to the letter. If they said one spoonful of salt and she inadvertently put in a little bit more she threw the whole dish away and started again. But her innate ability to master whatever she set herself to do and her love of making things, whether poems, dishes or curtains, led in time to her becoming an exceptional cook, and at her memorial service references to her meals were as frequent as to her intellectual curiosity or her toughness as a walker. In typically self-deprecating mode she wrote a little poem late in life which says much about the importance of cookery in her life and, like so many of her poems, leaves us wondering if what we are reading is celebration or lament:

The Cake-Baker

Each morning she awoke and baked a cake.
It gave, she said, a meaning to her days.
The cakes she baked she stored in air-tight tins.
When all the tins were filled she took the cakes
and fed them crumbled to the ducks and drakes.
Then baked more cakes to store in air-tight tins.
Cakes none but undiscerning ducks would taste.

She took typing lessons so as to type out Jean's stories and his thesis, and began to write poetry herself, in French of course, all of it lost during the war. Sacha loved driving and was usually the one at the wheel, with Jean clinging to the handbrake and yanking it up whenever she ventured over thirty kilometres an hour. In her seventies she still loved to drive and to drive fast, and, it seemed to me, my father's son in this at least, with a reckless disregard for the safety of herself and her passengers. I would beg her to slow down, as no doubt he had done, and she would say fiercely: 'I don't complain when you drive fast, do I?' 'But I'm frightened, Mum.' 'Well, so am I, but I control myself.'

With Tossi they would go off at week-ends to the still unspoilt towns and villages of the Côte d'Azur – Antibes, S.Raphael, S.Tropez – and for longer trips to the Alps. They would drive to Marseilles to take part in rallies of the Left and to attend football matches; they learned to play *pétanque*, the Provençal version of bowls; they made friends with local writers and artists.

Chief among these was Jean Giono, already famous as a regional novelist. He lived in Manosque, where he was born, deep in the heart of Provence. Apart from his father, Jean had never met a 'real' writer before, and he cultivated Giono assiduously. Giono too was not averse to adulation, and loved to talk about his impoverished childhood and the writing of his first book when, as a doorman at a bank, he would come home exhausted after a day's standing on duty and settle down at the kitchen table, his youngest son on his knee, and write. Jean told him about his own work and his ambition to write a short book outlining his views on life. 'Write it, write it,' Giono said. 'Why not call it *Lettre à Jean Giono* and I'll reply with a *Lettre à Jean Josipovici* and get Grasset to bring the two out together?'

Alas, Jean did his bit, but Giono, as might have been predicted, failed to produce his reply. Fame and fortune would not come so easily.

On Sundays they would stay in bed till lunchtime, reading Simenon and eating Swiss chocolates. If Marseilles was playing away they would tune in to the radio commentary, square off their sheets of paper, and follow their club's fortunes.

At that time too Sacha discovered the work of Raymond Queneau, which was starting to appear in the pages of the *Nouvelle Revue Française*. What she liked about him was his ability to be at once funny and serious, profound yet totally devoid of self-regard. After the solemnity, even the pomposity, of most of the serious writing she had encountered till then she found reading Queneau a breath of fresh air.

And she needed fresh air. Things were not going well between her and Jean. What Chickie had seen from the start she had begun to witness for herself. Besides his selfishness and self-absorption, he was also starting to have affairs with other women, sometimes with friends of theirs. Sacha was thrown back on herself, forced to recognise that her bid for freedom, for a new life, had been a foolish dream, unworthy of the realist she had prided herself on being. But if that was how things were, then the old questions returned: what was life about? How did one live it with dignity and responsibility?

The troubled circumstances in which she found herself perhaps explain her newfound passion for the works of Marcel Jouhandeau. That someone whose basic desires were after all both natural and simple, and who had come to think of her Jewishness as an important part of herself, should respond to a tormented Jansenist homosexual may at first seem surprising. Though Jouhandeau wrote over sixty books and was much admired by his peers, notably Paulhan and Gide, he has never made much headway in England and is now more or less forgotten even in France. His most famous book, *De l'Abjection*, was published anonymously (though everyone knew who the author was) in 1939, and I still have Sacha's copy. She has not underlined anything, but that this among all his books is the one which most deeply touched her is attested to by the fact that at some point during her time in England she began to translate it into English. What appealed to her in Jouhandeau was, I think, his fierce determination to be and remain true to himself, his feeling that God had made him as he was and that it would be a sin to try and force his nature into a mould acceptable to society: 'Were I the unhappiest of men, and should I pay for it with eternal damnation, I would prefer to be no other than myself, so impossible is it for me to renounce the truth: a hope, a memory, an emotion that I owe to it and by which I am confirmed in my stubbornness to remain in the being, in my being, to want nothing else in all the world than my own identity, my own singularity'.

Perhaps Jouhandeau's struggles with the flesh were hers as well. She never denied feeling or desire, but she never made the mistake of believing that to give in to these was the way to self-fulfilment. Her sadness at what was happening to her marriage was, I think, partly a sadness at discovering that others did not have similar views.

By the summer of 1937 Jean had completed his *doctorat d'université* and published it, as is legally required, at his own expense, under the auspices of the University of Aix-Marseilles, as *Fragments de vie interieure*. Sacha too completed her study of Nietzsche and Freud and received her *Diplome d'études superieures*, the only academic honour she was ever to acquire. Jean was busy on the interrelated stories he would eventually publish under the title of *Étrange comme la vie*, which came out in 1945 and is dedicated to the memory of his father. He felt it was time to move on. At the end of the academic year he and Sacha left Aix and bought – with Sacha's money – a house in Vence, a few miles from Nice, close to the Italian border.

Coline is a comfortable, roomy house, which stands in a large garden on the road leading out of Vence to the village of Saint Jeannet. When Sacha and Jean moved into it in the summer of 1937 they had as neighbours on the one side a young painter, Jean-Jean, and his wife, the granddaughter of that Dr. Cazalis who had been a friend and correspondent of Mallarmé: and on the other Claude Bourdet, son of the boulevard playwright Edouard Bourdet, and his wife, the Russian-born ex-tennis champion, Ida Adamov (a cousin of the playwright Artur Adamov), and their two children. It would be her friendship with the Bourdets that would save Sacha and me when the Germans entered Nice in September 1943.

In the cafés of the town they met a host of writers and artists: René Schickele, the anarchist Alsatian writer and erstwhile friend of Thomas Mann; Maxime Girieud, poet and translator of Juvenal; André Verdet, poet, painter and chronicler of the region who, like Claude Bourdet, would end up in Buchenwald as a result of his Resistance activities; Dorothy Bussy, Lytton Strachey's sister and the translator of André Gide, and her husband; and, of course, Gide himself. Learning of Sacha's admiration for Jouhandeau he urged her to write and tell him. 'Why should he be interested in my views?' she asked. 'Writers are always pleased to learn that someone likes their work,' replied Gide, 'especially if it is someone they do not know.' But she never did.

Jean was busy writing. Every morning, with the radio on – 'It helps me to think' – he sat at his desk, chewing his pen. Sacha did the shopping, cooked the meals, typed out what he wrote, drove them down to the coast. On holiday in the Alps they lost their way and endured a night in a blizzard trying to keep warm in the car. The dog helped.

I have a photo of Sacha, in white shorts, with Tossi on the lead, pine trees in the background; one of Sacha and Jean in shorts, each holding one of Tossi's paws as they try to get him to stand up before the camera; one of the two of them, most elegantly dressed, in front of the house, Sacha holding Tossi and Jean with a cat in his arms; one of Sacha posing in a tree; and one of the two of them in bathing-suits on a beach, the prow of a boat drawn up behind them, Jean looking at Sacha, who is a foot or two away and looking out into the distance. The sun seems to be perpetually shining on the Côte d'Azur.

It was not shining on their marriage. Jean had begun an affair with a close friend of theirs; Sacha found herself falling in love with a young man, Daniel Mars, of whom I know nothing except that when Jean found out he made such a row that she simply renounced him. 'It was when she had grown disillusioned with Jean that she fell in love with Daniel Mars', Chickie wrote to me after her death. 'I think apart from Jean, and you of course, who was the great love of her life, she was only really in love with Giorgio Nathan Rogers and Daniel Mars. She did not fall in love lightly.'

Why did she give him up if things were so bad between her and Jean? I asked her once but she just shrugged. It was, I suppose, just too complicated to explain. Besides, it was in the past, over and done with, there was no point in chewing over it again.

The sun was not shining on Europe either. No-one had much doubt now that war was inevitable. Before it broke there was news of Kristallnacht to strike terror into the hearts of Jews all over the continent, and then the invasion of Czechoslovakia and the German-Soviet pact. Curiously, though some foreign Jews settled in France who could afford it made plans to leave, Sacha and Jean do not seem to have contemplated it at the time. Reality is always hard to grasp.

When war finally came, in September 1939, it was, in a sense, a relief, after the unreality of the preceding years. Yet it was followed by the strange lull of the phoney war as France huddled behind its Maginot Line and awaited the inevitable confrontation, and Hitler calmly made sure his rear was covered by overrunning the Scandinavian countries before finally turning his attention to the old enemy. The result was devastating. Within days the German armoured troops had poured through the Ardennes and cut through Belgium. In five weeks from May 10 the Germans took almost two million prisoners and about a hundred thousand French soldiers were killed. A mass exodus to the South began, infecting the rest of the country with panic. By 12 June Pétain, now Deputy Prime Minister, was demanding an armistice. On 16 June Reynaud resigned in Pétain's favour, and by 25 June a cease-fire was in operation. A minor general, Charles de Gaulle, fled from Bordeaux to London and pledged to fight on, but in the chaos this went almost unnoticed.

The Germans, not wanting to waste manpower holding down a defeated country or to take the French into an alliance that would in time necessitate sharing the spoils with them, partitioned the country, keeping the most densely-populated and productive areas, the north and west, annexing Alsace and Lorraine, and allowing the south to administer itself – the so-called Free Zone. For many this was the optimum solution, a quick end to the war and a return to ordinary life. But of course for this to happen Britain would also have to reach an agreement with Hitler. Had she done so the bulk of the French nation would have breathed a sigh of relief and for all Jews living in France that would have been the end. Amazingly, for those watching events unfold from France, Britain held out. Not only did she refuse to do a deal with Hitler, she doggedly denied him the quick victory he needed. Unable to win air superiority the Germans couldn't launch a cross-channel invasion and eventually turned East to deal with Russia. A second long war, it became clear, was now in prospect.

Pétain and his deputy Laval prepared to rule the half of France the Germans had let them keep under the formula *Travail, Famille, Patrie*, a deliberate rewriting of the Revolutionary *Liberté, Egalité, Fraternité*. The Right, so long frustrated throughout the thirties, was finally in power. Those, like Claude Bourdet, who believed in democracy and could not bear to see France as a satellite of Germany, went underground.

Sacha and Jean, not only Jews but aliens, made plans to return to Egypt. They booked their passage on the last boat sailing to Egypt out of Marseilles, on 8 October 1940. Unfortunately that was the very day when, at six o'clock in the morning, in the maternity ward of Nice General Hospital, Sacha gave birth to her first child. It was a boy, as she had known it would be, and she called him Gabriel, after the poet Gabriel Gale in Chesterton's *The Poet and the Lunatic*, which she was reading at the time. There would now be no escape for them from Europe for the duration of the war.

There are six photos in the album which stand out from the rest. Their large format, the sepia tones and the elaborate signature underneath signal that this was a professional job, undertaken by a beach photographer in Nice. There are two of Jean, staring broodily out into the middle distance, looking for all the world like Gerard Philippe, and two of Sacha, her hair carefully pinned and rolled, one in which she is looking up and to her right and smiling, the other in which, her long neck fully visible and her lips set, she turns resolutely away from the camera. There are also two of the baby, a plump child with blond curls and a warm dark body, sitting on the sand in one, looking surprisingly thoughtful, the other in close-up. I don't know why they were taken or how much they cost, but there they are, a monument to the

skill and superficiality of the photographer where the adults are concerned, of his undoubted way with the textures of sand, skin and water in the case of the child.

And there are of course many snapshots of the baby: in Sacha's arms; with his teddy bear on the beach; clinging to a deck chair in the garden; sitting up in a mighty pram that looks more like a tank than anything else.

There are none of me with my father. Jean felt it was unmanly to be seen pushing a pram or carrying a child, a common enough attitude among European males at the time. (My great-aunt Pussy once explained to me that the only thing an Italian officer could be seen carrying without massive loss of face was the neatly-wrapped-up tart or cake he would have just bought, on his way home to lunch after Mass on a Sunday.)

My birth only worsened the relations between Sacha and Jean. She was more determined than ever to make the marriage work, but now Jean found it very difficult to have a rival for her attention in the house. She had less time now to type his stories, was unable to go out with him to the cafés or the cinema when he felt like it. He took to going out by himself more and more and their lives began to drift apart.

Rationing was becoming a problem. Anything one wanted could be obtained on the black market, but prices were rising steeply. My first memory is of Italian soldiers sitting on the grass verges at the side of the road and offering me fruit and sweets – no doubt I reminded them of their own children and younger brothers left behind in Italy.

Jean took off for Paris with Sacha's closest friend. Shortly after, she realised that she was pregnant again. She decided to let *Coline* and move into a *pension* in Nice.

The war was dragging on and, very slowly, the tide appeared to be turning. Clandestinely, people listened to Churchill and de Gaulle broadcasting messages of hope from London. But what promised to bring relief in the long run was to have dire consequences for the Jews of South-East France. In November 1942 the Axis troops had entered the Free Zone. Already by the summer of that year the Vichy regime had started rounding up foreign Jews. Now all Jews were ordered to declare themselves. Sacha had pneumonia at the time and the doctor suggested she wait till she had recovered; by then though the Vatican had forced the Germans to rescind the decree. Yet the first transport of Jews began to make its way to the camps in the East. This was the time when Saul Friedlander lost both his parents and Georges Perec lost his mother. I was more fortunate. The Italian troops occupied eight Departments of South-Eastern France, and they had a totally different attitude to the Jews from that of Vichy France. Despite the fact that Italy and Germany had linked their fates together Italy did everything in its power to frustrate attempts to round up and deport 'its' Jews.

Thus Nice became a haven for Jewish refugees. Amongst the motley collection of people washed up in the *pension* from all parts of France was the aged writer, Tristan Bernard.

'Dis bonjour a M.Tristan Bernard.'

'Bonjour M.Tristan Bernard.'

'Bonjour mon petit Gabriel.'

Hearing that the first word I had uttered was *ish*, he smote his forehead: 'I knew it! Living proof that Hebrew is the original language! The child said "man" in Hebrew before he could utter a word of French. Remarkable, madam, quite remarkable.'

The Allies pushed the Axis forces back in North Africa. On 13 May 'Army Group Africa' capitulated. In July and August the Allies seized Sicily and the Germans retreated to a line north of Naples.

'Bonjour M.Tristan Bernard.'

'Bonjour mon petit Gabriel.'

On 25 July Mussolini was arrested and the following day a Government without Fascist members was formed by Marshall Badoglio. Early in August Rome decided to evacuate troops from the Italian-held parts of France except for Nice and the surrounding area. By the end of August it had decided not to stop refugees entering Italy and made plans to evacuate the Jews of the region to North Africa.

'Bonjour M.Tristan Bernard.'

'Bonjour mon petit Gabriel.'

On 3 September an armistice was signed between Italy and the

Allies. It was to be kept secret until October so as to allow the evacuations to take place, but for reasons which still puzzle historians the Allied Ground Staff unexpectedly anticipated the announcement. This effectively scuppered plans for evacuation and placed the Jews of Nice in a mousetrap. On 4 September the Gestapo drew up plans for rounding up and disposing of the Jews of the region: they would close in from the periphery, pick them up, send them to various assembly points and from thence to Drancy and onto the trains bound for the camps in the East. Obersturmführer Roethke advised: 'It is necessary to appoint French antisemites to spy out and denounce the Jews who are camouflaged or hidden. Money should be no consideration (propose to pay 100 francs per Jew).'

By now Sacha, as well as having to care for a two-year old child, was feeling the effects of her pregnancy.

'Bonjour M.Tristan Bernard.'

'Bonjour mon petit Gabriel.'

On 8 September Eisenhower announced the Armistice with Italy. The Germans immediately seized Italian trains and goods. On 10 September they moved in to Nice. 'The "human hunt" on the Côte d'Azur in the Autumn of 1943,' one historian has written, 'surpassed in horror and brutality everything of this kind previously known, at least in Western Europe.' Denied access to lists of Jews by the Prefect of Nice (not all Frenchmen did the bidding of Vichy), who claimed that the Italians had taken them with them in their retreat, the Germans turned to more direct methods: they raided hotels and *pensions*, stopped men in the streets and stripped them to see if they were circumcised.

Sacha left the *pension* early that day with me in my push-chair. She had the feeling that she must be out of doors and behaving as ordinarily as possible. She began to walk along the Promenade.

By midday she was still walking, pushing the chair.

Someone clutched her elbow: 'Sacha! What on earth are you

doing here? Don't you know the Germans are rounding up the Jews?'

It was Ida Bourdet.

'I have nowhere to go,' Sacha said.

'Where's Jean?'

'He's gone to Paris.'

'You're on your own? With Gabriel? Where are you staying?'

Sacha told her the name of the *pension*.

'That's crazy,' Ida said. 'You can't go back there. You must come home with me straight away and tonight we'll get you some false papers. I have friends travelling to the Massif Central tomorrow. You and Gabriel must go with them.'

Claude, her husband, was in the Resistance, founded the journal *Combat*, was eventually caught and sent to Buchenwald, which he survived. After the war he became a leading left-wing figure, a thorn in de Gaulle's side. I recall a photo in the English press at the time of the Algerian War, of him with Camus outside the offices of *Combat*, which had just been fire-bombed by the OAS. In his moving account of his Resistance years, *L'Aventure incertaine*, he occasionally talks of his Russian-born wife and his children back in Vence. He does not say that at least two people owe their lives to her.

First they had to go to the *pension* to collect our belongings. Everything was quiet. The Germans, it turned out, had stopped two *pensions* up the street from ours, their trucks full; but no-one doubted they would be back – the Germans did not leave anything unfinished. ('But they were only boys,' Sacha told me later. 'We would see them in the street on the days before the big roundup. They were handsome young boys who simply did what they were told.')

At Ida's house all was activity: a false identity card for Sacha and for me, tickets, back-up papers. Sacha insisted she be in no way linked to me and asked, once inside the train, to be allowed to sit at the other end of the carriage, alone: 'I knew that if we were stopped and I was asked to account for myself I would most probably, despite my papers, say that I was Jewish. I felt that even though it would mean leaving you with strangers it was something I would have to do. There aren't many moments like that in life but I felt that this was one of them.'

Nowadays one can get from Nice to La Bourboule and Le Mont Dore in four hours. It took us eighteen. Amazingly, the train was not stopped. No Germans boarded it and asked to see our papers. Slowly it passed through the southern regions of France, out of the jaws of death and into the relative security of the Massif Central.

It was dark by the time the train reached Lyons, and it stayed in the station for a long time. I remember waking up and asking where we were. 'Lyons,' came the reply. I thought of lions and shuddered. I am sure I had no idea what was going on, but the fear of those around me must have seeped through to me, and even today any journey by public transport requires a bit of an effort.

La Bourboule.

The train stopped. The others helped Sacha with her luggage and handed me out to her. Then the train moved on, leaving her alone, heavily pregnant, with a two-year old child and her few possessions, on the empty platform.

La Bourboule is situated in a narrow valley some 1000 metres up in the Massif Central, the great chain of volcanic mountains that rises up to the north west of Lyons. When I visited it with Sacha in September 1967 in an attempt to exorcise for her the memory of those war years it had reverted to its old functions: long lines of French schoolchildren, scarves drawn up over their mouths and noses, wound their way from the baths to the drinking fountains, from the fountains to the *pensions*, for the mineral springs are what make this the foremost children's spa in France. In 1943, of course, there were no such lines, though here, in contrast to the rest of France, the pattern of rural life went on much as it had always done. This was the great advantage to the refugee. It was off the beaten track, so that the Gestapo and the French *Milice* were unlikely to visit, except occasionally in search of the maquis who hid in the wooded hills all around; and, being a farming country, food was more plentiful than in the barren south. It would still be expensive on the black market – Sacha was to exchange a dictionary for a pat of butter in the latter stages of the war – but at least it was available.

The first thing Sacha did was to go and see the mayor. She had decided that it was too risky trying to hide under false identities, that I was too young to be able to remember who I was supposed to be, and that the best thing was to tell the truth and throw herself on the mercy of the authorities. The mayor was sympathetic and promised to do whatever he could, and issued her with residence permits. When, a little later, she went back to ask him for a permit for Jean, who was coming to be with her at the birth, he granted that too without demur. Yet at the end of the war, when the reprisals against perceived collaborators took place, he was one of the first to be taken out and shot. 'Often they only used it as an excuse to settle old scores,' Sacha told me. It sickened her almost more than the German atrocities and confirmed her in her feeling that she never wanted to live in France again.

Armed with her residence permit she found rooms with a dour French family, the Redons. At least, she thought, I would be able to play with their two children during her confinement.

This is the only episode in her life that Sacha was reluctant to talk even to me about. I knew only that a little girl had been born who died shortly after. At Sacha's own death I realised with a shock that I did not even know my sister's name.

Once again Chickie obliged: 'You asked me about your baby sister. I think I know most of the little there is to know about her – she only lived for about ten days – she couldn't have left much mark on you – she must have seemed like some sort of illness Sacha had and then recovered from. But she left a sort of double-edged mark on Sacha. Partly remorse because she had almost starved herself to feed you and she knew she must have debilitated the baby – and partly relief because of a dream she'd had when she was only about twelve, that she was grown up and had a child of her own, a little boy, and they were in the garden, he was playing, with a hoop I think, and he came running up to her – and fell dead at her feet. And ever since she'd had you she'd dreaded that that dream was a premonition like so many others she'd had and that something would happen to you. So when Elizabeth [but can that really have been her name? I'll never know] died she felt this doom had been hers (though she was the wrong sex, but with premonitions such paltry details don't matter) and that you would survive.

'She wrote one of her best poems about that little girl – I only remember one line: "Petite fille de dix jours, petite morte pour toujours."

'The baby was born a few days after she got to La Bourboule'.

As often with Chickie, her memory is not wholly accurate. For after I got her letter I found a poem, in English this time, among Sacha's papers, which makes it clear that the line should have read: 'Petite fille de douze jours'. Its last lines are characteristic of the Sacha I knew: even at such a moment it is the nurse's false show of emotion which arouses her anger:

A Small Death

That wartime winter in France.
The bare quite comfortless room.
And the dying twelve-day-old
held in cold hands, my daughter.

I am acquainted with death
from my childhood, but as loss
not physical fact. I have
never seen anyone die.

And now I am mainly afraid
as, in the crook of my arm,
I clasp her close to impart
what heat my body exudes

until the death rattle stops.
Then: 'Prenez-la. Elle est morte.'
And the nurse, with feigned feeling:
'O, non, non! Ma pauvre dame!'

Idiot, I think. We both know
this is what we expected
since dawn when she vomited
blood and the doctor mumbled:

'Il n'y a plus rien à faire.'

After Sacha's death Rosalind Belben said to me: 'She once told me that
when the little girl died she only went on living because of you. If you
had not been there to be looked after she would have killed herself.'

I try to imagine those first months in La Bourboule and think:
if she could get through that and become the person I came to
know, then surely I should have no difficulty surviving her death.

There are two photos in the album which need to be looked at
particularly closely. They show Sacha standing up against a tree,

her hair swept back in the familiar style of those years, the strap of a bag cutting into her right shoulder and passing just to the left of her right breast. At first sight these are just another set of photos of a striking woman, but look a little more closely and you see in her eyes and the set of her mouth that something has happened. These are the photos of someone who has been traumatised, of someone who is keeping going because that is what has to be done, but for whom hope has been extinguished.

I don't know who took these photos or when exactly, but there they are, on the page in the album devoted to La Bourboule. There is one more of her, with me in a push-chair, but she is too far away for her expression to be visible. The other photos – there are not many – are devoted to me: with the Redon children; alone, in white shorts and a dark shirt, standing in a park; smiling and holding a sheet of paper in my hand; in a large whicker armchair with a little girl, on a balcony, with the sunlight falling across us as, totally absorbed, we bend over a book.

I don't know how long after the death of the little girl Jean
stayed in La Bourboule. Not very long, I think. But my only two
memories of him date from that time. Neither may be wholly
accurate. In one he stands over my bed and says goodbye – or
perhaps he does not say anything, I only have the sense that he
is leaving. The other is more detailed. I am out for a walk with
him and Sacha. We are strolling along a grassy path through a
park. We come to a pair of large wrought-iron gates. He puts his
hands round two of the vertical bars and pushes. Nothing happens.
'We'll have to climb over,' he says. This is exciting. A chance to
show what I am made of. I haul myself up and jump down on
the other side. I turn and see him pushing open the gate and
laughing as he and Sacha pass through. In my anger I bend down
and pull up a clump of grass. A blade of grass cuts my fingers.

Most days Sacha would take her rucksack and we would set off
for the farm. The farmer had six children, the third exactly my
age, so that he and his wife were only too pleased to exchange
the clothes I had grown out of for provisions to supplement our
meagre rations.

In the hotel room to which we had moved Sacha sewed and
cut, so that what clothes she couldn't exchange she enlarged. She
cut the letters of the alphabet out of wood and taught me to read.
She carved strange figures on the tops of stout sticks we had
picked up on our walks. She read to me from the few books that
were available and told me stories from the Bible: how Moses
outwitted Pharaoh: how David escaped from Saul; how Jesus died.

We moved again. In the new hotel, Sacha explained to me,
'nous aurons deux chambres comme une icante.' Qu'est-ce-qu'une
icante, Maman?'

She was perpetually hungry. Perpetually having to decide
which her body and mind needed more: food or cigarettes. With

cigarettes at least you could join up the butts of four or five and make an extra one. Almost as bad as the shortage of food and cigarettes was the shortage of books. There was one local bookstore, which had transformed itself into a lending library, but all they had was Balzac, so she read the *Comédie Humaine* from end to end. She had never liked Balzac and came to dislike him more and more as she worked her way through his grim novels in the course of those interminable months in that dark narrow valley.

She made friends in the hotel: 'There were some interesting people, washed up there by the war. There was one young woman I was particularly fond of. She was of Russian origin, had been abandoned by her lover. She tried to kill herself several times. Eventually, she succeeded.'

'One of the *maquisards* had a bad tooth. The *maquis* came into town, commandeered the local dentist and his chair. They let the dentist go when he had dealt with the tooth, but kept the chair. After that when one went to the dentist's an assistant tilted the upright chair back and one prayed he wouldn't grow tired or the chair break just as the dentist was at work in one's mouth.'

On some days, if the snow was firm, we would walk the five kilometres up the mountain to the Mont d'Or, the adult spa, and back. It was at La Bourboule that Sacha and I got into the habit of our long walks together, which we never abandoned till, in her eighty-third year, what she had always dreaded came to pass and, emerging from a series of minor illnesses, she found she could no longer walk without pain.

'Once we were out for a walk and you suddenly darted away up the side of a hill to where a large goat was tethered. Talk to it before you touch it, I called out. What shall I say? you asked. Introduce yourself. Gabriel David Josipovici, garçon. That was because, with your long fair curls, in Nice you had often been mistaken for a little girl.'

'Once we were on the way to the Mont d'Or in deep snow and

I was walking on ahead. Suddenly I realised you were no longer at my side. I turned round and you'd vanished. Then I caught sight of your cap bobbing up above the snow. You had stepped off the path and into a deep ditch.'

And then there was the radio. In the hotel people gathered closely round to listen clandestinely to Churchill and de Gaulle broadcasting from London. That mysterious country which in a sense she had been so familiar with as a child but had never got closer to than Berque-Plage, was once more playing a key role in her life. Because of England, because of Churchill, we were alive; perhaps because of them we would survive. The war was far from over, terrible things were going on, not only far away in Eastern Europe but right there in France, yet the tide seemed, to those who huddled round the set, to be definitely turning. The unthinkable was happening: Hitler and his armies were being pushed back on all fronts. Now it seemed just a matter of time before the Allies landed and France was liberated. But when would the day come?

It came on 6 June 1944. After months of rumours and counter-rumours the Allies finally landed in Normandy. On 25 August Paris was liberated. Three weeks later the Americans reached the German border. Meanwhile, on 15 August, a Franco-American force started to make its way up the Rhone valley. Allied flags were raised in La Bourboule, then quickly taken down again as it was rumoured that a fleeing German division was going to pass through. But the rumour proved unfounded and up went the flags again. By the end of 1944 the war in Europe was effectively over.

On 7 May 1945 Germany finally surrendered unconditionally. In La Bourboule as in the rest of France the victory celebrations were long and elaborate. There were greasy poles up which men had to climb to reach packets of food tied at the top, but even those who almost got there seemed to start sliding down just as they were reaching out for their reward. When the champagne corks popped I hid under the table in fear. Is that sound, I wonder, mixed up in my mind with the sound of gunfire as the reprisals took place and the mayor of La Bourboule, along with so many others, was shot?

With communication with the outside world once more re-established Sacha wrote to Chickie: 'Gabriel is, I think, turning out to be a success. The only success of my life.' Chickie for her part got some money out to Sacha, enough for boat tickets back to Egypt. In late September we finally left La Bourboule for Marseilles. The first boat on which Sacha was able to find berths was an English troop-ship, the *Arundel Castle*, due to sail from Toulon the following week. The only hotel she could afford had bugs in the beds and was so squalid we spent the days walking round the town, peering into the shops and restaurants. I remember an enormous fish, elaborately dressed, in the window of one restaurant, but nothing of what we actually ate. One day Sacha took me out to see the golden statue of the Virgin in the hills high above the city. It was, I suppose, the first of many sight-seeing expeditions we would undertake together, and now I think about it they perhaps always had the underlying sense: we are lucky to have survived; we are together; we will make the most of the life we have been given.

Finally, into a British army vehicle and the bumpy ride to Toulon.

The cabin had four bunks. The other two passengers, we were told, would be boarding at Malta. I tried each of the top bunks in turn before settling down for the night.

Sacha and I were already in bed when the boat docked at Malta. Two uniformed WAAFs entered the cabin, turned on the lights and began to dispose of their belongings. 'Look at these people!'

one said to the other. 'Sleeping in all the beds and leaving their dirty handkerchiefs under the pillows.' 'I'm sorry,' Sacha said from her bed. 'It's my son. He was so excited when we first got on board.'

Embarrassed, the WAAFs retreated to the bar.

Every day at sea there was safety drill. The boat might hit a mine at any time and everyone had to be prepared to take to the lifeboats at a moment's notice.

I found a few other children on board and we played hide-and-seek. That I spoke only French and they only English did not seem to be a barrier.

On the evening of 7 October 1945, as the ship was preparing to dock at Port Said the following day, the WAFs saw Sacha putting the few presents she had bought in Marseilles by my bunk as I lay sleeping. 'Is it a birthday?' they asked, still anxious to make up for their *gaffe* on the first evening. 'Yes,' Sacha said. 'He'll be five tomorrow.'

After rummaging in their bags the two ladies produced some bars of chocolate and laid them alongside the other presents. Not only that. They spread the news, and the following day there were dozens of bars tied to various parts of the deck and we children were let loose to try and find them and climb up to get them. So, as the boat docked in the harbour at Port Said, the war ended for me with the sheer excitement of searching and climbing and then eating this unimaginably sweet, this delicious new food.

'Faut pas en manger trop, tu te sentiras mal.'

'Oui Maman.'

'Voilà. Nous sommes arrivés.'

'C'est ça l'Egypte?'

'Oui Gabriel. C'est ça.'

III   EGYPT

Identities

Eleven years
had elapsed
when I returned
to my native land.

So much had I changed
in that time
my friends
did not know who I was.

Nevertheless
they willingly
trusted my word
assuming no doubt

an imposter
would have taken more pains
to resemble
the one they remembered.

I am an imposter.

That was the hardest thing about returning: no-one, not even Chickie, seemed to have any conception of what she had been through.

Later, in England, she would say to me: 'Nowadays when I see women of thirty-five or forty they seem to be on the threshold of life, almost youthful. When I returned to Egypt after the war I was thirty-five but I felt like an old woman, my hair was white, my life over.'

*   *   *

At first we shared a small flat Chickie had recently moved to in Maadi with Albert and the two girls, Monica, who was thirteen, and Anna, a year younger.

Maadi, where, all those years before, the Russian Vice-Consul, Mr. Vinogradoff, had lived with his beautiful wife and unpleasant little boy, and from where the two little orphans had been kidnapped by their grandfather, was built as a garden city at the turn of the century, mid-way between Cairo and Helwan. The Delta Land Company, which had developed the site, was financed by the large Jewish banking families, the Cattaouis, the Tilches, the Mosseris, all related to Chickie and Sacha via their mother. Their grandparents' money had, however, been frittered away by their uncles, and they were left with two ancient buildings in Boulac, an unsavoury suburb of Cairo, some items of furniture, and the complete Grand Larousse Encyclopédique bound in red leather, which for some reason we inherited and which lived, for the duration of our stay in Maadi, behind the glass doors of the handsome inlaid bookcase.

Maadi was built on a grid system, round the railway line which linked it to Cairo and Helwan, with the Nile to the west and the desert to the east. In 1945 it consisted mainly of villas built in a bewildering variety of styles, for the Italians, Swiss, Germans,

French, English and Scandinavians who had settled there in turn hired architects (who had been trained in France, Italy, Germany or Scandinavia) to realise their dreams. These villas were set in large gardens. A central canal made irrigation a simple matter and every garden had its plentiful supply of guava and mango and apricot trees, as well – the English gardens in particular – as a wide variety of flowers and, of course, bouganvillia and wisteria clambering over the house. Flame and jacaranda trees had been planted alternately on many of the streets by the early planners, and the banks of the canal were lined with giant eucalyptus trees. Today the canal has been filled in, ostensibly to cut down the mosquito population, but in the process robbing the town of a natural axis and filling it with swirling dust. But Maadi today is anyway nothing but a suburb of Cairo, the gardens have long been sold off to developers who have put up five or six storey buildings in nearly all of them, and a whole new city, with close on half a million inhabitants has grown up where in the fifties there was only desert and Victoria College.

*   *   *

Chickie's flat was much too small for two families and we all soon moved to a house much closer to the station and the Sporting Club, the hub of the social life of the town. A legacy of English colonialism, these clubs had only recently even allowed Egyptians to become members. I remember sensing Sacha boiling when we overheard someone at the club saying they did not know what the place was coming to, it was now full of 'ces tarbouchards'. 'Q'est-ce qu'un tarbouchard maman?' 'C'est quelqu'un qui porte un tarbouche, chéri. Les gens qui parlent comme ça sont mal elevés.'

Sacha was not alone in feeling like that. The nationalism which had been rumbling for seventy years and which had been given impetus by the First World War was now an unstoppable tide. It seemed that whenever Sacha arrived in a country that country's historical clock would begin to tick in double time. It had happened in France in 1935 and it happened again in Egypt in 1945. If the ten years that followed 1935 were the most turbulent in France's history since the Revolution, then the ten years that followed 1945 were the most turbulent in the entire history of Egypt as a modern nation: 1948, the first war with Israel; 1952, the officers' coup that got rid of Farouk and turned Egypt into a Republic; 1956, Suez. Sacha was there for all of it except the climax of the Suez saga.

*　　*　　*

At Groppi's, the big Cairo pastry-shop where Sacha would sometimes take me, I would slip the lumps of sugar unaccountably left unguarded in a bowl on the table into my pockets to show Sacha when we got out. 'Tu n'as pas besoin de faire ça, tu sais. On en a assez à la maison.' 'Comment ça ce fait. Maman?' 'La guerre est finie.' 'Alors je les remets?' 'C'est pas la peine. Mais n'en prends pas la prochaine fois.'

In Cairo too I saw my first film, *Robin Hood*. I just could not believe, as I sat in the darkened cinema, Sacha reassuringly beside me, that it was possible to experience so much pleasure, so much excitement, for so long. It was wonderful and never-ending. And when we emerged into the bright Cairo afternoon there was not even the regret that it was over, for Sacha said I could go back and see it again whenever I wanted. 'Demain alors?' 'Non, pas demain. Mais la semaine prochaine si tu veux.' We may indeed have gone back, but it is that first experience I still remember.

Naturally Sacha sent me to a French school, since I only spoke French. But she was horrified to discover that they were giving me homework at the age of five and that there were no organised games. A child who's been through the war needs to play with other children and not have to worry about work, she felt, and took me out and sent me to the little English school by the canal to which Anna and Monica went. At first I was utterly miserable. I would cry when she left me and she would find me in tears when she came to pick me up. After a few weeks she said: 'Do you want to go back to the French school then?' 'Oh no,' I said. 'But you seem so miserable.' 'Non Maman. C'est seulement quand je te vois que je pleure.'

So at the little English school I stayed, and though at first Sacha and I naturally spoke French together gradually we began to communicate in English, so that by the time we came to England and I had to pass my A-level French and we tried to practise speaking French together it felt forced and artificial and we quickly reverted to English. Today, in England, I still speak to Anna, who also lives here, in French.

* * *

Chickie and Sacha were not getting on. They had not lived together since Chickie had left the grandparents' house to get married. As the elder she had always been used to getting her own way and now, with a husband and a house, she saw no reason to change. Sacha, on the other hand, felt that she had lived through enough and had taken enough difficult decisions on her own not to have to submit to a bossy older sister. Both of them violent in their love and their rage, an emotional violence quite foreign to the Cattaouis but perhaps derived from their Rossi grandfather or their Rabinovitch father, it was only a matter of time before something was said that could not be unsaid. Albert, always emollient, tried to keep the peace, but it was clear that the arrangement could not last. Sacha found a ground-floor flat in Road 9, with a veranda giving on to the railway line. When the trains went past the noise was deafening, but it's surprising how quickly human beings adapt. Soon we were no longer even aware of the trains, though when guests came they would stop talking and stare at us in disbelief as they thundered past. There were compensations, though. Beyond the railway line the fields of *durra* or Indian corn stretched away into the distance, and on clear days one could just make out the tall masts of the feluccas sailing slowly up and down the Nile.

At once Sacha fell ill. She had held out throughout the war because she had to, and now the accumulated anxiety of those years, the effects of malnutrition, and relief at having got through safely with me finally caught up with her. The doctors diagnosed a return of her chest problems, plus general mental and physical exhaustion. Chickie was all attention, and, with the help of a devoted servant we had at the time, made sure I was fed and got to school every day.

Gradually, Sacha recovered.

*　　*　　*

The summer of 1946 we spent in Alexandria, where Charlotte, Sacha and Chickie's half-sister, lived with her baby daughter Nell, and where old friends like Joe and Nadine Suares and Joe Tilche were keen to see us. Sacha made new friends, including a giant Russian sculptor, Alexandre Naglowski, who had a boat and would take us out into the bay and let me dive overboard and swim in the warm clear water.

There is a photo of Sacha and myself in a garden in Alexandria, taken that summer. Sacha is in a long loose dress made of some dark material with large white spots, and I am in shorts and barechested, holding her hand. It is difficult to make out her expression, but it seems serene, and her hair, despite her insistence that the war had turned it white, seems as dark as ever. Did she dye it? It was not in her nature. Perhaps it is a trick of the light

or perhaps she simply exaggerated, seeing a few white hairs and becoming convinced that her whole head was white. A kind of peace hangs over the scene, with the lush vegetation rising behind us and the gentle light playing over the two figures. It is as though at long last it was possible to relax after the traumas of the past six years.

Another photo, taken on the terrace of the flat in Road 9, shows Sacha looking quizzically up and across a table laid for breakfast, me sitting next to her and about to bite into a piece of bread, Alexandre standing facing the camera and looking nervous, and, next to him, a dark bearded man who is looking down at his hands. Beyond, one can make out the railway line and the fields of *durra* with a row of trees in the far distance, hiding the Nile. Alexandre is looking nervous because he has just acquired a camera that can be preset. He has done just that and rushed round to form part of the group.

As well as being a sculptor and the owner of a boat, Alexandre was a keen amateur photographer. There are several photos in the album which he took of me and of our dog Lala on the banks of the central canal, and they convey wonderfully well the pleasures Maadi offered to a child. 'As for Sacha's other loves,' Chickie wrote to me, 'I don't think she had any besides Giorgio and the young man in France. I expect she told you about the affair with Alexandre Naglowski which I know she rather enjoyed, but she

immediately broke off with him when she got the impression you resented it – only to hear you say when Alexandre's visits ceased: "We rather miss the old fellow, don't we?"'

*   *   *

Road 9 was a very busy road. I remember Sacha waking me one morning, kneeling by my bed and saying: 'Lala's been run over. He's dead.' It was my first encounter with death and loss. But there was Sacha there to share the pain. I think it was the first time I became at least partly conscious of the two of us as a unit, going through life together, getting by in spite of everything.

Of course if I had Sacha it could not be said that she 'had me' to share things with in the same way. That would not happen for many years. But then, as she told Rosalind, had it not been that she had someone to look after in difficult times she would not have had the will to live.

There would be many more deaths, mainly of animals, to draw us still closer together.

*   *   *

Sacha took a job at Astra, the milk company. She had to be at the shop by five-thirty in the morning to get the milkmen on their rounds, but she was free by eight, in time to make my breakfast and send me off to school, after which she would go back to the shop for the rest of the morning. Throughout our time in Egypt, apart from a few months early on, when she was ill, we had been the only European household without servants. Partly because we were so hard up, but mainly because Sacha hated the thought of ordering someone else about simply because you were better off than they were. She would laugh, imitating them, at the ladies who sat, beautifully dressed, in their apartments, pointing out specks of dust to the servants, who would rush around trying to remove them.

When I was not at school the chances were that I was at the Club. Chickie had a lodger, Saïd Chaâbane, who had been an international footballer, an inside forward, as they were called in those days, in the Egyptian national team. Noticing that I was gifted he spent a good deal of time teaching me the basic skills of ball-control, passing and shooting. Even the memory of Robin Hood paled beside the pleasures of being coached by Saïd Chaâbane.

In the summers there was the pool. It must have been in 1947 that we established the routine that was to last more or less unchanged till we left in the summer of 1956: after lunch and a short siesta we would go down to the pool (I might have been there already by myself in the morning to play with my friends while Sacha shopped and went to see Chickie – but had she then stopped working at Astra's?), where Sacha would sit with the other mothers while their children trained. We had most of us been taught to swim in the same way by the same person, tiny wizened old Ibrahim with his shapeless clothes and too-large face. He put a rope round your waist and pulled you through the water, encouraging you to make swimming motions with your arms and legs. Then suddenly one day, right out at the deep end, the rope was no longer there and you had to make those movements for real if you were to get to the safety of the poolside. After that initiation we graduated to the proper coaches, who changed every two or three years and came in the afternoons from Cairo. They would drill us for a couple of hours of crawl, backstroke, breastroke and butterfly, starts and turns, ending with a few relays the length of the pool – 30 metres or, to be more exact, 33⅓ yards, since the pool, like the rest of the club, had been built by the English. There was a balcony upstairs above and cabins on the western and northern sides, and there the mothers sat and had tea and chatted and watched over us.

Sacha herself hardly ever swam, and when she did it was in a stiff breaststroke, keeping her head well above the water. Despite her history of illness she would have made a fine sportswoman, and it is sad that no-one ever bothered to teach her the sports she loved watching, especially tennis and swimming. Once, out in the desert, I tried to teach her how to kick a ball, but as I bent down to show her how to draw back her foot she let fly and hit me in the forehead. 'What happened to you?' I was asked as school. 'My mother kicked me.' My friends stared at me in disbelief: 'Your mother?' 'I was trying to teach her to kick a ball and she kicked me instead.'

Even in England, in our first years here, I remember going with her to watch the great Australian swimmers in an indoor pool in London, and her excitement when Dawn Fraser broke the sixty second mark for the hundred metres. I think it must be from her I've inherited the feeling that if two athletes or two teams are competing and it's possible to watch, then all else has to give way – though Sacha drew the line at rugby and golf and even I balk at Formula One racing.

*   *   *

What did Sacha think about in those years? There are no poems and very few photos from that period for me to interrogate. The simple business of getting by, day by day, no doubt (for we were always hard up); but probably relief too at having survived and brought us both to safety, and anxiety about the future. But at least for the first time in her life she had a clear goal: my fulfilment. When, in later life, we quarrelled and I accused her of being over possessive, she drew back, I puzzled: 'Am I? I suppose because I never had parents to be concerned for me I don't know what it means to feel that someone is possessive.' And I could see her point, and recognise that her love and total dedication were infinitely more important than the occasional feeling they generated in me of her making too many demands, but that did not nullify the feeling.

*　　*　　*

After Lala there was Rex, who adopted us and lived with us for six months and then disappeared for a month and then returned and was spotted with us as we passed a house on the outskirts of Maadi by a man who demanded to know what we were doing with his dog, but then, realising that Rex had made his choice, retreated with good grace and left us in sole possession of him. And then there was Judy, the poor little epileptic bitch with St. Vitus's dance and the permanent shakes; and, at various times in those years, various other dogs as well. Sacha gradually acquired the reputation of being 'the mother of the dogs' ('*umm el kilab* – occasionally '*umm Gabriel*). It was said that when people arrived at the little Maadi railway station from Cairo they would enquire where they could find the 'mother of the cats' if they wanted Chickie (she had forty-two at one time, much to the disgust of her husband and daughters), and the 'mother of the dogs' if they wanted Sacha – and they were quickly pointed in the right direction.

*   *   *

But dogs caused problems. We had moved from the flat in Road
9 across the railway line to a basement flat in Road 6. On the
ground floor lived a school friend, but, occupying the two top-floor
flats, were the owner of the building, his wife, children and grandchildren, amounting in all to more than twenty people. If one
of the family was ill they would call in the local medicine man,
who would slaughter a turkey in the garden, chanting spells. The
entire family wore *galabiyehs*, which always, for some reason, drove
the dogs to a frenzy. There were constant rows: 'Look, the dog
has torn my *galabiyeh*, has savaged my cap (both quite possibly
true), has bitten my little girl (not true).' All this screamed out
at Sacha by large and powerful and often hysterical men, who
towered over her as she stood at the basement door leading into
the garden, occasionally taking swipes at her head with their feet,
as she attempted to calm them down and promised to pay for the
damage, while insisting they had made a mistake, her dogs had
been shut up all day, they only went out on a lead, never bit
anyone.

This must have been when the first Arab-Israel war was under
way or had perhaps just finished, and anti-foreign feeling was
running high. Sacha always maintained that there was very little
anti-Semitism to be found in Egypt and that if you wanted to
look for the finished product you could not do better than turn
your spotlight on the French *petite bourgeoisie*. However, when a
flat fell vacant on the other side of town, near to where Chickie
had just built her own house, and she found she could afford the
rent, she moved us there with great relief.

*   *   *

Moving flats, which we seemed to do with monotonous regularity in those years, consisted of hiring a man with a cart, onto which all the furniture would be piled and tied down, and we would then walk along behind it with the dogs to make sure nothing fell off in transit.

Sacha made each flat the most comfortable and *homely* home possible. I think that is why, though we were constantly on the move from my first to my twenty-third year, in three different countries, I have never felt an exile. Never having had a country to be exiled from, I now see, each home we moved to, no matter how small and mean, was transformed by Sacha into my native country. Her sense of order and of regularity without rigidity, her instinctive ability to transform even the dingiest habitation into a place of brightness and calm, meant that wherever I lived with her was home.

On Sundays, as a special treat, she would take me to have lunch in the enormous bright dining-room of the Club, with its crisp white table-cloths and napkins, quiet, efficient *suffraguis*, and delicious food. I always chose the same dish: chicken with rice and white sauce, and the taste of that dish even today – Anna occasionally makes it for me – always brings those Sunday lunches back to me.

The other treat was going in to Cairo to buy carpentry tools and, later, the book I had saved up for every month, and to end up at the open-air Groppi's, that wonderful garden in the lee of the house where she had grown up, and where the toast came, already buttered, in little closed circular dishes. When you lifted off the lid and took out one of the four thick semi-circular slices of toast it was suffused with butter and melted in the mouth. Almost as good was the milkshake that invariably went with it, sucked slowly through a straw as the new saw or chisel was unwrapped and examined.

* * *

In 1950 Jean wrote to say he was remarrying and wanted a divorce. Sacha took me down with her to the courts in Cairo, where she waited for hours before her case was called. As we shifted in our seats in the heat Sacha felt something hard against her hip, rummaged about and brought out a book. It was, of all things, *The Albatross Book of Living Verse*, edited by Louis Untermeyer, printed in Great Britain (I have it in front of me as I write), no date, over six hundred pages in excellent condition, ranging from medieval lyrics and border ballads to John Crowe Ransom and T. S. Eliot, and concluding with someone I have never come across elsewhere, Merrill Moore, born in 1903.

Finally, her case came up. The lawyer motioned her forward, the magistrate looked down at his papers, then up at her: 'Sacha you bitch?' he asked. 'Yosipovitch.' Ah, yes, 'Yosipovitch.' Then it was over and we were out in the hot crowded streets of noonday Cairo.

Jean was marrying Viviane Romance, the ageing French film star. He was going to write films for her to act in. The papers were full of profiles of the famous Egyptian writer who was marrying a famous French actress.

*   *   *

English books were available in several bookshops – one of them, I learned not very long ago, owned and run by Marina Warner's father, burnt down in the anti-Western riots of 1952. Egypt, however, for Europeans who had always lived there, was, culturally, primarily a fiefdom of France. If you read Faulkner it was because Sartre said you should; a new novel was a new French novel. Albert had become the librarian of the Club Library and he did his job, as he did everything, meticulously and assiduously. In 1951 he brought home the work of a new writer everyone in Paris was talking about: Samuel Beckett. Chickie was more interested in Jung and alchemy and her long-standing endeavour to reconcile this with Coleridge's views on the creative process, but Sacha and the circle of ladies who gravitated round Albert passed *Molloy* and *En Attendant Godot* from hand to hand.

Sacha, though, much to Chickie's disgust, was spending most of her spare time reading the books I was reading: 'I started my education all over again with you, from scratch: from Grimm's fairy tales to Enid Blyton and *Just William* to Biggles and finally to Conrad. I wanted us to be able to talk about books together and I much preferred reading English books to French ones anyway.'

Joe Tilche had given her a one-volume Shakespeare when we were in Alexandria and she read it, as she had read the Bible during the war, from beginning to end: 'Of course I found so many of the phrases which Nanny had used and which didn't seem to belong there, in the narrow columns of print, because I had only ever heard them spoken out loud: I can call up spirits from the vasty deep. Ay, so can I, but will they come? Timon is dead, who hath outstretched his span. Some beast read this: there does not live a man. Golden lads and girls all must, As Chimney-sweepers, come to dust.'

*   *   *

All Chickie's friends were in awe of her, insisted that she was a genius, could not be judged by the same criteria as other people. As well as her mind, they admired her unconventionality, for she had had a lover for many years, who regularly came to the house for lunch and whose daughter was her own daughters' best friend. Sacha on the other hand had returned from France alone with me, her marriage a failure, her body and spirit broken by the war. Chickie naturally felt she could tell her how to live her life and Sacha naturally resented it. Their quarrels were spectacular, but they never lasted very long. In the end they were too close for any lasting disagreement to occur. But Sacha felt it couldn't go on. Sooner or later she would have to get away once more.

*　　*　　*

At Christmas Charlotte and Nell would come to stay, and on occasion Joe Tilche would pay a flying visit from Alexandria. We acquired a cat, Batlaimous or Ptolemy in the Egyptian pronunciation (which made him catlike – Batly for short), to go with the dogs. His favourite spot was the bidet, on top of the dirty clothes Sacha kept there prior to giving them to the *makwagui* or laundryman. We would come home to find him asleep on his back on the pile of clothes, a beatific smile on his face.

I had started going to secondary school, Victoria College, which had recently been built in the desert beyond the flood barrier on the eastern edge of town. During the war the school had moved from Alexandria, where it had opened in 1901, to Cairo, in the general evacuation, and taken over the Italian school. After the war the governors felt there was room for two schools, one in

Alexandria and one in Cairo. The only trouble was that the Italians wanted their school back, so a new school was built, right on our doorstep. It opened just as Egypt was convulsed by the Officers' Coup, hardly the best welcome for the new headmaster, A. G. Elliot Smith, who had until then been Headmaster at Cheltenham College (and who was to leave in even more critical circumstances, given just a week to pack his belongings after the Suez War). Like Ida Bourdet, though less dramatically, he was to play a decisive role in Sacha's life and mine.

To pay my fees Sacha applied for a job at the school. Since she had no degrees apart from her useless diploma from Aix, she was put in charge of the pre-school boarders in the afternoons when they had finished their lessons. First she had to supervise them at play, then watch over their home-work. It was rather more trying a job than the equivalent in a school in England would have been. Many of the boarders came from rich Gulf families, and there was always the chance that they might be kidnapped, either by criminals for ransom or by one or other side of the family in dispute with the other. In addition there was the hazard that arose from the boys themselves. You had to keep a constant watch over them or they would be quite likely to maim or even kill each other. One day a child rushed up to Sacha and told her to come quickly, Mahmoud was killing Abdallah. Indeed, he had him pinned to the ground and was waving an enormous rusty iron nail, long as a dagger, above his chest. Sacha tried to drag him away. 'No, Miss. I kill him Miss. He said bad words on my father.'

Sacha rather liked their wildness and fearlessness, as she always did, in man or beast, but had to admit that she was very relieved when the day ended without further incident.

*　　*　　*

When she was not looking after the boarders she would do things with me. We would go out in search of a specially malleable mud out of which elaborately-shaped pots could be made, entirely by hand, without a wheel or the need for a kiln, and allowed to dry in the clear air. At one time I became obsessed with bows and arrows and we would go out into the desert, find some spot where we could set up the target, and take it in turns to shoot. Sometimes we would go out for picnics with some of the other mothers and children, either in the shady groves around Victoria College or out to the sulphur springs of Helwan. And then in the summers

of course there was the regular routine of the pool. On some evenings films were shown in the open air at the Club. Nothing as good as *Robin Hood*, of course, or perhaps I had simply lost my filmic innocence. There were a great many Hollywood musicals of the forties; indeed, this seems, in retrospect, to have been the staple cultural diet of my childhood and adolescence.

At first I had difficulty following what was going on. 'Why is he not speaking to her?' I would whisper to Sacha. 'Because he loves her,' she would whisper back. 'But if he loves her shouldn't he be speaking to her?' Disapproving shshshsh's would come out of the darkness around us, but I needed to understand. 'Shouldn't he, Mum?' 'He's upset because he thinks she doesn't love him.' 'Why does he think she doesn't love him?' 'Because she won't speak to him.' 'Why won't she speak to him?' Shshshshsh. 'Because she loves him.' 'But if she loves him why doesn't she speak to him?' 'I'll explain to you later."

*   *   *

There were interclub swimming competitions, with races for the under twelves, under fourteens and under sixteens. Sacha and her friend Frieda, an Austrian married to an Egyptian officer, whose son was a fine swimmer and just my age, would come along in the club bus to the Sporting Clubs of Gezira, Tewfikia, Maâref or Heliopolis. Once a year the championships of Cairo and then of Egypt were held in the Olympic pool at the National Sporting Club in Gezira Island, week-long events with heats and semi-finals and finals. The clubs as well as individuals were in competition with each other, and though they had to vouch for the ages of their competitors and, if asked, produce their birth-certificates, it was well known that some of the under twelves, for example, were touching fourteen, and some of the under fourteens would never see sixteen again. When this was too blatant and affected my chances of victory Sacha would go and complain. She was always complaining about the slights I received or she thought I was receiving, while I cringed and pretended I didn't know her. But I suppose she had experienced enough discrimination in her life and was determined to stand up for my rights.

Most Europeans went to the cooler climates of Europe for the summer, but it was out of the question for us, so that the summer meant the pool. Winter meant football matches and spring tennis tournaments. Before an important race or match I usually found it difficult to sleep. I would go to bed conscious of the fact that I needed a good night's sleep to be at my best the following day, and that of course was the best way of ensuring that I couldn't get to sleep. On those occasions Sacha would drag her mattress into my room and lie down alongside my bed and we would talk in the dark about the next day or about other, quite different things, her own childhood, her Nanny, the names she and Chickie invented to make their lives more exciting, until I would eventually drop off to sleep. I knew that my friends' mothers did not behave in the same way with them and that ours was a special bond: after all, there had always been only the two of us.

*   *   *

What do you want to be when you grow up?

I had ceased to want to be an engine driver, or, if that was not possible, God, and had decided I wanted to be a farmer because I liked animals. But I don't think I ever really believed it. In truth I did not know what I wanted to be. I read everything that came my way, I did so well at school that I kept skipping class, I played with my friends and trained and practised as hard as I could to improve my swimming and tennis.

It was growing clearer by the day though that there was no future in Egypt for anyone who was not a Moslem. I doubt if Sacha had ever thought otherwise. Egypt had just been the place where her sister and whatever she had known happened to be, so that it was the natural place to return to after the war. But now? Oh, Sacha would say, he'll probably go to university in England. But that was still a long way off.

*   *   *

By the central canal, next to the club, was a group of eight bunga-lows, arranged in a square, with three houses to each side. We had always admired them when we walked past them and often indulged in the fantasy of living in one of them. One day Sacha learned that perhaps the most beautiful, which gave on to the canal, had come up on the market. It belonged to a Swiss firm, Sulzer Frères, who had used it to house their executives, but now they were in the process of building a new house for that purpose and were selling it, though with the proviso that they would be able to stay on as tenants until the other house was ready. Sacha acted at once. She sold the Boulac tenement house and bought both the bungalow and a villa split into two flats further along the canal.

But Sulzer Frères stayed on. Sacha begged, threatened, cajoled, but even when one director left another was promptly installed. It seemed as if we had bought the house of our dreams only to find that we could never occupy it.

And then suddenly they were gone. The new house was ready and ours was now free for us to move into. So once again we hired the removal man and his cart and tied the furniture down and followed behind with the three dogs and Batly complaining loudly in his basket.

*   *   *

My memories of Egypt are coloured by that house, although we only lived there for two years. Like the other bungalows it had a covered verandah running round three sides, supported by wooden pillars up which climbed the bougainvillea and the wisteria Sacha refers to in her poem. On the side giving on to the road that crossed the canal at that point via a simple wooden bridge there was a large apricot or *mish-mish* tree. The children passing on their way to the Arab school further down the road would pelt it with stones as soon as any fruit appeared on the branches. Sacha would go out and plead with them to wait until the *mish-mish* were ripe, but though they nodded sagely as she spoke they never changed their ways.

One night she was woken by a noise outside her window. She peered out and saw a white form in the *mish-mish* tree. Who is it? she called: '*Min?*' '*Ana*, me,' replied a sheepish voice, and the night-watchman slowly clambered down.

On the other side of the house, in a more secluded position, was a lawn and a mango tree and a number of flower borders. A gardener came once a week, when it was the turn of our district to have the water, taps would be turned on and the garden would lie under three inches of water for the rest of the day. Once or twice a year Ahmed Doki, the old cook from the grandparents' house, would come for the day, see Sacha and Chickie, receive a tip, cook a meal, and fall asleep in the garden. And once, sitting on the lavatory, I was suddenly horrified to see a snake sliding in through the high window. I rushed out of the house pulling on my trousers – I don't know where Sacha was, probably at work or at Chickie's – and sought help from my friend the doorman at the Club. He called over a friend of his who, he said, was an expert. Together we went back to the house, but there wasn't a trace of the snake. 'It is the guardian of the house', the man explained to me. 'It is very sacred. If you harm it its mate will come and exact revenge. It is better to leave it be.' That summer, though, I seem to remember, I was permanently constipated.

Every evening the milkman came, with his large cylinder full of the rich buffalo milk that always had to be boiled before use and produced a rich cream, and once a week the iceman came, bearing his column of ice on his back. He set it down, then hacked off what you needed to fit into your ice-box. We never acquired a fridge, though we did one fine day move from primus stove to butagas, cleaner, less noisy, but liable to blow up at any time. And on certain days of the week the fishmonger did the rounds, cycling along the streets with his huge flat tray of fish on his head. 'Mummy, why can't we have fish any more?' Chickie's daughters would ask. 'Because I've quarrelled with the fishmonger.' 'Why?' 'I can't remember.' 'Aren't you going to make it up then?' 'Yes, but not just yet.'

*   *   *

As well as Rex and Judy we had acquired Sambo, a large handsome red setter, but darker than most, indeed almost black. I can't remember how he came to us, but Sacha adored him. Unfortunately Rex was terribly jealous of him and the two of them often fought, especially of course when Judy was on heat, having to be separated by Sacha at the cost of deep and painful bites to her arms and legs. He was also even more prone than Rex was to tearing at *galabiyehs* and savaging headgear. Sacha loved him for his wildness and independence of spirit, just as much later in England she was drawn to such different but powerful personalities as Stockhausen, Boris Becker and Stephen Berkoff.

The lorry-drivers were always on the look-out for dogs straying onto the road, finding it great fun to try and kill or maim them without endangering their vehicles. So Sacha took to exercising the dogs in the early mornings, before the lorries were on the roads. She would set out on her bicycle, take them out beyond

Victoria College and then round the southern end of Road 9, near to our first flat, where the baker Gavrielides had his oven. There at seven in the morning one could buy bread fresh out of the oven and Sacha would purchase four of those crisp round rolls with a smaller round on top known as Kaisers, which she would bring home for breakfast. But she would often return with her knees and elbows scraped and bleeding, since even at that time of morning Sambo had to be kept on his lead and it is not the easiest thing to stay on your bicycle with a powerful and excitable dog at the end of a lead.

Eventually Sambo went too far and actually bit an Arab boy and had to be put down. Sacha grieved terribly. Shortly after I found Paavo, named by me after my great hero, the Finnish long-distance runner Paavo Nurmi, though he was not much of a runner himself, being small, stout and covered all over with thick brown yellow and white fur. He had a habit of lying on his stomach with his legs spread out behind him like a frog which endeared him to everyone. Even Rex seemed to rather like him, no doubt because, unlike Sambo, he was never a threat, and because he had such a sweet temper.

There is a photo in the album of Sacha with Batly in her arms in the garden in front of the bungalow, and one of me in the same spot with the two dogs, Rex and Paavo. No doubt I took the one and she the other. A warm light plays over the leaves of the trees and creepers behind us and over the stones at the base of the verandah. *This*, one feels, is what life should be like.

*   *   *

The bungalow was wonderfully roomy. Too roomy, Sacha decided, and made over the big room on the right as one came in to lodgers. A painter friend who was involved with the communist circles which were active in Egypt in the mid-fifties, asked if she

could take in 'someone she knew'. Sacha agreed, on condition that she herself remained in the dark as to who this person really was. She turned out to be a quiet, cultured and charming young woman, who was out so much one was hardly aware of her presence. One day she asked if her husband could come and stay for a few days. Surprised, since there had never been any mention of a husband, Sacha agreed. One night, soon after he had arrived, I was woken by voices at the front door and then the sound of men in the house. Sacha came into my bedroom and explained that it was the police but that there was nothing to worry about. It seems they had been keeping an eye on the young woman for some time and decided to make an arrest that night. When Sacha tried to stall them at the door by saying she knew of no 'masmeselle', she had a married woman and her husband as lodgers, they simply pushed past her and asked which room she was in. They knocked and marched into the room, saw the two people there and turned to one another in congratulation: they had netted, quite unexpectedly, for they had come only for a minnow, one of the biggest fish in the pond.

He was given twenty-five years in prison and she got five. In the course of her sentence, Lydia later told Sacha, she had lost her idealism and decided to go back to her musical studies when she got out.

After that we had a plump, warm-hearted Greek girl who taught in the junior school at Victoria College. The police did not return.

*   *   *

I had taken my O-levels and done well. Sacha went to see Elliot Smith and had a talk with him about my future. 'I want him to go to Oxford,' she said. 'There are other English universities you know,' he said. 'No,' Sacha said, 'I want him to try for Oxford. Is there any chance of his getting a scholarship? I could never afford the fees.'

She said Oxford not out of snobbishness but because Oxford and Cambridge were the two universities she had heard of and there was still the belief that Oxford was for the arts, Cambridge for the sciences. Elliot Smith promised to make enquiries and a few months later called her in again. There were no scholarship to be had from Egypt, he said, but if I were to take my A-levels in England, at an English school, then I would be eligible for a State Scholarship. Were we living in England I would have gone to a state school and not had to pay, but the catch was that I could not go to a state school unless I was already living in England and would not be able to enter England unless I was already enrolled at a school. The only option he could suggest was that I spend my last A-level year at a fee-paying school, which would take me in on his recommendation. He had been Second Master at St. Paul's and Headmaster of Cheltenham College and would, if Sacha wished, see if he could get me into one or other of those schools as a day-boy for one year. Would she like him to go ahead?

Yes, she said. Go ahead and see what you can do.

Two months later he called her in once more. He had had no luck at St. Paul's but had found me a place as a day-boy at Cheltenham College, starting the following September. Sacha had just six months to prepare for our departure.

She had never felt at home in Egypt, had, I think, found the residual colonialism difficult to live with and the weather debilitating. That was why, unlike Chickie, who has always loved the place and lived there all her life, Sacha had agreed with such alacrity to move to France when she got married. That attempt to be free of Egypt had failed, for public and personal reasons. Was there a sense now that perhaps she had simply mistaken her destination? That it was England, the imaginary country of her childhood, not France, with which she had never felt much affinity, she should have headed for? That what she had failed to do for herself she might do for me? Probably she did not think in such abstract terms at all. She was too busy trying to deal with all the practical problems her decision had unleashed. She herself had no passport, her Nansen Pass having been surrendered when she arrived in Egypt in 1945 and never returned to her; I had no passport; she had to sell two houses and spirit the proceeds out of the country without arousing suspicion, since the authorities were clamping down on the movement of capital out of Egypt; there was the furniture she had inherited to consider; and, above all, the dogs.

Friends urged her not to burn all her boats, to keep one of the houses and her furniture in case she might want to return. But Sacha never compromised. Egypt held no future for me and so none for her either. She did not know what would happen to her but she would make sure I got through my schooling and then to university, ideally Oxford. One couldn't look backwards all the time: one had to take decisions and then stick to them.

Joe Tilche, ever the avuncular adviser, told her he would be able to get the money from the houses out to Geneva, but that she would lose about one third in the process. She told him to go ahead. The problem of my passport was soon resolved: enquiries revealed that Jean had become a French citizen, so, with a French father and having been born in France, I was automatically a French citizen. Her own passport was more of a problem. She hired an Italian lawyer who had known her grandfather to try and obtain an Italian passport for her. It would cost a bit of money, he said, but it could be done; the only problem was that since Italy didn't recognise divorce she would appear on her passport as Signorina Sacha Rabinovitch and thus, since French passports no longer included the names of the parents, we would, officially speaking, not be related to each other at all. Since there was no alternative she told him to go ahead.

Now came the problem of the exit visas. Again, it looked as if history was going to conspire to thwart her plans. In July Nasser had nationalised the Suez Canal and Egypt was in a state of tension with France and England. Probably it was my French passport that was complicating things, holding us up. Every day, throughout that hot July and August, Sacha and I took the little train down to Cairo and then traipsed to the Square of the Republic, to the labyrinthine building where visas were issued. Every day we would have to wait for hours in a hot stuffy office with a dozen other applicants. Every day, when our turn finally came, the fat sweating officer behind the desk would study our papers, look things up on his files, and then announce that he couldn't give us the relevant document till we had acquired another document, for which we would have to go to another room in the building. The next day the same ritual would be played out in that other room, and at the end of it we would be told that we had to get a further document, from another room. And so it went on. Sacha tried pulling all the strings she could: my cousin Monica had married an Egyptian basket-ball champion who, like the entire Egyptian basket-ball team, was an army officer, and he had a friend, another player, whose uncle was married to someone whose father was head of the visa section of the Home Office; the Italian lawyer had his own contacts, and urged her to be optimistic; the French Embassy told us to keep calm, that they were sorting things out. But nothing seemed to unlock the door. Meanwhile, in the dingy, sawdust-covered corridors of the vast building, with peanut-vendors and cold-drink salesmen at every corner, we would come across the same faces day after day as desperate Europeans tried, like us, to find a way out of Egypt.

My father, on learning that we were coming to Europe, had written to say that on my way to England I must come and stay with him and his film-actress wife in their luxurious house in Cannes. I had reluctantly agreed, but, rather to my relief, the plan had to be cancelled as the days went by and no visas were forthcoming. The question now became: would we get out in time for the start of my school term? And even, though we tried not to think about it, would we *ever* get out?

Suddenly the exit visas were ours. Instead of sending us to still another room in search of still another document, one day one of the fat officers looked in his files, took out two pieces of paper, stamped them hard and handed them to Sacha. 'What do I do now?' she said. 'You go to the central office and they will issue you your visas.'

So now, with the two houses sold and the visas to hand there was just the question of leaving the furniture to Chickie and Monica, and, saddest of all, leaving Rex and Paavo with Chickie, who had promised to look after them. Judy had died earlier in the year, drowned in a small puddle in the course of one of her epileptic fits, and Batly must have died some time before that (I try to remember but meet only with darkness). The other dogs we had acquired, and whom we felt much less attached to, Sacha had put down.

I repressed all feeling and simply lived from day to day. What Sacha was thinking I never knew. At that age I did not even think about it: she was old and wise, she had always taken the decisions, she would see us through. Now, though, when I look back and think that she was considerably younger than I am now, a woman alone with a child, about once again to take their lives in her hands, and with no idea of the outcome, I marvel at her courage.

*　　*　　*

We left Maadi almost exactly eleven years after we had arrived, and spent the last few days in Alexandria, from where we were to take the boat. I remember a day's outing to Agami, the magical beach resort outside Alexandria, which consisted of nothing but a few wooden chalets, white sand, fig trees and sea, where I had once spent an idyllic week with a friend whose parents owned one of the chalets. Old friends of Sacha's rallied round. Joe Tilche came with us to the boat and saw us on board. When he left we waited in trepidation lest at the last moment the police come to arrest us for slipping money out illegally. But no-one came, and at last the ship steamed out of Alexandria harbour where so many years before I had dived off Alexandre's boat, and headed for Venice.

*　　*　　*

Sacha had decided that we would spent a week in Venice, since we were landing there, so that I could get to know the most beautiful city in the world, a city she had always loved. But as we traipsed up and down the canals and over the bridges I could think only of the friends and the life I had left behind, and of Rex and Paavo. I was wretched company. When mealtimes came round we would peer into the restaurants we could afford and

Sacha would suggest going in. 'There isn't any room.' I would say. 'Yes there is, there, at that table.' 'But there are already two people sitting there.' 'But it's a table for four.' 'How do you know they aren't keeping the other places for friends?' 'We can always ask.' 'No, I'm embarrassed.' 'Well then, where do you want to eat?' 'I don't know. Not here.'

Paintings and churches did nothing for me either. In Egypt one went to the cinema and that was about it. I had never been to an exhibition or a concert and only once to the theatre. I didn't know what to look for and nothing I saw made any impression on me. Of course I was apprehensive and unhappy. But it never struck me that Sacha too had lost the dogs and, as the person with the responsibility, must be anxious and probably frightened as well.

Things improved when we left Venice for Geneva. As soon as the train started to move into the mountains my heart leaped. At the sight of mountain torrents I was filled with joy. I must have known what mountains were, since I had spent two years at La Bourboule. But since then, apart from a month on Mt.Trudos in Cyprus with the Boy Scouts, when I was ten, I had not set foot outside Egypt. My body, it seemed, hungered not for art or architecture but for mountains and streams and meadows. I gazed out of the train window, taking it all in.

There were fresh problems when we got to Geneva. All the banks were shut for the local holiday, the Feast of S. Genevois (or was it the Petit Genevois? I can't remember). And because it was a public holiday all the hotels and *pensions* were full. Sacha and I wandered from street to street in search of accommodation, until a man fell into step beside us and told us his sister had a room to let. Were we interested?

No bugs in the beds this time, though the district did not inspire confidence. Sacha, however, had made her decision, and, as was her way, thought no more about it. We left our things in the room and set out to see if we could take a boat trip round the lake.

I remember that afternoon on Lake Geneva far better than all our days in Venice. Everything enchanted me: the boat, the blue-ness of the water, the little towns we could see along the shores, the blue mountains rising up on all sides. Years later Sacha and I went to Brittany on holiday and one afternoon took a boat to visit the islands of the Lake of Morbihan, of which, the guide-book told us, there are as many as there are days in the year. As we got on board we looked at each other: we had both had the same memory: Lake Geneva.

The next day Sacha went to the bank to deal with her affairs. Everything was in order, as Joe Tilche had promised. Then it was on to Paris, to see her mother's brother, her uncle Guido. I was getting more and more anxious about school and took in little of Paris except for the uniform greyness: grey skies, grey buildings, grey river, grey suits.

On 13 September 1956 we boarded the train at the Gare du Nord en route for Calais and Folkestone and London. On the boat, as we handed in our passports to be checked, we were told to wait. When the other passengers had been dealt with – the boat had by now docked at Folkestone – we were called into a small room and told to sit down. Two officials began to question Sacha. She produced the letter from the school which showed I was due to spend a year there as a day-boy, starting at the end of the month. 'And you?' they asked her. 'Why do you wish to enter?' 'I've come to look after him,' she said. 'But someone else could look after him, couldn't they?' 'He doesn't know anyone else.' They tried another tack: 'Would you like to stay in England?' 'Yes,' Sacha said. So they gave her a visa for one month instead of the routine three-month tourist visa and told her she could apply for an extension to the Home Office. 'Now hurry along,' they said, 'the train's waiting.'

It was, we later learned, the first fine day that summer. Sacha and I gazed at the fields rolling by. I think I was too numb with anxiety to respond very much. I wonder now if Sacha was thinking of her childhood and *The Wind in the Willows* and *Puck of Pook's Hill*, and feeling that at long last she had arrived (but her passport now said: one month only) at the place she had in a sense known all her life.

Later, when friends of ours complained about England, its philistinism, its drabness, its Puritanism, she would bridle: 'If you'd lived as I have in countries – Italy in the twenties, France in the thirties, Egypt in the forties and fifties – where the rule of law is never something to be taken for granted, you might not be so quick to condemn England.' And when, as happened more and more frequently, policemen were convicted of forging and suppressing evidence, she would shrug and say: 'That happens everywhere. At least here some of them get caught and convicted.'

*　　*　　*

At Victoria we took a taxi for Paddington. We were going to spend the first week in Gloucester with Pat David, my old history teacher from Victoria College, and his family. They had a flat in the Cathedral Close because he was now teaching at the King's School, and had offered to put us up till we found something in Cheltenham.

There was almost an hour to wait for the train so we went into the station buffet, found a table and sat down. It was at that moment, I think, that it hit both of us that we were in England at last. At first we just looked at each other, not quite sure what it was about the place that had struck us as so peculiar. And then, simultaneously, we both got it: though the room was full there was hardly a sound to be heard; everyone was speaking in whispers.

Inevitably our own voices dropped. 'Why are they talking like that?' I whispered to Sacha. 'Perhaps that's how they always talk in public places,' she whispered back.

We gazed round the Paddington Station Buffet. 'I think we have to go and queue for our tea,' I whispered to Sacha. 'You stay here with the luggage. I'll get it.'

IV   ENGLAND

The Cathedral bells kept us both awake that first night. And, I suppose, the excitement of arrival. Then Sacha had to get busy again, go over to the school with me to talk to the housemaster, find us temporary accommodation – with the threat of expulsion hanging over her she could not think of anything even semi-permanent. She eventually found us rooms with one of the science masters, within easy walking distance of the school. The house was gloomy, the family cold and correct. It didn't impinge upon me too much as I was settling into the routine of school, which included putting on a starched collar and school tie and blazer as well as the mortar-board we all had to wear even in town. Sacha, resourceful as ever, discovered the public library and began to read her way through the English classics. She always maintained that England did not boast enough about its two wonderful free cultural provisions, the public libraries and the Third Programme. 'How can people take them so much for granted?' she would say, and then later, as they both started to decline: 'They made all the difference to me in those first years in England, when I couldn't afford to buy books and records and wouldn't have known what to buy anyway.'

She was still waiting for news from the Home Office when, in late October, the Suez War broke out. Almost immediately afterwards the long-awaited letter arrived: the authorities had given Sacha's case careful consideration but could not in the end see their way to letting her stay in this country. However, she would have ample time to settle me with a family for the remainder of my year at school.

Sacha had a bad cold. She rang the Home Office and fixed an appointment for the following day. When she finally got to see the official her nose was streaming and she had to blow it almost continuously. 'There's going to be another world war,' she said to him, coughing and blowing her nose, 'this is no moment to separate parents and children. We survived Hitler, we survived Nasser and are you now going to tear us apart at a moment like this?'

The man got up from behind his desk (those fat officers in Egypt had *never* got up from behind their desks: their desks were their fortresses) and came round to her chair. 'Please don't cry,' he said nervously. 'I'm sure there won't be a world war.' 'That's what they said the last time,' Sacha said to him, sniffing and blowing her nose, 'and look what happened.' 'I'll tell you what we'll do,' the man said, resuming his seat and fiddling with his pencil, 'we'll reconsider your case. And even if the decision is still the same, don't worry, we'll give you plenty of time to settle your son before you leave.'

'If I hadn't had that cold,' Sacha always said, 'I doubt if I'd be living in England today.'

For indeed, six weeks later she received notification that she had acquired a one-year residence visa, with strict injunctions against taking any paid employment. 'And once you've got one year,' my father's cousin Stella in London assured her, 'you'll get automatic renewal. Especially if Gabriel gets his grant.'

So we were able to leave the depressing house of the science teacher. Sacha found a tiny cottage in the grounds of a large manor house on Battledown Hill. The owner, Mrs Tanner, lived in a flat in the manor house and let the rest of it as well as the cottage. In her younger days she had bred race-horses and one of her old horses, Denmark, roamed the grounds. We had both got bicycles, though even at the end of that year it was only on rare occasions that we were able to cycle all the way up the hill without having to get off and walk the last bit. As one entered the grounds the gradient levelled out and as Sacha cycled in on her way back from the shops Denmark would come loping forward and shove his nose into the basket at the back to see if there was an apple there for him. Downstairs consisted of the living-room/kitchen, entirely dominated by an ancient Aga stove, which was our only source of heating and cooking, and upstairs there were two small bed-rooms and a bathroom. Sacha, typically, chose the damper and colder of the two bedrooms. There were no bookshelves, so we set the few books we had on the window-sill in the kitchen. This became a problem in the Spring, when the window was open, for Denmark, ever nosy, would peer in and, in order to see better, imperiously sweep the books to the floor.

Sacha gradually learned to cook on the Aga, not an easy thing to do when you've been used to primus stoves and gas, and made worse by the fact that we had never heard of firelighters and would often find that the Aga had gone out in the night and had to be relit with newspapers and the sticks we rushed out to pick up from the grounds, but which, of course, as the winter wore on, grew damper and damper.

Yet these were trivial difficulties. Sacha must have felt a sense both of relief and of pride. Her gamble had so far paid off. Those who had hedged their bets and left money and property in Egypt had had it all sequestrated or frozen. Victoria College was closed down, along with all the French and English schools, only to reopen under the elegant and ironic name of Victory College. She had obtained permission to reside in England for at least a year, and so did not have to worry about where she might live and how I would get on without her. Now, in a sense, it was up to me. I had to try to get into university and obtain a State Scholarship. I didn't dare to think of what might happen if I failed in either of those two aims.

The school had entered me for an Oxford College, St Edmund

Hall, which I had never heard of. This was not surprising, since the only colleges I had heard of were Christ Church, because of Lewis Carroll, and Balliol. St Edmund Hall at the time, under its new Principal, J. N. D. Kelly, was trying to establish itself as a force in its own right after seven centuries of living in the shadow of its larger neighbour, Queen's. One way Kelly planned to do this was by establishing it as a major sporting college, and already it boasted more rugby and rowing blues than any other college. This was a help to me as I had always been good at sports. 'The best tennis-player of his age I have ever seen,' wrote the headmaster of Cheltenham College in his reference for me, and no-one was to know that he rarely watched a game of tennis. It must have done the trick, though, for I was invited to Oxford after sitting an entrance exam I had completed in a sort of daze.

Sacha came with me, partly to give me confidence and partly to see the place she had dreamed about for so long. The bus wound its way slowly through the Cotswolds. I kept looking at my watch. Here was another moment of decision for us, my equivalent, as it were, of her Home Office ordeal. We located the college and Sacha went off to have a cup of coffee while I awaited my turn. I can't imagine what they made of me, Kelly and Graham Midgley, the English tutor. I remember only that they kept asking me what English novelist I most admired and I kept saying Dostoievsky and they kept saying English novelist, Mr Josipovici, and I kept saying Dostoievsky, vaguely aware that something was profoundly wrong but unable, in the heat of the moment, to put my finger on it.

A few weeks later the headmaster informed me that St Edmund Hall had offered me a place, but only for 1958, as I would have been just seventeen by the following October and they felt I would be too young. Perhaps they thought I might have read some English novels by that time.

Snow had fallen on Christmas Day, the first snow we had seen since leaving France. The Davids had asked us to lunch in

Gloucester and we gaily went down to the station only to discover that in England everything, even the trains, came to a standstill on Christmas Day. That and the fact that all the schools in the country seemed to be English were the oddest facts about this odd country in which we had landed. We phoned Pat David and he drove out to pick us up.

On week-ends Sacha and I went for walks around Battledown and Cleve Hill. As Spring approached we were amazed at the number and variety of flowers bursting into bloom. Sacha, after all, had never lived further north than Provence. I must have bought a camera because there is a photograph of Sacha standing in a skirt and pullover by the old disused swimming pool in the manor grounds. There are one or two of me in the same spot,

obviously taken by Sacha. The school reports said that I would do well if I didn't work too hard – only an English school would say a thing like that, Sacha remarked. We had decided that if things worked out and I got my State Scholarship we would move to London, where I would have the chance, in the year between school and university, to catch up on the things I had never done in my life, like going to art galleries and concerts and actually getting the feel of life in a big city.

That summer, after I had taken my A-levels (and the O-level Latin Oxford insisted on, and which I tackled with the help of a crammer who told me, wisely, that he could, in the short time at our disposal, either try to teach me Latin or get me through O-levels, but not both), my cousin Anna came to stay. She had had a terrible car accident in which her fiancé had been killed and she had been badly concussed, and had come to Europe to try and recover. She brought us news of Rex and Paavo, who had settled down with Chickie and her animals and seemed quite happy, she said.

When I had arrived in Egypt I was five and she was twelve. For a year or so she played with me and treated me like a younger brother. Then, inevitably, she found better things to do with her time and when I left, at fifteen, I was still a little boy and she was a young woman. Now, a year later, I had grown up and we were once more on an equal footing. She joined in our walks over the hills and I have a photo of her with us and Mrs Tanner's granddaughter, her horse and rabbit, posing in front of the manor house.

By August the results had come and we knew that I had made it. So, with the state now committed to spending on my education, it looked as if we would both be able to stay in England. Sacha's gamble had payed off and the worst was now behind her.

Stella, Jean's striking red-haired cousin, her two younger sisters and her old mother, Albert Josipovici's sister, were all living in London. She insisted we stay in the large house in Holland Park she and her second husband, Didi, shared with her mother, while Sacha looked for a flat to rent. Stella and Didi (who had changed his name from Harari – he and Stella were cousins – to Harcourt) had built up their own wine business, which they had then sold to the Army and Navy Stores, where Didi was now Wine Manager. His great passion, though, was music. He never went to concerts but endlessly played his innumerable records on his excellent hi-fi system, conducting vigorously from his armchair, while in the next room Stella tried to persuade Sacha that I ought to change my name. 'What about Josephson?' 'But he doesn't want to change his name.' 'You know, Sacha, I've been in this country for a long time and I know what I'm talking about. Believe me, going around with a name like that could be a real hindrance. What about David? Couldn't he just drop the last name and call herself Gabriel David?' 'But Stella, he doesn't *want* to change his name.'

Eventually Sacha found a flat, furniture and fittings for sale at £1000, rent £10 a month. Sacha had already dug into her small capital for my school fees and now decided there was no alternative but to dig again. After all, we had no furniture and even if most of what we were buying was rubbish, some of it was tolerable and most of it was necessary. The flat itself consisted of two large bedrooms on the ground floor of a Victorian villa in Putney and, down a flight of steps, a coal-room, a living-room and a kitchen flush with the long thin garden that ran down to a high wall on the other side of which was the East Putney tube station. Today, like much of the street, the villa has gone and been replaced by a badly-designed block of flats. It is not only in Egypt that architectural vandalism thrives unchecked.

A close friend of Chickie's, who had been in Egypt during the war, lived not far away in the Upper Richmond Road. She had built up a thriving business in interior decorating and advising rich Egyptian Jews who distrusted their taste on how to decorate their homes. Since Sacha didn't have a work permit she suggested she come and work for her making lampshades and restoring broken-down chairs and the like. Sacha had always been skilful with her hands but had no experience of this kind of work. 'Join an evening class,' Billee said, 'learn how to do it, and meanwhile there are lots of other things you can help me with.' So while I wandered round London getting to know the museums and galleries and the city itself she went to her evening classes and then worked away at her chairs and lampshades either at home or at Billee's, where I would sometimes go and fetch her.

We had both discovered the Putney and Wandsworth public libraries, which were every bit as good as the Cheltenham one. Most afternoons we would walk on Putney Heath or cycle out to Richmond Park. All her life, until the ill-health of her last years prevented it, Sacha tried, if she was not working at a nine-to-five job, to take an hour's walk after lunch. We would turn up Carlton Drive into Putney Hill Road, past the Girls' High School and on up to the Heath, fantasising about who might live in the strange turreted Victorian follies which lined the road. Very occasionally, for we were conscious of our dwindling capital, we would go to a concert or a play. Thus we went with Stella's sister Claudine and her husband to that performance of Bartók's Fourth Quartet where Sacha told me to shut up and just listen, and, shortly before I was due to start at Oxford, to a performance of Eliot's last play, *The Elder Statesman*, at which we were both convinced the author had been present and which we both found deeply disappointing. Then I packed my bags and once more found myself at Paddington Station, but this time waiting for the train to Oxford.

*   *   *

'Here was I,' Sacha said to me later, 'having devoted my life to getting you to Oxford and no sooner were you there than you started bombarding me with letters about how awful the place was, how depressed you were, and how much you hated it. You can imagine the effect on me.'

Of course at the time I couldn't. Parents are there to be complained to, and when one is feeling cheerful one does not write home. I never once asked myself what effect my letters would have on her, only hoped for sympathy. After all, she had always been there to provide it.

Not that I was particularly unhappy. Universities are ideal institutions, so one is always likely to be disappointed in them. I had imagined long conversations with like-minded people; all I found, the time being October 1958, was excited talk about the Manchester United air crash. Gradually, though, as with the little English school in Egypt, I began to settle down and make friends. Looking back, I wouldn't have wanted it any different. If I was not blissfully happy at least I was given enough free time to discover who I was and what I most wanted to do, and the chance to stroll through one of the most beautiful cities in the world every single day.

In a sense I knew already what I wanted to do. In the year between school and university I had begun to write in earnest. I had written my obligatory first, autobiographical novel, and had had the critical acumen to throw it straight into the dustbin. I had also written a few stories, one of which I had left with Sacha when I went up to Oxford. She wrote at once to say she thought it was good, a cut above the other things I had shown her. Emboldened by this I sent it to *Encounter*, which I had started taking when still in Egypt. When, after six months, they had still not acknowledged it, I wrote again to ask them to dig it out and send it back. To my surprise they replied at once, saying they were giving it serious consideration and would let me know their decision soon. When the verdict did come it was negative, but Sacha's endorsement and the interest of the editors of *Encounter* gave me new confidence. I had always known she would be totally honest and always tell me when she thought something was bad, but I suppose I had thought she might naturally be prejudiced. Now I felt that her judgement was sound and I knew I would always be able to rely on it. Her response to that story in effect changed the nature of our relationship. It brought us closer together, but no longer as mother and son, more as two friends following the same path.

*   *   *

Meanwhile, her permit had been renewed for another year, but this time with permission to work. She had enjoyed her time with Billee and learning how to make things, but the pay was bad and she thought she might try to get work in a bookshop, where her languages would come in useful. Didi discovered that there was a vacancy in the bookshop of the Army and Navy Stores, and, after a brief interview, they took her on. Within a week, though, they had moved her to the magazine counter by one of the main entrances. This was an advantage in some ways, in that she was her own boss, responsible for the ordering and sale of all magazines, accountable only to the Book Manager, a fussy little man called Mr Joy (who went on to write a memoir of his time in the book trade, called, if my memory serves me right, *Joy of Books*). The disadvantages, however, were numerous. She had to be on her feet all day except for half an hour for coffee and half an hour for tea and an hour at lunch, which had to be taken either before or after the period 12.30–1.30, when things were at their busiest. During that hour all she could see was a multitude of hands thrusting money at her, and of faces shouting questions at her or abusing her. What seemed to incense customers most was that, having paid good money for their copy of *Playboy*, they would open it on their way out only to discover that the centrefold was missing. The culprits were most often the window-dressers, with whom Sacha had an excellent relationship and who, being paid, as they felt, far too little by the management, thought they were entitled to the odd pin-up without having to pay for the entire magazine.

The other major headache was those journals that were not sold on a sale-or-return basis. Here it required nice judgement to decide how many copies to order: order too few and you had unsatisfied customers who might desert you for good; order too many and they stayed on your hands, so much money down the drain. Thus Sacha would have to decide whether in the week to come new revelations about Princess Margaret were likely to sell more copies than new photos of Elsa the lioness. If she got it wrong Mr Joy made it clear that he was not too pleased.

The other person who felt no compunction about telling her what he thought of her was Frank the doorman. 'Don't be so bloody servile, Sacha,' he would say. 'It's a bleedin pain earin you sir this and madam that.' 'Well,' Sacha would reply, 'what do you want me to call them?' 'Call them love,' Frank said. 'But they're not my loves.' 'Never bloody mind. Just call them love and stop suckin up to them with all this sir and madam business.'

'What a strange country England is,' Sacha said when she told me the story. 'In France if you enter a shop you automatically say Bonjour Madame and Bonjour Monsieur and are answered in kind. Why can't the English do the same?'

Between Frank the doorman's cubicle and the magazine counter was a recess where coats and hats could be left. Once, when I was home for the holidays, Sacha came back almost in tears. A well-dressed man had left his coat and umbrella in there and, on returning with his purchases, had called out to her: 'My coat and umbrella – the dark one on the first hook.' When she handed them to him he turned round and held out his arms. She did not move. 'Well?' he said, turning his head. 'Get a move on, will you?' Sacha still did not budge. When he realised that she had no intention of acting as a valet he turned on her in fury, seized his things and said: 'I will inform the management of your insubordination, my good woman.' Sacha shrugged and returned to her kiosk. A little later Mr Joy came down: He would not have his staff being rude to the customers. 'I'm not paid to help them on with their coats,' Sacha said, 'I'm paid to sell magazines.' 'In this store you're paid to put the customers first,' he shouted, 'and don't you forget that.' But she heard nothing more of the incident.

In the winter she would have to wake up when it was still dark and, by the time she got out of the store in the evening it was dark once more. And in the three years she worked at the Army and Navy Stores she caught the same tube almost every morning at East Putney and every evening at St James's Park, and saw the same faces coming and going, but no-one so much as smiled at her, let alone said anything. Once, she told me, as the doors opened and everyone poured into the train at St James's Park, a man and a woman she had often seen standing on the platform rushed for the last vacant seat. The man just made it and sat down in triumph, whereupon the woman lifted his bowler hat off his head and cried: 'The winner!' Sacha laughed out loud but everyone else pretended they hadn't seen.

When she got home she was so tired she rarely had the strength to cook herself a meal but just made herself a cup of tea and a piece of toast and crawled into bed with a book. Often she was so weary she couldn't get to sleep and spent most of the night reading.

Sometimes, when it wasn't raining, she would walk in the mornings to Putney Bridge Station over the railway footbridge to get some exercise and see a bit of sky. One evening she heard a programme on the Third about Yeats at Coole Park. It was punctu-ated by strange booming sounds she could make nothing of. Next morning, as she was walking over the footbridge, she suddenly heard the very same sounds and, looking up, saw five swans flying low over the bridge, and understood.

Another programme on the Third introduced her to a poet she had never heard of but who became very important to her, Wallace Stevens. When, years later, I gave her his letters, which had just been published, she was deeply moved by his stoicism, his silence in the face of personal disappointment and his ability to remain enchanted by the ordinary and the everyday to the end of his life. A poem she wrote in the late seventies suggests how much he meant to her:

Friends to Tea

No more than two I would have loved to meet,
friendly, for conversation round a table.
But oh the tricks time plays! Space we can cheat
while time's divides are insurmountable.

Name-dropping it might seen to drop the name,
five letters long, over five centuries old,
of one whose *dolce stil* that earned him fame
still warms the cockles of dull hearts grown cold.

Then I would choose that connoisseur of cadence,
aristocrat and wizard of the word,
who yet befriends me in his fleshly absence
with voice distincter than are voices heard.

Ah yes, that Florentine, that Yank will be,
If I can wind back time, my guests for tea.

It was during her time in London, in fact, that she started
writing again, this time in English, not French. She sent me a
poem of which she remained fond all her life, one of her many
meditations on a biblical subject:

Lot's Wife

In the bustle and confusion of departure,
the excitement of leaving,
the formality of farewells was forgotten.
She went unheeding.

They travelled swiftly in the darkness, her feet
on the sand trod lightly,
but her steps waxed wearier and weightier
as dawn loomed whitely.

Wandering in weariness she fell to thinking
and began weeping
for those who unsuspecting in the doomed city
lay sleeping.

Lagging a little she lamented the lost land
of her childhood,
then, turning her tear-wet face for a last greeting,
small and alone she stood

suddenly screaming: 'All warmth is draining from me.
I am petrified with cold.'
While Lot plodded on, head bent, never turning, doing
as he had been told.

I don't know if it was those 'trods' and 'waxed' that put me off, or
the idea that my mother should be doing anything so undignified as
writing poetry, but I wrote back airily from Oxford to say that surely
she meant Eurydice. I don't mean Eurydice, she wrote back furiously, I mean Lot's wife. Get hold of a Bible and read the story.

I don't think she ever quite forgave me for that. But I was
going through the phase when one's parents embarrass one simply
by their existence and where at the same time one thinks one
knows everything and everyone else, especially one's mother,
knows nothing. Perhaps too I sensed obscurely that she was talking
about herself, about the pain of exile and the fear of being abandoned, which would never leave her till the end, and must have
been implanted in her by the early loss of both her parents, and
co-existed with her otherwise extraordinary mental and physical
toughness, and simply didn't want to know.

Now I think back on that period in her life I see how lonely
she must have been, and how her mental toughness, developed
in her childhood and honed in wartime France, must once again
have been sorely tested. And yet our adult relationship was forged
in those years: our respect for each other; our dependence on
each other; my half-acknowledged shame at that dependence; her
half-acknowledged fear that I, like everyone else she had ever
loved, would sooner or later abandon her; and the plain fact that,
because of what we had been through together and because of the
people we had turned out to be, we found each other better
company than anyone else. When Sacha came down to visit me
on some week-ends I would show her around Oxford with the
pride of possession, then take her back to my digs for lunch or

tea. I introduced her to the friends I had made, and when I came up to London with them to go to concerts of new music, in which I had become very interested thanks to my friendship with Gordon Crosse, the music scholar at St Edmund Hall, she would join us after work and then often put us up in the flat in Putney.

I don't think I quite understood the extent of her pride in me. I took it for granted and it formed the ground of my being, but it was only much later that I understood how very deep and selfless it was. She was not proud of what she had made of me; she was proud simply to be associated with me, and never ever tried to mould me into her image of what I should be like. And I, for my part, robbed her of speech in conversations with my friends, taking the words out of her mouth, often answering for her when she was asked a question. I did this quite unconsciously, of course, and she submitted to it with good grace, almost as though that was to be expected. It was only much later, when we had been living in Lewes together for a long time, that friends sometimes said to me: 'Let Sacha speak, for goodness' sake!' and I realised the habit I had got into of thinking of us almost as one person: she was what had made everything possible, the ground of my being, and I was the spokesman. Looking back on it now I wonder how she felt about this, whether there were times when she felt stifled by me, or whether, in her natural shyness, she was actually relieved.

Of course now I am doing it again. Now she can no longer speak for herself. Even though I am giving her poems and the photos I have of her, I am still commenting on them from the only point of view I know, my own. I try to see her for herself, to see her as she was, and I am both the best- and the worst-placed person to do it. It is my hope, of course, that if I simply go on her reticence will shine through, in all its quiet strength.

*   *   *

During my first summer vacation I had planned to go to Italy with a friend, but when it came to it he found he couldn't go. Would Sacha come with me? At first she said we couldn't afford it, but in the end I persuaded her. We decided to take the train to Rome, spend a week there, followed by a week in Florence and then a stop over to see her aunt and uncle in their grand house in Bologna, ending up with a week in Venice. Always game, Sacha made light of the interminable rail journey – we had decided we couldn't afford couchettes – and then walked with me in the boiling heat of an Italian summer from one end of Rome to the other. The fiasco of that earlier visit to Venice was forgotten. I discovered I was rather good at planning sightseeing trips and that I had a passion for the art of the Middle Ages, which Sacha, who had never been exposed to it, found she shared. She on the other hand knew classical Rome well and was keen to share her knowledge and her memories of earlier visits with me.

In those days if you did not drink wine or order a main course you were not very welcome in Italian restaurants, no matter how modest. I recall innumerable instances of sitting, exhausted after a long morning's walking, waiting to be served our pasta, while other people, who had arrived long after us, were fussed over and served at once. All too often we would gradually reach a state of such fury that we would walk out, even though we knew that it would only mean waiting again in another restaurant.

In Bologna Sacha was reunited with her uncle Charles, her mother's younger brother, who, after dissipating the family fortune, married a rich Bolognese and retired to Italy. Sacha was very fond of Lola, his wife, who seemed equally fond of her. Charles we hardly saw because he kept strictly to the routine he had established when still a young bachelor: he would get up at eleven in the morning and spend two hours making his bed – no-one else was allowed to touch it. Then he would dress and come down to lunch, return to his room for a siesta, spend another hour or two getting dressed to go out, and leave the house in the late afternoon to go and play cards at his club, from which he would return in the early hours of the morning. We were leaving for Venice at 10.30 and he made us the enormous concession of coming down to say goodbye – perhaps sensing it would be the last time he and Sacha would ever see each other. In Venice the Festival of Contemporary Music was in full swing and we went to hear a large number of new works, including an electronic piece by Berio which felt very strange, given as it was in La Fenice, and no performers on whom to focus ones attention. This time it was I who dragged a tiring Sacha around the city, anxious to see everything there was to see.

*   *   *

Back in London Sacha returned to her old routine: wake at 5.30, feed Ginger, the fat neutered tomcat we had acquired from Billee (our first English pet), take a long slow bath, have a quick breakfast, do the few household chores, leave the house at 8.00, get back at 6.30 if she had not stopped at the Westminster Library to renew a book or get out another, feed Ginger, make herself some toast and tea, and get into bed. I was writing fewer desperate letters. I had by then moved out of college and into digs as far from the centre of Oxford as I was allowed, which meant half-way up Hinksey Hill, and had decided that no-one in Oxford had any feeling for literature and that the main virtue of the place was that it left me plenty of time to read what I wanted and get on with my own writing. My letters to Sacha were now full of injunctions to read Langland or Sterne, and when I came home I brought her as many books to read as I could manage, for I was avid to discuss my new enthusiasms with her and she in turn, starved of company and conversation, was more than ready to follow up my suggestions. Though her work at the Army and Navy Stores wore her out, she was quite capable of staying up half the night to read *The Faerie Queene* (which she liked) or *Paradise Lost* (which she disliked).

I had given up all sport, feeling that it took up too much time and energy, sold my tennis rackets, football boots and tracksuit, and one day in Putney, while Sacha was out at work, I burned the scrapbook which she had lovingly put together out of newspaper cuttings and photographs of my swimming and tennis achievements. When she came home and found out what I'd done she was more upset than I could have imagined: 'It wasn't yours to burn, it was mine, mine.' 'There's no point in being nostalgic about the past,' I responded, 'it's the future that's important.' 'You don't know what you're talking about,' Sacha said, and indeed I didn't. Looking back at the incident now I think it was precisely because the past still had such a hold on me that I chose this dramatic and brutal way of breaking free of it. I now know that the past does not let you go so easily. Yet it was the first of many such gestures, carried out in the spirit of a Pascalian wager, and which I was only able to indulge in, perhaps, because deep down I always felt that she was there to provide an essential continuity, that her presence somehow guaranteed my past, however many tokens of that past I destroyed. It has taken her death to make me understand.

She had made one or two friends at the Army and Navy Stores, who occasionally asked her to dinner, and old friends passing through would look her up and, once in a while, beg for a room for a day or two. Once she told me an old admirer of hers from Egypt, who now lived in Paris, had rung up and invited her to the theatre. She had never particularly liked him but she went out so rarely she accepted. 'Can you believe it?' she said to me afterwards. 'He tried to hold my hand!' I couldn't, of course, to me she was well past the age when that sort of thing might even have been thinkable. And yet now I work it out, she was only forty-seven or eight, and he was probably a year or two older. A strange way to behave, but not as totally incomprehensible as it appeared to me then.

By and large, though, it was a lonely existence. She had achieved her main goal, which was to give me the opportunity to live a full and rich life, to be to some extent at least in control of my own destiny, but what was there for her to look forward to? Pride in whatever I achieved, I suppose, and the sense that it was to some extent her own achievement as well. And probably the thought that she would at least never again have to fear for her life and mine.

It may have been at this time that she wrote two more biblical poems, very different from each other in feel, but both suggesting something of what she was going through, as well as being marvelously deep readings of the biblical material:

Jonah

I am that Jonah
who sailed for Tarshish
and slept through the storm
eyes shut tight as two fists.

Death like Tarshish
was a refuge from fate.
But in my fish-belly sea-grave
I repented. I was saved
for the fate I had fled.

No man can escape from his fate.
Therefore in Nineveh I prophesied:
The destruction of Nineveh is at hand!
knowing that the city would be spared.
The city was spared. And I wept

for the terrible futility of my fate.
'Nothing is futile' said the flourishing gourd.
'See how my greenness gladdens,
how my death will distress you.' And it died.

Alive, Alive-o

I am Lazarus who died.
They buried me in my grave
and then I was raised from the dead.

They rejoiced when I came back.
The men shaved their stubble of beard
The women discarded their black.

As for me a coldness
clings to my skin
and the place stinks of death.

But it is not my flesh
alone that exudes
corruption and stench

for I've seen the look in their eyes
and I know that they too
only pretend they're alive.

I am Lazarus who died.

*   *   *

My views about the future underwent a radical change in the first
term of my last year at Oxford. Farmed out to an outstanding
tutor, Rachel Trickett, herself a novelist and a woman of wide
sympathies, a friend of Erich Heller and the American composer

Virgil Thompson, I suddenly began to feel that I might be able to combine my writing with academic work. Sacha and I made tentative plans. After three years away from home I had begun to discover that Sacha was in fact the best friend I had, the person with the nearest intellectual interests to my own, and the one whose whole outlook and way of life I felt most attuned to, perhaps because of all we had gone through together. But it was not only that, it was at least in part a most fortunate congruence of minds. It seemed absurd that if I returned to Oxford the following year to do graduate work I should spend money on a room and be deprived of her companionship while she went on living in Putney and going out to what I had begun to realise was nothing but drudgery and humiliation. We decided that if I did well enough in my Finals to get a grant to stay on in Oxford for two or three years she would give up the Putney flat and move down to Oxford, where she might be able to get a job at Blackwell's or Parker's, both of which had large foreign books sections.

As soon as Finals were over I took off for France to stay with my French girlfriend at her family house near Lille. Sacha would receive the card I had filled in and left at the Examination Schools, and which would be stamped with my degree. I would ring up the day it was due to arrive and learn our fate.

But on the fateful day a telegram arrived in France for *me*. I opened it feverishly, only to be faced with an enigmatic message: 'Congratulations dear ba stop mum.' What did it mean? What was dear ba? And did Sacha's omission of my degree mean that she was trying to sugar the pill, congratulate me for getting a degree when we both knew that only a First would do, for only that would ensure my getting a grant to go on with graduate work? I couldn't phone her, for she was out at work all day, so we whiled away the time as best we could till the evening, periodically rereading the telegram to try and wrest its meaning from it.

All was revealed as soon as I was able to make contact with

her. Yes, she said, of course I had got a First, hadn't I received her telegram? Yes, but you said nothing there about a First. Didn't I? No, you just said congratulations dear ba – what is dear ba? Dear B.A. Oh, I said, I see. But why didn't you put down First? I thought I had, she said.

Later she told me about that morning. She had waited for the postman, feeling that if she was late for work once in her life it wouldn't be the end of the world. She had heard the card drop through the letter-box and gone upstairs to pick it up, then felt her legs go weak under her and had sat down on the floor beside it. It was turned with the address on top and for a while she just stared at it, not daring to turn it over. Then, quickly, she did so, and there, rather smudgily, but unmistakably, was the stamped number: I. She was so relieved that she sat for a while longer, her eyes closed, holding the card. Then, on the way to work, she stopped at a post-office and sent the telegram.

* * *

I came back from holiday. She had decided it was time to take the dwindling remainder of the money out of the Swiss bank and try and buy a house in Oxford. But when we went down the following Saturday to take soundings we quickly found that any house in a part of Oxford we liked would be well beyond our means. So we turned our attention to the countryside around Oxford and, the following Saturday, found a thatched cottage for precisely the sum we had, in the village of Eynsham. We made a bid for it and it was accepted. The week after that Sacha went round the Oxford bookshops to see about a job, while I waited for her at the Tackley, a nice reversal of the first day for both of us in Oxford, four and a half years before, when I had come up for my interview at Teddy Hall.

She returned after some time with excellent news. She had first gone to the antiquarian bookseller, Rosenthal, in the Broad, for someone had suggested the work there might be more interesting. Mr Rosenthal, she said, had looked at her across his desk, taken another look at the name on her letter, and said: 'One of us I presume?' She confessed that indeed she was. 'Have you done anything about provisions for your burial?' he asked. Sacha was taken aback. 'No,' she said laughing, 'no I haven't.' 'Don't laugh,' he said solemnly, 'these things are very important.' Sacha was silent. 'As for the immediate matter in hand,' Mr Rosenthal went on, 'I'm sorry but we haven't any vacancies.' Both of them got up and he escorted her to the door. 'Don't leave it too late with the other matter,' he said. 'Goodbye.'

The interview at Blackwell's went more quickly. They had a vacancy and would be pleased to take her on, starting on 1 October.

We returned to London and Sacha handed in her resignation at the Army and Navy Stores. Then a hitch occurred. The estate agents rang to say the house we had made a bid for had been taken off the market. It was by now too late to try and buy another before moving down, so we decided to rent a flat while I went out househunting in the days before my B. Litt. course got under way. The only flat we could find was on the first floor in a quiet but unprepossessing street between the Cowley and the Iffley roads. How was Ginger going to manage? He had always been used to a garden. We noticed that beneath our kitchen window the downstairs flat had a roof sticking out, presumably over another kitchen. We asked the occupants if they would mind terribly if we made some kind of rope ladder which would allow Ginger to get from our kitchen to their roof, from which he could jump into their garden, and fortunately they found the idea so amusing they gave us their permission. Sacha did her last day's stint at the Army and Navy Stores, said goodbye to her friends and to Frank the doorman – 'You're all right, Sacha. I'm sorry you're going –' and came home on the rush-hour tube for the last time.

A few days later, with the furniture in storage, we left the Putney flat, Ginger complaining vociferously in his cat basket, which Sacha carried, while I carried the two suitcases we had allowed ourselves. He went on complaining all through the tube journey, but by the time we got on to the train at Paddington he had obviously decided we were not going to let him get out, no matter what sort of a fuss he made, and he had better save his breath.

So Sacha's four years in London came to an end.

The day after we arrived in Oxford Sacha started to work at Blackwell's and I set off in search of a house. Amazingly, the very first house I saw was not simply suitable, it was what I might have dreamed of if I had allowed myself to dream of such things. Along with the bungalow by the canal in Maadi it remained our favourite house: simple, aesthetically pleasing, perfectly suited to the climate and topography, and comfortable.

Armed with a key and map provided by the estate agent I had taken the bus to Woodstock, eight miles north of Oxford, walked down the hill and up the other side, and arrived at a row of six stone cottages set at right angles to the road. No. 57, to which I had the key, was the fourth from the road, and as soon as I saw it my heart leapt. The walls were several feet thick, there was a stone cellar with a large domed ceiling, large flagstones in the two downstairs rooms, broad and solid beams in the two upstairs rooms and the attic. And it was only just over half the price of the Eynsham house. I got the next bus back to Oxford, asked the agent if we could keep the key overnight, and went round to Blackwell's to tell Sacha. She agreed that the best thing would be for her to come out with me to see it as soon as her day's work was over.

On the way out I tried to describe it to her, and of course wondered if I had overlooked some crucial drawback which she would spot right away. But no. Her response was as enthusiastic as mine. We explored it more thoroughly and debated about what work might need doing before we moved in. We tracked down a builder in the village and he agreed to come straight over and give us some estimates. Yes, he said, he knew the house, had even played in a band that used to meet in the domed cellar when he was young.

While he and Sacha were discussing what needed to be done I strolled up to a little gate set in a high wall, just yards from the house, went through and found myself in a huge park, with a stretch of water glinting below me in the evening light. I rushed back to the house: 'There's a park with a big pond in it just yards away!' 'Pond!' said the builder scathingly. 'That's Blenheim Park and that's the lake that is. Right on your doorstep. And that there gate's free, for the villagers, not like the other in the town, see?'

Even without Blenheim Park as our back garden the cottage filled us with joy. And this time there were no hitches. Before Christmas we were able to move in, Ginger and all. The actual back yard ran along the row of three cottages nearest the Park, and in our part of it an outside lavatory still stood, though a bathroom had been installed inside. We removed the lavatory and fenced off our portion, and Ginger was able to step straight out of the kitchen into his very own garden.

Things were not going too well at Blackwell's, though. Sacha found herself caught in a power struggle between one of Sir Basil's sons and the head of the foreign books section. She also found the paternalism of the establishment barely more congenial than the capitalist ethos of the Army and Navy Stores. On Christmas Eve, for example, all the staff were told that they should line up and shake Sir Basil's hand and wish him a happy Christmas. 'After he shakes hands with you you will be given a pound,' Sacha was told. She laughed in disbelief, but it was no joke. Moreover, to ensure that no-one came round twice and thus doubled their

Christmas bonus, senior staff were posted to keep a look-out. 'Unbelievable,' Sacha said.

In the New Year tension in the department got really bad. Sacha walked across the street to see if there might be a job at Parker's. She was interviewed by the head of the foreign languages department, Mr Braun, a remarkably cultured and intelligent Viennese Jew, who explained that the actual shop was closing for refurbishment but that they would be moving to Walton Street where they would continue to do mail-order business, and he did indeed require an assistant. A few weeks later she moved into her new job.

As soon as we had moved down to Oxford I had started to invite my old tutors to meet Sacha. Rachel Trickett was the first to come to dinner, had three helpings of the first course and then exclaimed in amazement when Sacha brought in the main course. 'I made such a fool of myself,' she said to me later. 'I had no idea there was another course coming. I wasn't yet used to Sacha's generous hospitality and only taken with how delicious the pasta was.' Two of my tutors from Teddy Hall also came, Graham Midgley, who had interviewed me all those years before, and the young American research fellow, Del Kolve, who had taught me in my first term and fired me with his passion for the Middle Ages. In Woodstock Graham and Del, who were both six foot, had to bend as they entered so as not to crack their heads on the lintel, and after lunch on Sundays we would all go into the Park by the little gate and walk round the lake and talk. When there were no guests Sacha and I would go for longer walks, right round the extensive grounds of the Park, or out into the surrounding country, or we would cycle out into the Cotswolds, stopping to look at churches as we went. Sacha would cycle to work on Monday mornings, for there was an excellent bicycle track all the way from Woodstock to the outskirts of Oxford, leave the bicycle there to do her shopping in her lunch break during the week, and then cycle back on Friday evenings. The other days she would walk through the Park and out by the main gate and along the High Street past the wooden stocks to the bus stop. Where on the London underground no-one ever spoke to anyone, here in the country she quickly made friends with most of the regular bus-users. A little boy who got off at the Catholic school half-way to Oxford became her special friend. If he was there first he would keep a place for her, and spend the journey telling her his views on life. 'The trouble with the Popes,' he told her once, 'is they're so old. They should elect a young pope and then you'd see the changes.'

I was not getting on too well with my B. Litt. Much as I had enjoyed my time as an undergraduate, I found being a graduate a miserable affair. Partly this was built into the situation: one is between worlds, no longer simply getting through weekly assign-ments in a carefree way, but not doing any meaningful job either. One swings from feeling that one has all the time in the world to feeling that one will never have enough time to do all the reading that needs to be done even if one worked all day and all night. But the Oxford set-up didn't help. Helen Gardner's notion of a research student was of a budding professional who had to be trained to enter the inner sanctum. I had never thought of reading and talking about books as entering a profession and was horrified at what I was experiencing. However, Woodstock helped put all that behind me. I loved walking the grounds of Blenheim, shop-ping for the evening meal which Sacha would cook when she got home, talking to her about my day and hearing about hers and then, after supper, sitting in front of the log fire – 'villagers' had collecting rights in the Park, we discovered – and reading or listening to concerts on the radio.

And we acquired our second pet. Or rather, as with Rex in Maadi, a pet decided we were the right people to settle in with. We had been for a walk to the village of Wootton and were passing a farmhouse when a little long-haired black cat ran along the wall, jumped off and rubbed itself against our legs. We put it back on the wall and resumed our walk. But the following week-end, having decided to repeat the walk, the little cat appeared again. This time though, as we were talking to it, a lady came out of the house and called out: 'Do you want him?' 'No thank you,' we shouted back, 'we've got one of our own.' 'He's not mine,' she shouted. 'Some people came in a car last week and left him here.' 'No thanks,' we said again, slightly shaken by this information, and walked resolutely on. But the cat had other ideas. He jumped off the wall and began to follow us, rubbing up against our legs, skipping away when we bent down to pick him up, but never straying too far from us. We turned off the road and into the field that ran along the stream that eventually fell into the lake in Blenheim Park. The cat came with us. It was a mile and a half back to Woodstock and we kept expecting him to lose interest and go back, but he stuck to us. At the main road I stooped and picked him up, and this time he purred happily. Ginger, however, was not so pleased. He took one look at our new acquisition and hunched his back, spitting. But his heart didn't seem to be in it, as though he too recognised a *fait accompli*. The assurance of the little cat was astonishing. He sniffed carefully round the house, then lapped up a bowl of milk, waited for Sacha to sit down and jumped on to her lap, purring. Within a few days Ginger had reluctantly accepted him, or rather her, for we gradually realised that we not only had a female on our hands, but a pregnant one at that.

One Sunday, not long after, Graham Midgley came to lunch. As he was sitting in the front room after lunch he suddenly said: 'A cat has just flown past your window.' We rushed out into the front garden and there was Miss Black, as we had come to call her, after the English teacher at the little English school by the canal in Egypt, slightly winded but otherwise unscathed. It was typical of her that, having found herself shut up in an upstairs room by mistake, she didn't howl or scratch but leapt onto the sill of the open window and then jumped out.

No sooner had Graham left than she went into labour and gave birth to two kittens. I persuaded Graham that the Teddy Hall kitchens needed mousers, and though one ran away the other went on to win a prize for the best working cat in Oxford, a term designating not so much the doing of work as the non-domestic category. Miss Black, however, went on to have many more kittens before Sacha finally accepted that she should be spayed. We had found it harder and harder to find homes for them and eventually ended up with two of them, a magnificent tiger-like creature called Squeaky because of his unfortunate voice, whom Sacha loved as she always did the wild and handsome animals we acquired, and a rather retarded little creature no-one wanted. Miss Black would bring in live shrews from the Park for them to play with, spitting at us furiously if we tried to rescue them. Ginger, who, if he accepted her, was nonetheless extremely jealous of her, would sometimes amuse himself by patting a ping-pong ball round the room, getting more and more excited as he began to lose control of it, his face getting squarer and squarer, his whiskers straighter and straighter till the moment came when, abandoning the ball altogether, he would rush after her and pummel her as he had been doing with the ball, then quickly retreat into a corner with a sheepish look on his face as she screamed and fled.

The winter of 1962–3 was one of the worst this century. Already in November, as we walked through the Park, we could see the cobwebs frozen on the branches of the trees. On New Years' Day we came downstairs and found, when we opened the front door, that three feet of snow had piled up on the outside. The following day, when Sacha went down to work, she had to wait almost an hour for a bus and arrived frozen at Parker's. The snow hardened and the weather just kept getting colder. 'You want to have a run round the Park before your breakfast,' Sacha's little friend advised her on the bus. The lake froze over and Graham would come out and skate on it, a strange eighteenth century figure in his dog-collar. I had acquired a scooter and would make my way gingerly down to the Bodleian and then sometimes give Sacha a lift back in the evenings. Though it was bitterly cold on the back of the scooter she preferred it to waiting interminably for the bus.

Meanwhile, we had both become British. September 1961 marked five years since we had arrived in England. Every year we had had to go and register at the local police station, and every year Sacha had to apply to have her visa renewed. After five years we could apply for British nationality. A policeman came round shortly after we had done so and asked Sacha if she could read and write in English. She laughed. 'Don't laugh,' he said, 'if you can't they won't give you a passport.' When the moment came we had to swear allegiance to the Queen on the Bible and Sacha surprised me by asking for a Hebrew Bible or at least an Old Testament without the New. I had not realised she felt so strongly about these things.

I had started applying for all the academic jobs that were advertised. I was interviewed for a number of Junior Research Fellowships at Oxford and it was made clear to me that I was both ignorant and confused. I also went to the new University of York for an interview in thick fog, and didn't enjoy the experience, and then to the new University of Sussex, whose syllabus had immediately appealed to me, and where, at the interview, for the first time, I felt I was not so much being tested as invited to take part in an interesting intellectual discussion. I knew at once that this was where I wanted to be, and knew that I would feel even more depressed than I had been in the other instances if I didn't get the job.

I needn't have worried. A week later a letter arrived saying I had been offered the job. I rushed round to tell Graham the good news, then leapt on to my scooter and hared round to Walton Street. 'I've got it!' I said to Sacha. 'Sussex have offered me a job!' For both of us it was the end of long years of anxiety.

When I went down to Sussex to have a talk with David Daiches he asked me how my research was going. 'Not too well,' I said, 'I don't think I'm cut out to be a scholar.' 'Do you think there's a book there somewhere?' asked David. 'There might be,' I said. 'Don't worry then,' he said, 'you'll have plenty to do preparing for our courses here.'

So it came about that by the middle of that freezing February I had to all intents and purposes said goodbye to Oxford. My supervisor tried to persuade me to finish my B. Litt., but I could see no point in it. Sacha too, who hated to see anything left unfinished, since it smacked to her too much of the easygoing attitudes of people in Egypt, which had always driven her to distraction, tried to persuade me to complete it. In later years she admitted I had been right to trust my instincts and go my own way. 'When it comes to decisions about your work you usually seem to make the right choices,' she said. 'I'm not so sure about your personal life.'

She told Mr Braun that she would be leaving at the end of the academic year. We had decided to let the cottage till we saw what the housing situation was like in Sussex. I wrote to the University Lodgings Bureau and said I was looking for rented accommodation for a year for myself, four cats, a rabbit (the gift of a friend who had decided the grass Sacha had sown in our little back yard needed cropping) and a mother. When I met the Lodgings Officer at a party the following year she told me my letter had led to much mirth in the office, but I felt I was only stating the facts.

177

We had come down to Brighton, armed with lists supplied by the Lodgings Office, and eventually found a hideously furnished bungalow in Rottingdean, with breathtaking views of the sea and clocks in every room. The owner was letting it cheaply for the winter months, and we agreed to be out by the end of June.

The fact that I now had a job meant that we could afford a car. We bought a fourth-hand mini and I learned to drive. I passed my test just in time and we bundled the rabbit and the cats into the car and set off on the three-hour drive to Brighton. It was now almost exactly seven years since that sunny day when we had landed at Folkestone.

The first thing that happened when we got to Rottingdean was that Squeaky vanished. Had he, in his independent way, tried to get back to Woodstock? Was he seized by a fox as he explored his new garden? (We saw a number of foxes in and around the village that winter). Sacha mourned him silently, as she had Bimbo.

Then, barely a couple of days after I started teaching, my American girlfriend wrote to say she could not bear being at Johns Hopkins, where she had just started as a graduate student, that she was handing back her grant and coming to England on the next boat. At Southampton, where she arrived a week or two later, they gave her a month's visa. The only way to resolve the mess her life seemed suddenly to have fallen into seemed to be to get married. We both tried to pretend that once we were married things would sort themselves out, but I resented her for having, as I saw it, forced this upon me, and she felt my resentment and grew even more wretched. Getting married solved nothing. On the contrary, it made matters worse. I tried to pretend that nothing had happened and get on with my new job; she, with nothing to do, bereft of the academic work which meant so much to her, grew desperate. She decided to go and stay with friends in Rome for a while to see if distance would bring clarity, and when there she tried to trace my father, who had divorced Viviane Romance and was said to be working for a film studio in Rome, though letters sent there by his aunt in London were returned with 'not known at this address' on them. She had no success. On her return, since matters had not improved between us, she decided to go back to the States. Fortunately everything worked out for her. She was given back her grant, she moved from Johns Hopkins to Yale, where she had been advised to go from the start, and her academic career has since blossomed. My main feeling was of immense relief. 'Do you want to talk about it?' Sacha asked. 'I don't know,' I said, 'I just want to resume my life.' Later she said: 'I should have told you not to rush into it, but I felt I had no business meddling. Besides, what son would listen to a mother saying that?' Of course she must have wondered if things would have turned out differently if she had not been there, but I doubt if they would. At best we would have struggled on for a few more months and then most probably parted much more acrimoniously than we did.

At the end of the year we left the hideous bungalow in Rotting-dean and moved to a university-owned house in the village of Kingston near Lewes. The core of the village was charming, 'nestling at the foot of the South Downs', as the estate agent jargon had it, but the university houses were part of a newly-built estate carved out of what had once been an apple orchard. The open plan design of the houses and the total lack of trees meant that one felt one was on show all the time, and I found it trying to see the same faces when I got home as I had seen all day at the university. At least Sacha got to know the wives and children of some of my colleagues. Delegations of children would arrive demanding to see Cobweb, the angora rabbit, and Sacha would then show them the scratches he had made on her arms as she tried to comb him. But he was a terrible nuisance, always escaping and getting into the neighbours' gardens and eating their lettuces. One morning as I tore after him across one garden after another

I saw one of the neighbours at the window aiming a gun at us. Cobweb, however, was undeterred.

Sacha and I laid turfs on the enormous expanse of back garden, backbreaking labour and the start, she later said, of the arthritis which, in her last years, made it almost impossible for her to hold a pen. We walked over Kingston Hill and across the ridge to Lewes, two miles away. Sacha would often walk there to do her shopping, have a cup of coffee and then walk back. She had also taken her driving test when we were in Rottingdean, not having driven since before the war in France, when going over thirty kilometres an hour was considered daring and if you saw another car you waved. There were rather more cars about now and the hills and roundabouts of Brighton were not the easiest course on which to pass a test, but the examiner grudgingly acknowledged at the end that she had passed – but only just, he said. 'That's all I want,' Sacha said.

We had had Ginger since the first years in Putney and no-one knew what age he was when we had got him. Now he fell ill, wouldn't eat, his fur lost its shine, and died. We buried him in the garden and then went for a walk over the hill.

One day my colleague Peter Burke stopped me in the corridor and asked if my mother would be willing to translate a book from the Italian, a study of the philosopher Francis Bacon by Paolo Rossi, which he had persuaded Routledge to bring out in England. When I got home I said to Sacha: 'You know you said you'd like to do some translating? Well, I've got something for you.' I showed it to her. 'Oh no,' she said, 'I couldn't possibly, it's much too learned and difficult.' 'Of course you can,' I said. 'Besides, you'll have to do a sample chapter for the publishers anyway, so why not give it a go?'

Routledge were satisfied with the sample chapter and she got down to the book in earnest. It was a large and imposing tome, *Francesco Bacone: Della Magia alla Scienza*, written in typical Italian academic style, the author never using one word when two could be found. But she discovered that the discipline was congenial and began to get great satisfaction out of the feeling that she was actually able to do it. When it was completed she sent it off to Routledge. She heard nothing for a long time, and then, eventually, a brief note of acknowledgement arrived. When the proofs came, however, she found, to her horror, that someone had gone through her typescript systematically changing all full-stops to commas and vice-versa, regardless of syntax or meaning. At first she tried to correct the proofs, but it soon became clear that nothing short of a complete resetting would do. In fury and despair she sent the uncorrected proofs back and told Routledge that unless they restored her original punctuation they could remove her name from the cover. With hardly an apology they restored the original text. The book came out to respectful reviews and then, to her delight and utter amazement, her translation was awarded the Florio Prize for the best non-fiction translation from the Italian for that year.

By then we were no longer in Kingston. We had both begun to feel that though we thought we could live in any conditions, those of a middle-class English open-plan estate were so unreal it was driving us mad. By herself Sacha would have stayed on, for her instinct was always to get through life without complaining, but I persuaded her to move and in the summer of 1965 we found a house in Lewes. It was to be the last of the many moves Sacha made in her unsettled and complicated life.

There is in the album a photo of Sacha which I have often interro-
gated since her death. It was taken by Nell, Charlotte's daughter,
my half-cousin. Sacha is standing by the sea wall in the undercliff
walk somewhere between Rottingdean and Ovingdean; there is a
hazy sea and sky behind her, and a helicopter, just visible, is flying
off into the distance. She stands firmly there, her hair shortish
and curly, in an open-necked man's shirt and open windcheater,
a broad smile on her face. She looks healthy, weather-beaten and
happy. It is as though she had earned the right to happiness, as
though the hardships and sorrows of her life had not broken her
but had, instead, fulfilled her. In the phrase of Vauvenargues her

great grandfather Elie Rossi was fond of quoting: 'Si le bonheur m'avait élevé dans ses bras, il m'aurait étouffé, et je n'aurais pas eu la force d'étouffer le malheur.'

'The last thirty years of my life more than made up for the pain of the first fifty,' she said to me at the end. And, several years after we had moved to Lewes: 'For the first time in my life I feel at peace. I have no fears for my safety or yours. I have no financial worries any more. And we even have a car!'

Of course there were problems. There was the tragedy of Pilly, of which I shall speak in due course. There was her health. I hadn't quite realised till we started to live together in Woodstock how unrelenting was her cough. Sometimes she would pass the whole night racked by it. She would get up and take her linctus and go back to bed and as soon as she was lying down it would start again. Sometimes I felt I just had to do something for her and would get up and make her a hot drink and bring it up to her, and at some point I would fall asleep, but when I woke up she was still coughing. Doctors who examined her for the first time threw up their hands in horror: 'You need a lung transplant, Mrs Rabinovitch!'

At any rate she should give up smoking. But that she could not do. 'It's not that I suffer when I don't smoke,' she would say, 'or feel desperate for a cigarette, it's that I feel so stupid. Life just isn't worth living in that condition.' In her seventies, when we would reach the top of a particularly steep ascent in the Dolomites and sit down to recuperate, admiring climbers less than a third her age would ask her how old she was and then whistle and ask how she did it. 'Twenty cigarettes a day for fifty years,' she would say.

Actually she was boasting. She had cut down to ten or less, and in her last years was even down to five. When the cough was particularly bad she would stop for a day or two, and when it improved, start again. The house we had moved into had no central heating and we had brought along the paraffin heaters we had always used, but the first thing Sacha did with the money Routledge paid her for her translation was to get central heating installed. After that her cough improved a bit, and towards the end of her life the doctor recommended a spray used by asthmatics, which certainly made her nights more peaceful, but irritated her throat. And, going to concerts with her remained a slightly anxious undertaking. She would be fine while anything loud was being played, but if we had got on to Webern or a late Beethoven quartet the cough was sure to manifest itself. She would quickly stuff a cough drop she had already unwrapped into her mouth, while irate concert-goers cast disapproving glances in her direction and I, I am afraid, shrank to the other edge of my seat and pretended I had nothing to do with her.

Apart from her cough there was me. No doubt Sacha, whose whole life had been devoted to my happiness, was concerned about me and remained so till her death. Early on she would have liked to see me married and with children of my own, and must have wondered if she was the reason for my not marrying and to blame in any way. She knew that I too would have liked to marry, but without giving her up, which was perhaps to ask for the impossible, and why it never happened, and again she must have wondered if she was to blame for that. She explored her feelings in a poem called, simply, 'Sonnet for a Son':

Am I a vampire feeding
on your flesh, gradually bleeding
you to death, perched precariously
on your heart, on your heart vicariously
living? Am I a Pelican Mother ripping
open her breast to extract dripping
with blood her heart so that her young
may feed? Perhaps it is only among

legendary creatures that we find
such singleness of purpose and of mind.
Ambiguous humans have the power
to be devoured and to devour
simultaneously, for the human brain
makes of each human contact twofold pain.

Was it my weakness that kept me by her? Had she, in her desire to protect me after what she felt had been the traumatic years of my earliest childhood, made me dangerously dependent on her? Or was the whole Freudian vocabulary and mind-set of devouring mothers and submissive sons only a cliché by which the west had become enthralled? I was certainly the best friend she had ever had, and she, to her surprise, had turned out to be the best friend I could have hoped for. Perhaps our relationship was a miracle which needed to be nurtured rather than denied. After all, every close relationship has its tension and in her silent dogged way she must have thought that only time would tell whether we had both made the right choices and whether our lives would be impoverished or enriched by them. 'Riddles,' as she was to say in a later poem, 'are for asking. They are better left unsolved.'

In the summer of 1966 I suggested to Sacha that we drive down through France and revisit all the places we had lived in during the war. I was curious to see for myself what Sacha had so often told me about, and I also hoped that by so doing we might be able to exorcise for her the horror of those years. We decided to visit La Bourboule first, then drive down to Vence, and finally pay a visit to her aunt Pussy who, with her husband Pino, now totally paralysed by a stroke, lived in San Remo, just across the border from Nice.

I found that La Bourboule, far from being the gloomy, depressing place of Sacha's memory, was a charming if rather dark-stoned spa town high up in the volcanic mountains, filled with chattering French schoolchildren, sent there to take the waters. Even Sacha had to admit that it was quite different from how she had remembered it. We walked out to the farm where she had bartered the clothes I had outgrown for food, but Sacha was unwilling to go in and find out if the same family still lived there. In Vence though we did call in on the house next to *Coline* on the off-chance that Jean-Jean and his wife would still be there. Not only were they, they even found the books Sacha had left with them when she had moved down to Nice with me in 1943, and I put a box of them in the boot of the car. In San Remo, while Sacha talked to Pussy I shut myself up and wrote my first novel, a children's book about Ginger. The discovery that I could simply invent from day to day and not have to rely on a preformulated plot, helped me, as I had hoped it might, with my first serious novel, *The Inventory*.

I asked Sacha if she felt the trip had helped exorcise the past and she said she thought it had, to some extent. I suppose it simply made the past a little more real, and so a little more bearable, but she did not try to talk to me about my sister and I was reluctant to ask. It did establish though that pattern of revisitings which were to be such a feature of the last part of her life.

Back in Lewes I struggled with *The Inventory* and, when it was done, left the typescript with Sacha and went up to London for the day. I had no idea if it would make any sense to anyone else, all I knew was that I had at last managed to write in a way that satisfied me. When I got back in the evening I went into the kitchen where she was cooking and kissed her. She said at once: 'It's remarkable. I read it at a sitting and was totally absorbed.'

I was so relieved I found my legs wouldn't hold me up and pulled out a chair and sat down, although I knew she didn't like people in the kitchen while she was cooking. At dinner she carefully qualified that first statement, as she was to do with all my work, making several suggestions and criticisms, all of them practical and doable. Nothing she said could eradicate the feeling produced in me by her first words. They flowed through my body like waves and sent me to sleep more deeply contented than I think I had been since those days in Egypt when I would come home happy and exhausted after a successful race or game of tennis.

The next day, fired by her belief in it, I began the novel again and finished a second draft just as my term's leave from the University was coming to an end. In the next few months I produced four more drafts and finally felt that I could do no more.

Sacha read it again and said it was a great improvement on the version she had seen and a book she would always love. I felt there was no point in having an agent for a first novel, drew up a list of the publishers I would most like to be published by, and started sending it out.

So began a long series of disappointments. Sacha would wrap up the parcel and send it off and six weeks later it would come back, the letters of rejection growing shorter and shorter and less and less encouraging, until finally, with the eleventh publisher, the breakthrough occurred. Raleigh Trevelyan at Michael Joseph wrote to say everyone in the office loved it and they would like to make me an offer. The letter arrived just as I was taking Bimbo for his early morning walk, and I read it as I went. As soon as I saw what it said I rushed back to the house and thrust it at Sacha: 'They've taken it! They've taken it!' She hugged me while Bimbo wagged his tail and tried to draw our attention to the fact that he hadn't yet been given his breakfast. As with the Sussex job and the permission to stay in England, it felt like a joint success.

Bimbo. Once we were settled in Lewes and I felt happy with my job we had both felt it was time to get a dog. In Egypt of course we had never gone out to get dogs, they had, as it were, simply happened to us. But this was England, and there were no strays – or so we thought till I found Pilly. So we made enquiries and found a dog-home in Sussex. At first they tried to palm off a beautiful but rather violent animal on us. He was, they admitted, not altogether reliable, had been known to bite children, but once in a good home he might well change his character, and if we didn't take him he would have to be put down. This was blackmail and we almost succumbed to it, but luckily common sense prevailed and we said that we simply couldn't take the risk. A few days later they phoned to say there was a three-year old dog who'd been brought to their attention, whose mistress had gone to Africa and left him with her mother, who now had to go into hospital.

Would we like to have a look at him? We drove to the address they gave us and were introduced to a melancholy brown-eyed labrador. 'He's been moping since my daughter left,' the lady said. 'What he needs is people who can exercise him as my daughter did. He's a lovely dog, very gentle and well-behaved. His name is Bimbo.'

Not a name we would ever have chosen ourselves, but there it was, it couldn't be changed. We looked at him and he sadly returned our look. 'Bimbo,' I said, and he wagged his tail. Yes, we said, we'll have him.

That night he slept in my room in the dog-basket we had bought for him. His nose seemed far too long and I suddenly felt terrified at the thought of what we had taken on. But I need not have worried. Along with Rex, of whom he came to remind me more and more, he was, I think, the dog I have loved the most. And when we acquired Pilly, a giant Scotch collie, his nose came to seem almost snub. And he was certainly well-behaved, the best brought-up of any of the dogs we have had, no doubt because it was not we who had reared him. I would take him out to dinner and he would curl up under the table and keep absolutely still, though, as ten o'clock, the time of his evening walk, approached, he would lift up his head and if I glanced at him begin to thump his tail against the floor. 'Yes, boy, in a minute boy, in a minute.' With a deep sigh he would let his head drop onto his front paws and close his eyes. But as soon as I moved he would be up and at my side, tail wagging furiously, joy in his eyes.

Sacha and I took turns to walk him before breakfast and last thing at night. Often Sacha would take him shopping with her in Lewes and, if I wasn't teaching, I would accompany her when she took him up on the Downs on his longer, afternoon walk.

A year after he had come to us we acquired our second dog. I had been up to London on a Saturday afternoon in late June to see the Picasso sculpture exhibition at the Tate, and was walking down the Vauxhall Bridge Road, when I saw a dog dart across the street, run along the pavement, then dart back, oblivious of the traffic, which was sparse at that time of the day and week, but still dangerous. I crossed the road to take a look at him. He was not very big, with a head the size of his body and a rat-like tail and the thinnest nose I had ever seen on a dog. He was panting and his eyes were big with fear and confusion. I bent down and he let me stroke him. I took him into a couple of shops and asked if anyone knew who he belonged to. 'Never seen him before today,' I was told. 'But he's been running up and down the pavement and across the street ever since this morning.' 'The best thing you can do,' one shopkeeper said, 'is take him across the river to the dog's home in Battersea. Over the bridge and turn right.'

I had no intention of doing that, for the dog's sake and mine. I asked for some water for him, which he drank down furiously and then seemed to forget all about, and then for some string, which he let me tie round his neck.

I resumed my journey to the Tate. He was surprisingly docile. I had decided to tie him to the railings and just nip in quickly to have a look at the show before taking him home, but he had other ideas. No sooner had I tied him up and taken a step back than he let out a pitiful howl. People began to turn and look at us. I decided to try another tack. I asked a lady sitting on a bench in the garden if she would mind looking after my dog for a few minutes while I went in and had a look at the exhibition, but she turned away quickly, as if I was propositioning her. I tried a man at the next bench but the response was similar. Finally I stopped in front of two German ladies who sat smiling through my speech and then said of course I could leave the dog with them, they would be there for at least another half-hour. I charged round the show, somehow taking it in far more intensely than I would have in normal circumstances, and hurried out, suddenly feeling that I would emerge to find the ladies and the dog gone. But no, there they were, just as I had left, them, the dog fast asleep at their feet. I retrieved him, thanked them, and walked back to Victoria. He sat on my lap for the duration of the journey, at first following every movement made by a fat boy who sat opposite, reading a paper and methodically transferring greasy chips from a paper bag to his mouth. At East Croydon the boy got out and the dog suddenly relaxed on my lap and with a sigh fell asleep. He was extraordinarily light. I carried him off the train at Lewes and he hurried up the hill after me as though he had known me all his life. At the door I picked him up again and went through the house and out into the garden, where I guessed Sacha and Bimbo would be. As I came out, saying: 'Look what I've brought you!' she came towards us, saying – for she had been listening to Wimbledon while gardening –: 'Pilic has beaten Emerson!'

So we called him Pilic. Pilly for short.

Like Rex with Sambo and Ginger with Miss Black, Bimbo deeply resented the intruder, then grudgingly accepted him. It helped that Pilly was still almost a puppy and went on looking up to Bimbo as long as we had them both. On the Downs Bimbo would forget any animosity he might have and the two of them would run and chase each other for hours, weaving intricate patterns round us as we walked.

One walk Sacha was very fond of was called The Red Dog Walk. We would go over the Downs to the nearby village of Offham, cross the main road and start back towards Lewes along a path that wound its way through trees and along a little stream. At whatever time we seemed to go in the afternoon we would nearly always, at some point, see, in the distance but coming in our direction, the ominous shape of a huge red dog. It was always with its owner, a stout man with a red face, but always a few yards ahead of him, and the question always was: would it rush forward and attack our dogs before its owner would call it to heel? We would grab our dogs and push them behind us, certain that this time we had tempted fate once too often, but on every occasion, at the last moment, its owner would call out sharply and the dog would stop and wait for him to catch up with him and put him on the lead. We would cross each other on the narrow path, the dogs rearing up and barking furiously, and then looking back at each other and straining at their leads. Yet the walk was so varied and of such an appropriate length that we went on tempting fate until one day there was no red dog and we never saw him or his owner again.

Chickie came to stay. She had been in London in 1965 when Anna's second child had had to be operated on for a hole in the heart. The operation had passed off successfully and Anna, her husband and two children, were now all in Portugal. But in 1969 the child had to have a second operation and Chickie had come to be with her daughter. Before that she came to Lewes for a few days.

One day I had been up to London and when I returned I learned of the drama that had taken place that afternoon. Sacha and Chickie had taken the dogs up onto the Downs for their afternoon walk. At the top of the path they had seen what they thought was a wounded bird flapping about. Pilly had run ahead to investigate, then veered sharply away. Bimbo, more curious and more foolish, had gone up to it, then suddenly backed away with a howl. It was not a bird at all but an adder, which slithered away into the undergrowth. When Sacha and Chickie got to Bimbo he was rubbing his nose furiously with his paws and crying out plaintively. They examined him and at first could see nothing, then made out two little red marks, one on either side of his shiny black nose. 'Stay here with him,' Sacha said to Chickie, 'he mustn't move or the poison will spread, I'll run back and get the car.' 'No no,' said Chickie, terrified that Sacha's dog might die on her, 'it's good for them to walk.' So they dragged and cajoled Bimbo, whose nose had by this time swollen to the size of a tennis ball, back to the house. Sacha rang the vet who said to wrap him up in a blanket and bring him straight round, she would get a serum ready and inject him as soon as he arrived. By the time they got him back home he was asleep in his basket, the swelling had subsided slightly, and there was hope that he would survive. But both Sacha and Chickie were very shaken.

He did indeed survive, but, though we did not realise it at the time, the shock had affected his heart. A few months later he began to slow down and within two years he was dead.

Anna's little boy died under the second operation. Sacha's birthday was one day after Anna's and my birthday was on the same day as Dino's, Anna's first son. Dimitri's death made Sacha feel even more strongly that fate had decreed a curious symmetry between their two lives.

That summer we took the two dogs on holiday in the new minivan we had bought instead of the old mini I had learnt to drive in. We found a bed and breakfast place in Lyme Regis that would accept two large dogs and spent the days walking along the cliffs and bathing in the coves. Bimbo was quite fearless but Pilly was scared of heights and scared even more of water. I would swim with Bimbo while Sacha and Pilly sat on the beach, but soon Pilly would grow restless and run along as far from the water as possible but staying parallel to us, howling pitifully till we emerged. His sheep-dog instinct was so strong that when a group of us would go for a walk on the Downs if one part of the group got separated from the other he would run between the two groups barking his silly high-pitched bark and trying to get them to join up again.

At the end of the week we decided to drive slowly back to

Lewes, stopping somewhere in Wiltshire for the night. But this time we found that no guest-house would have us with two dogs. I would go in and ask if they had a room for the night and, if they did, if they accepted dogs. If they said yes I would explain that I meant two large dogs, whereupon they would shake their heads and turn us away. In the end we found ourselves driving back to Lewes through the night. We passed through Winchester at two in the morning; the moon was up and the Cathedral lay there like a great sleeping beast. We arrived home at four, and while Sacha took in the luggage I gave the dogs a last walk round the block before we all collapsed into bed. I fell asleep at once, but by seven o'clock the next morning there was Bimbo sitting up and staring at me, thumping his tail on the floor as soon as he saw I was awake and looking at him.

Rain or shine the dogs had to be taken out. If the weather was really foul the person who stayed at home would have towels ready for the one who had been out. The dogs too had to be rubbed down, not only to save them getting colds but also to stop them making a mess of the house. There had never been that problem in bone-dry Egypt. This was the time, too, when the Government decided to change lighting-up time, and for the whole of that winter the person who did the pre-breakfast stint went out in the dark, with the yellow street-lights shining and more often than not a cold wind blowing in from the sea. The reward was that there was a moment when one would be facing due East, and, with luck, would see the sun rising over Mt Caburn above Glynde.

I caught mumps from the son of a friend with whom I had been staying in London and for a while Sacha had to take the dogs on all their walks as well as looking after me. She had asked the doctor if there was any chance of her catching it and he had laughed, saying that the possibility of one adult passing it on to another was about one in ten thousand. But of course she caught it, and much more violently than I. Never a good patient, she lay in bed moaning and groaning, while I walked the dogs, did my teaching, and looked after her. My first play too was being done at the University and Sacha was devastated not to be able to see it.

It was shortly after this that we began to notice that Bimbo was slowing down. He would be the first to the door if either of us made a move to take the dogs for a walk, leaping up and biting his lead, but as soon as we set out he would fall behind. It was pitiful to see. He so much wanted to be part of the walk, to run with Pilly and play with me, but he simply couldn't summon up the energy. We would stop and wait for him, then try to cajole him up the hill. Sometimes we shouted at him and told him he was a lazy pig, and he seemed to agree with us, looking at us with his big sad brown eyes, but unable to move at more than a snail's pace.

I was away in Dijon, teaching at a summer school, when I got Sacha's letter telling me of his death. It is, I think, the only long letter she ever wrote to me. She knew I would want to know everything and she hated the phone even more than she hated writing letters, but it must have cost her a great deal. She told me how one day Bimbo had simply refused to go out at all. Alarmed, she had called the vet, who said to bring him straight round. When they got him on to the operating table Miss Breeze examined him and found that his heart was hardly beating at all. Sacha reminded her of the incident with the adder and she nodded, then asked how old he was. We'd had him for three years and had been told he was three when we'd got him, so Sacha said six. Miss Breeze shook her head. 'Look at his teeth,' she said. 'He must be at least ten, probably more.' What must have happened was that his owner, at the time we had made enquiries about him, understandably keen to find him a good home, had lied about his age. And who could blame her. We might not have taken him had we known he was seven or eight, not three, and so would never have got to know him, so in a sense it was fortunate that she did lie. 'What can be done?' Sacha asked. 'You could take him home,' Miss Breeze said, 'but I don't think he'll last more than a day or two and he is already in some pain and discomfort. It might be kinder if I put him out of his misery now.' So Sacha held him while she injected him, and felt him go limp, then left him for Miss Breeze to bury and went home and wrote to me. It seemed unfair on both of us that I should have been absent both when he was bitten by the adder and now at his death.

Pilly had grown into a magnificent Scotch collie, just like the film star Lassie. People would stop me on the Downs and ask about his pedigree and I would have to confess I did not know.

But now, a few months after Bimbo's death, he had his first fit. He had been acting strangely throughout the day, panting heavily and walking around restlessly. Sacha and I were in the kitchen having supper when suddenly we heard a crash and sounds as though a violent fight was taking place. We rushed to the source of the noise and found Pilly in my study, on the floor, foaming at the mouth and with his legs thrashing wildly. We tried to hold him and talk to him soothingly and reassuringly, but he was beyond help. It seemed like hours that we knelt there beside him, but at last he lay quiet, breathing heavily, his muzzle and beautiful white chest filthy with saliva, his hind legs covered with urine. He had not lain there long like that, while we tried to clean him, when he suddenly tried to stand up. We helped him and he stood, very wobbly and apparently completely unaware of where he was. We coaxed him out into the garden and tried to get him to do something, but he just stood there in a daze, so we eventually brought him back inside. We laid him on his bed and he seemed to go to sleep, but a short while later we heard the dread sounds again and rushed in to see him thrashing about once more. And so it went on through the night. Sacha and I took it in turns to stay with him while the other snatched a few hours of sleep. We wondered how his poor body could cope with the violence of the spasms that racked it and seemed to be tearing him apart, but all anxiety blurred into a weary waiting for the night to end. First thing in the morning we rang Miss Breeze and she came straight round. She examined him – he was asleep again – and said the only thing was to give him a massive sedative which would let his body rest for a while. It could be a brain tumour, she said, in which case there was not much hope, or it could be poison, in which case it looked as if he might pull through.

He did. Forty-eight hours later he was back to normal, though a little dazed and shaky. We were shattered by the horror of what we had been through and the lack of sleep, but enormously relieved that he seemed to have survived. Over the next few weeks we waited anxiously for a recurrence, but nothing happened and gradually we began to think that it must have been poison and that the episode was thankfully behind us.

It wasn't. Six months later the sound we had been secretly dreading recurred: a thud as of something falling somewhere in the house, and then the thump of legs kicking out of control. We rushed upstairs and there was Pilly on the floor in one of the bedrooms, thrashing about, his muzzle flecked with saliva. Once again we went through the routine of trying to hold and calm him, and once again it had no effect. Once again, when it was finally over, we tried to clean him up and lead him outside. Once again the measures were only temporary. It was as if his body exhausted itself with the spasms and then gradually regained enough strength for another fit to wrack it. Once more we took turns to sleep and watch, once more we rang Miss Breeze and she came round as soon as it was light. Having given him another injection, however, she said that the best thing would be for him to have a brain scan. She gave us the address of a vet in London who would do it, we fixed an appointment and drove him up.

The scan was indecisive. There did not seem to be a tumour, but there did seem to be something wrong somewhere. Reluctantly Miss Breeze came to the conclusion that he must be epileptic. I began to read into the literature and discovered that, as with so much medicine, the profession seemed unsure of many things connected with epilepsy, though drugs had been developed for humans to help them cope with it. There was even a school of thought that felt it might be hereditary. In many cases it was a childhood illness which eased off as the patient grew into adulthood.

And so a new pattern was established in our lives: a pattern of uncertainty, of waiting for something we knew was going to happen but could never determine when. It was clear that Pilly was epileptic, that he suffered from the *grand mal*, not, like our little Judy in Egypt, from the milder form known as the *petit mal*. The fits could come on at any time, it was impossible to know what would trigger than off: a bitch on heat in the neighbourhood, my return after a few days away, a change in the weather. Without warning he would fall down and the fit would be upon him.

Netta's son Ricardo, visiting England for a vets' congress, had had a look at him and confirmed the diagnosis, but told us that it was worse for the onlookers than for the patient, who was oblivious while it lasted. Nevertheless, there were times when I would be lying reading on the sofa in my study with Pilly lying beside me and I would feel a tiny tremor go through him and I would look into his face and see terror in his eyes. A human epileptic knows at least what is the matter with him, but the sadness here was the sense one had that he had no idea, probably no memory of how it had gone before, knew only that some alien and terrifying force was about to take him over.

The aftermath of the fits was almost worse than the fits themselves, certainly even more uncanny. He would often get up, very wobbly, and stagger to a corner of the room, pushing his long thin nose into the joint of the two walls and standing there until we gently led him away, though even then, as soon as we let him go he would often gravitate back to his corner. And clearly after a fit his jaws or teeth would trouble him, for he would bite at his bowl when he had emptied it or, if we were at table, stand up on his hind legs and put his forepaws on the table and bite at the plates, though normally he would not dream of trying to eat our food.

Yet having an invalid in the house, which is what it was, once again brought Sacha and me together more closely. She began to sketch again and in the evenings would often sketch me reading with Pilly lying beside me, or sketch him alone as he lay asleep on the carpet or in one of the chairs. When Pilly died she put away the sketch-book and never took it out again.

But she was getting more and more exhausted. I would go away occasionally to stay with friends but she never left his side. I didn't know how long she could go on like that, and I wondered too if it was any sort of life for Pilly himself. Sacha and I talked it over and finally asked Miss Breeze to put him down. Always reluctant to do that, she suggested we try one last remedy: put him on human anti-convulsants and see if that worked.

It seemed to do the trick. His fits became less violent and occurred less frequently, and they didn't last as long. On the other hand, as is always the case with drugs, they affected his entire personality. He had been the liveliest and most playful of dogs, but now he slowed down, lost his zest, his bounciness. We took him to Ireland, the only country on return from which one did not need to put a dog in quarantine, and that was a success. But we couldn't pretend it was a normal life. And we still waited anxiously for those sounds.

Miss Breeze had warned us that one of two things might happen: that we might gradually be able to wean him off the pills as he grew older, or that one day they would simply cease to have any effect and he would revert to the bad old days. Sadly, it was the latter of these two possibilities that occurred. We had been staying in a friend's house in London while a play of mine was being put on. The house was close to Holland Park and we walked him in the park every day and things seemed to be fine. But the day we returned to Lewes he had a massive fit. Once again Sacha and I took turns to be with him, once again I found myself, stupefied with tiredness, dragging him round the block in the middle of the night, the lights out in all the houses and the street lamps shining yellow and unnatural, then cleaning him, getting him onto his bed, getting into mine, falling into a heavy but anxious sleep, only to be woken by hearing him struggling with another fit. In the morning Sacha and I looked at each other. We both knew the end had come. For once Sacha couldn't face it. 'I'll take him,' I said. We rang Miss Breeze, I got him into the car and to the surgery. As always he was docility itself – unlike Bimbo, who would have done anything rather than let a vet get close to him. We laid him down on the operating table and I held his head and stroked his soft cheeks and ears while she gave him the lethal injection. Very calmly he fell asleep and then died. I left him with her to bury, got into the car and drove home.

As with Lala, as with all the other dogs and cats who had been a part of our lives and then died, we each had the other to turn to as a source of comfort. But we both knew deep down that Pilly would be the last dog we would ever have.

Sacha, by her death, seemed to have taken my life with her as well. Because of the strange circumstances of our existence she had been the only witness to all the important events of my life. Now, with that witness gone, it was as though the past had begun to grow dim and dissolve. Until that moment I had not realised the importance of witnesses. And the importance of stories. When Sacha told me stories about her childhood and youth she was doing so in part because she herself had never had any parents. When she told me stories about my childhood it was because I had no brothers and sisters, aunts and uncles and grandparents, who had known me from my earliest years. Now she is gone and I have started to tell her story I find a kind of calm descending on me and I know why: by piecing her life together I have begun to reconstitute my own.

This is more than the therapy of confession. It is not the wounded spirit that is being healed, but, in a way I could never have anticipated, my body that is returning to me. That is why a memoir would never have been enough. A memoir would have left me to wallow in my sorrow; writing the life of another, of that other, was what I needed to do, and I now see why.

Intense intellectual and emotional effort, such as is required to write any book, often has a sort of magnetic effect. Disparate elements are suddenly brought into the same orbit and as a result

new insights are acquired. The day I suddenly grasped the meaning of witnessing I found myself in synagogue – an extremely rare
occurrence – for the *bar mitzvah* of a friend's son. And there in
the ordinary Sabbath service I read and heard the words: 'Remember us, O Lord – *zakhrenu adonai*.' Jews pray to God to remember
them! But of course! A people without a land, a people dispersed,
need a witness, they need someone to remember all that has
befallen them and made them what they are. And since no
human being could fulfil that role, they have a God, and their
deepest fear is that that God will forget them and they will simply
vanish.

Writing about Sacha and reading at the same time the memoirs
of other children of Holocaust survivors has also made me see
what is unique about this story: the war and her survival was
perhaps the most important thing in her life, but it was only a
small part of it; partly because of who she was and partly because
of the peculiar circumstances of her life, that life is more rich and
complex than that of many survivors. And only I can tell it.

Sacha had talked to me about Bressanone and the Dolomites ever
since she had begun to tell me about her childhood and youth.
Now the moment had come to go there. She was emotionally and
physically exhausted, and I felt that only a total change would be
able to restore her to good health. So long as we had dogs Ireland
was the only foreign country we could visit, but now, suddenly,
we could go wherever we wanted. 'We'll go to Merano,' Sacha
said, 'and then, if there's time, to Bolzano.'

We drove to Strasbourg and then to Ulm and up the fine road
that leads into the Alps. As we approached the mountains and
the air began to change I experienced the excitement I had felt
on that train journey from Venice to Geneva all those years before.
Merano, though, was a huge disappointment. It was full of grand

hotels, bands played in the public gardens along the river, and everywhere crowds surged, eating the famous Merano grapes out of paper bags. Kafka, I remembered, had spent some miserable days there in 1911 or 12 in a *pension* whose clientele consisted mainly of anti-semitic colonels and aristocratic old ladies. 'I thought the atmosphere would appeal to you,' Sacha said, admitting that she too was disappointed. After a single night we fled to Bolzano, the capital of the region. That was much better, less touristy, less crowded, but it was still too much of a big city for me, though one could see the mountains all around. After three days there Sacha suggested we drive out to Bressanone for the day.

As soon as we entered the little walled town I knew this was what I had been secretly waiting for. We strolled round, had a cup of coffee in the main square, and I said to Sacha: 'But it's beautiful, why didn't we come here right away?' 'I don't know, I thought you'd be bored,' she said. The truth was, I think, that she was terrified I wouldn't like it. It had meant so much to her, she had such strong memories of it (as had Chickie, when I talked to her about it, many years later), that she would have found my disliking it almost too much to bear. Once again, though, we found that our tastes coincided. It was not just because it held memories of her youth that she had been fond of it, but partly at least because of what it was. Because it's a walled town developers can't spoil it; because of the two rivers running through it and meeting in the middle of it, it feels like a mountain village; yet it has a grand Bishop's Palace, an extraordinary painted cloister with well over a hundred late Gothic frescoes, cafés, restaurants, swimming pool and tennis courts. In a few minutes one can get out into the apple and pear orchards which surround the town, and in half an hour's strenuous climbing one can reach the first of the little villages that dot the mountains round about. 'Why don't we cancel the Bolzano room and move here for the rest of the holiday?' I suggested. 'I'd like that,' Sacha said. We found a room in the oldest part of town, Stufles, and went back to Bolzano to fetch our things.

In the next few days Sacha and I had some memorable walks up into the surrounding mountains and Sacha rediscovered many of the places she had known fifty years previously: hotels she had stayed in with Chickie and Pussy and the grandparents, the Elefante and the Excelsior; the pastry shop where they had been in the habit of dropping in between breakfast and lunch, still run by the same family; the ice-rink where she had fallen and bumped her head and heard the strange reverberations. It made her happy to show me these places and talk to me about them, as though her coming here with me, now that I was a relatively successful writer and academic, and we were firmly settled in England, redeemed the past in some strange way, as though without her early suffering she would not be there now, with me. And it was true. I too was happy and excited to see at last what I had heard so much about. It made Sacha more real to me, as well as tugging at my heart as I sensed that there were so many paths her life could have taken, so many ways for me not to have existed, and yet here I was and here I was with her – two English tourists in a little Alpine town. Life at that moment did seem like a miracle and a blessing.

One morning I went into her room and found her lying on her bed, looking up at the Plose through the open window. 'See that little white chapel on the hillside up there?' she said. I went to the window and looked out. 'I could see that little chapel from the room in the Excelsior I shared with Chickie half a century ago,' Sacha said. 'It must have faced in exactly the same direction.'

On the last day of our stay we decided to take the funicular to the top of the Plose and walk down into the town. We should have known better. Going down a mountain is always worse than going up it, and five hours of unremitting descent reduced our feet and ankles to a bleeding pulp, without our even having had the satisfaction of climbing to some high spot. The next day we set out on the long drive to Dieppe, exhausted and in pain, but vowing to return as soon as we could.

And we did return, almost annually, until Sacha ceased to be able to walk and finally even to want to travel. As soon as we were there we would begin to feel well: our lungs expanded, our hearts lifted. At first we would spend the entire fortnight in Bressanone itself. We had found a beautiful absurdly cheap hotel, giving straight onto one of the rivers, and would go to sleep to the sound of the water running over the stones. We would walk up to the villages in the hills, get the key to the church from the adjoining farm-house and study the completely unknown Gothic frescos which covered the walls and ceilings. Once, when Anna had come on holiday with us, we found one of the churches open, went in, and as I closed the door behind me the lock snapped to with an ominous click. I tried to open it but it was firmly shut. I rattled the door but nothing happened. 'Don't worry,' Sacha said, 'there'll be another door.' But there wasn't. 'Perhaps we could try ringing the bells,' Sacha suggested, but we couldn't see how to get to the ropes. It was a Friday afternoon and no-one was likely to enter the church for at least twenty-four hours. Within fifteen minutes we were start-ing to feel cold. I went back to the doors, thinking that if I could get them swinging I might be able to break the lock. They swayed and creaked and the noise got louder and louder, but the lock held. Finally we heard a voice shouting: 'What's going on here?;' 'We're locked in!' we shouted back in relief. 'Wait!' the voice said, then there was silence. We embraced each other with relief, but then as the minutes ticked by we began to wonder if they were going to leave us in there all night as a punishment. But no. There was another flurry of noise, a key was turned in the lock, and a large peasant woman stared in at us. 'My son locked us in,' Sacha said. 'Well, you're not locked in any more. Get out!'

After several years of annual visits to Bressanone we began to feel it would be nice to spend a few days in the higher mountains. Sacha suggested the Lago di Carezza, where she had also been as a girl, and where she had met Giorgio Nathan Rogers. Soon we got into the habit of spending a week there after a week in Bressanone, and walking in the dramatic bare landscape of the Rosengarten. On one memorable ten-hour walk we found at the end that the only way forward was down what looked like a sheer drop, and that it was too late to go back the way we had come. 'Don't take your eyes from the path immediately ahead of you,' Sacha said, knowing that I suffered from vertigo. I lowered my eyes but could see only sharp grey rocks with, here and there, patches of red on them that I at first took for the blood left by falling bodies, but then realised must be markers for the 'path' we were meant to follow. Gingerly I began to inch my way forward and down. Every few metres there was a metal rope set in the rock. Sacha, at seventy, shimmied down these like a monkey; I followed, laboriously, holding my breath, trying not to look up and out. Hours later, as it seemed – but it can only have been twenty minutes or so, we finally reached a little path that ran round the side of the mountain. We stood there, trembling a little with the effort, and looked at each other. 'Goodness,' Sacha said, 'you *are* pale under your tan!' 'Am I?' I said, my hand going up automatically to my cheek. I turned and looked back and up at the way we had come. 'Look!' I said to Sacha. She too turned and followed my gaze. 'Oh!' she said, and promptly sat down where she had been standing. 'I think I'll just stay here for a few minutes,' she said. 'My legs feel a bit wobbly all of a sudden.'

One day, going from Bressanone to Chiusa, a daylong walk, but fairly easy, we found ourselves looking up into a valley opposite towards some beautiful, pencil-thin peaks in the distance. 'We must come here next year and see if there's a hotel in that valley,' I said, and we did indeed do that and found just the kind of hotel we liked, in the tiny village of S. Pietro. It had been in the same family for generations, handed down from daughter to daughter, and the current owner, no doubt like her mother and grandmother before her, had seemingly only one wish: to make her guests as happy and comfortable as possible. Sacha and I took to going there every year after that, sometimes with friends, and in the end not bothering to stop first in Bressanone. Partly this was because the hotel there had changed hands after the brother of the two old ladies who ran it had died, and partly because we felt we had exhausted its attractions for the time being. As the years went by Sacha settled into a routine of walking one day and resting in the gardens of the hotel the next, and even in her early eighties she still came up with me on the three and a half hour walk to the Refugio Genova, from which a whole new stretch of mountains could be seen. One of my favourite photos of her in her old age shows her sitting in the hotel garden, a book on alpine flowers and her packet of cigarettes on the table beside her, smiling her inward smile: contentment.

Robin Lee was a mature student, in his mid-twenties and already a published poet when he came to the University in 1969. We first got to know him when he wrote and asked to see me: he wanted advice on whether he should stick it out at Sussex or leave. The University had disappointed him, his teachers, he felt, knew nothing about literature, his fellow-students even less, and he wondered whether he wasn't simply wasting his time. I persuaded him to stay and in the course of time he became a good friend not only of mine but of Sacha's as well. He was the only person apart from me she would show her poetry to, and he was a far better critic of poetry than I was, homing in on a word or phrase that was the root of the problem with unerring instinct. He was subject to fits of depression which, he knew, had both physiological and psychological roots, and in his childhood and adolescence had several times tried to kill himself. There were days when something was clearly wrong, when he would sit silent in the midst of a group of friends, then abruptly leave and go home. His girl-friend would sometimes ring me in despair, saying he had been lying in bed for forty-eight hours, unable to speak, his jaw sometimes literally locked. When he was well he was the most witty and charming of companions, brilliantly inventive, always ready to learn, at once profound and light of manner. At the end of his first year he played the lead in a play I had written for the students, and did it brilliantly. He began to relax with some of his fellow-students and with the younger members of faculty. In his final year he got down to some really serious work and was rewarded with a First and the chance to go on to an MA and possibly research work. But towards the end of his first year as a graduate things began to go wrong. Even though he was awarded a Junior Fellowship, which would have allowed him to do some teaching the following year, even though he was writing better poetry than ever, the days when he was out of action were increasing. His girl-friend left him, having finally understood that he had no intention of getting married, and he took it very badly. We had often talked about suicide – Alvarez's book on the subject had recently appeared and we both agreed that it was full of Romantic twaddle. One did not kill oneself, that was the easy way out, one lived out one's life in all its pain and confusion and, if one was a writer, used one's gift to cope with whatever life might offer.

And then Robin killed himself. His mother rang one night to tell me what had happened. I went into Sacha's bedroom – she was still reading and coughing – and told her. Like all Robin's friends we were not only devastated but riddled with guilt: should we not have done more for him? How had we not seen that this might happen? Why had we not been more available, less wrapped up in our own affairs? His mother asked me to act as his literary executor, along with the poet Herbert Lomas, a friend from pre-University days, and going through his books and papers was an unexpectedly horrible ordeal. I had only ever experienced the deaths of beloved animals, and animals have the good sense not to store possessions in the course of their lives.

After her death I found this poem among Sacha's papers:

The End of an Ordinary Day

At the end of an ordinary day
the intermittant buzz
interrupts the monotony of bedtime ritual.
Across fifty odd miles
of dual-carriageway
an unfamiliar voice
on the unreceptive eardrum
telescopes time and space
as we connect what it has to say:
our gentle courteous friend
took his own life this day
in his high room
eight miles away.

A few weeks later Sacha and I got away to Bressanone – the only time we went in April, the snow still thick on the mountains all around, though we managed to get a few walks in. Neither of us though was in a walking mood; we comforted each other and I wrote a piece called 'He', the nearest I could get to an *in memoriam*, and which helped me regain my balance to some extent (I don't know when Sacha wrote her poem). But all was not well between us, and as soon as we got back home we began to quarrel again. I had just broken off an engagement to someone Sacha was extremely fond of and taken up with an actress who was performing one of my plays that was then on tour. As a result she had left her husband and was living in her parents' London flat while they were in the country. Sacha could not understand what I was up to, and, indeed, neither could I. The excitement generated by having one of my plays put on always had a strange effect of me, and now Robin's death added to the dangerous mix of emotions. For the first time I saw Sacha's face set at moments in a strange way, so that I felt I did not know the person I was talking to or screaming at. She was not my mother, or, indeed, anyone I had ever known. And with this new face on she would rush out of the house and I would run after her, seizing her arm, asking her where she was going, begging her to be reasonable. But she would shake me off, turn away, mutter that she was going to kill herself. 'What do you mean kill yourself?' 'Let me go!' 'I won't till you calm down.' 'Let me go, you've no right to hold on to me like that!' 'Stop trying to blackmail me.' 'Let me go, let me go.' And so on.

I don't know if Robin's death had anything to do with it. They say that one suicide sets others in its train. It had certainly broken a barrier inside her. But then she had always been afraid that she would go mad, like her father, that perhaps the strains of syphilis were at work in her as well and would surface one day. And the sense, I suppose, that after all she had tried to do for me and all the hopes she had had for me, I was turning into someone she didn't know or like, someone – it came out one day – like my father, was just too much for her.

'My soul surpasses my ancestry,' writes Leon Wieseltier in a book that has recently come my way, a book he wrote in the aftermath of his father's death (one day after Sacha's, as it happens). 'My father imbued me with my purposes,' he goes on, 'but my purposes carry me beyond my father. In the heart of the family, there must be a wise alienation, a standpoint stricter than the standpoint of love.' These are wise words, but sometimes wisdom is impossible to follow. That is perhaps the basis of tragedy. In *Le Cid*, which I saw recently, the authority of the father is like a great block of basalt that comes down into the souls of sons and daughters, leading to disaster. My relations with Sacha did not lead to tragedy, but the ties that bound us together were far too close for that wise alienation of which Wieseltier speaks to be possible. I thought of leaving Sacha but in the end

I could not do it. I felt I would never be able to live with myself if she did indeed kill herself, and I felt too that I loved her too much to want to see her in the state she was in. At the same time I had no desire to move in with the actress, who had anyway by that time decided to go back to her husband. Gradually everything calmed down. We both accepted that terrible things had been said. In some ways we grew closer, but at the same time we both recognised that something decisive had happened, that we could never re-establish the relationship of total trust we had enjoyed before. Periodically thereafter furious rows would flare up between us, periodically I would see that terrifying unknown face settle over the known and loved one. Then it would vanish as suddenly as it had come and life would resume its course.

Our life was not a tragedy. Sacha was too wise for that, and she had, like Wieseltier's father, 'imbued me with my purposes', which did indeed carry me beyond her. But I often wondered, in the next twenty years, if it had been my weakness or my strength that had led to my making my life with her, whether, by going away a long time before, I would have given *her* the freedom and strength to move beyond me. And I see now that my often compulsive involvement with women throughout my life, my desire, after barely a week's acquaintance, to marry them, and my consequent horrified withdrawal as I realised what I was committing myself to, may have had more to do with my fear of being left alone after Sacha's death than with the desire to escape her. But who can really tell what would have been for the best? We can never stand outside ourselves and see 'the truth'; we can only struggle to do the best we can with what we have been given. Alone, Sacha would no doubt have spent the last years of her life as a dignified and not unhappy old lady. But her life, I am sure, would have been a lesser thing; and so would mine.

In the early seventies I wrote a radio play called *A Life*. I was young and it was not a very good play. I did not even really know what it was I was trying to do. But now, as I try to write about Sacha and to understand what it is I am doing, I think back to that play and its title. I realise that what interested me already then was the fact that in the ordinary course of things human lives are so spread out over time that we never have any sense of their individual *shapes*. Only the narrative of a life, and a reasonably brief narrative at that, as Samuel Johnson understood and as modern biographers do not, can go some way towards capturing this. If it works, the brief narrative of a life can bring into the light of day what would otherwise remain dark, can draw out the mysterious interplay between chance, character and destiny which tragedy once made manifest on the stage. That is why autobiography is so unsatisfactory. A person can never grasp the trajectory of their own life, not only because that trajectory is not over till that life ends, but because a life is more than what one can say, it is more than one can think. It can only be lived, not told – not told by the liver, that is, but only by another.

Of course I cannot tell if I will succeed, only others will be able to determine that, but this, I begin to see, is what I have been trying to do here and why, though I have used that title before, I will call this book *A Life*.

It is difficult, though, to write a life when nothing happens. It is easy to write about great sorrows, great escapes, but the daily round, which is the predominant life of men and women, is difficult to present. Yet, as Sacha's life brings out so clearly, the times when things happen are usually times of deep unhappiness, and human beings perhaps really only come alive, as opposed to simply surviving, when nothing much happens. To tell her life and to tell it so that all may recognise themselves in her it is necessary to tell both parts, to convey what it means to live a life of simple iteration as well as of decisive, unrepeatable events.

Sacha put as much effort into the maintainance of routine as she did into our survival in France during the war. The two are not perhaps unrelated. Despite what was going on around us she wanted me to lead as normal a life as possible, and no doubt wanted it for herself as well. Of course she had a naturally tidy mind, a natural tendency to prefer order to chaos. But that tendency was, I am sure, exacerbated by her own wretched disordered early life. So, for as long as I can remember, lunch was always at 12.30, tea at four, supper at seven. This was her routine in Lewes, and mine too if I was at home. No matter what happened during the day, she always seemed to have the supper ready precisely at seven. This made for friction if I was late and hadn't warned her. Much more was at stake than a meal getting burned or growing cold. But she was no fanatic, merely felt – rightly – that creative work could only be done against a background of order. I suppose as she got older she held more and more passionately to her routines, but I am convinced that she was essentially right to think that routine, while it can deaden if made the substitute for thought and feeling, can actually enhance the possibilities of life if consciously embraced. It is like poetry: the rules are what makes things happen.

Michael Wadsworth, who officiated at Robin's funeral, was an Anglican priest, a classicist and a semiticist, who had come to Sussex to teach Religious Studies after working with Geza Vermes in Oxford. Shortly after his arrival he announced that he would be starting classes in classical Hebrew for anyone who was interested. I joined up and Sacha begged me to teach her in turn what I was learning in the class. Soon we had mastered the basic elements and started to read the narratives of the Hebrew Bible. Sacha, in a sense, had been a frustrated linguist all her life. She had learnt enough Middle English to read not only Chaucer but the *Gawain* poet, and then enough Old English to read *Beowulf*. Now she would be able to read the Bible, which she had always loved, in the language in which it was written, a language she had never had the chance to learn, for neither her parents nor her grandparents had any acquaintance with it, despite the fact that her grandmother still fasted on Yom Kippur. But the language, for her and for me, was not totally unfamiliar, since it has a great deal in common with Arabic, which she had heard all her life and which I had studied at school. Sacha now suggested we meet at our house, once a week, to read the Bible and talk about it, and these weekly meetings, with Sacha dispensing coffee and biscuits, became another aspect of beneficent routine.

Sacha was in her sixties when she began to learn Hebrew and in her seventies when she got down to classical Greek. A new Cambridge Greek course had just come out, and a member of our Hebrew Bible reading group suggested she turn her attention to that – and then, he said, we could get a Greek reading group going. Sacha pressed and chivvied me to such an extent that within two years we had reached the end of the course and were ready to read Homer. By now the Bible group had begun to disintegrate, partly for want of teachers and partly because many of the original members had moved elsewhere. So, imperceptibly, a Homer reading group replaced it, still meeting one evening a week at our house. Sacha was an assiduous preparer and now took to reading her Greek at night when her cough kept her awake. Her memory was so acute – I would ask her for the names of students I had taught many years previously and which I just couldn't recall and she instantly remembered them – that though her grasp of grammar remained rudimentary she was able to keep the crib covered during our sessions (something even those with some classical training were reluctant to do) and hardly ever faltered.

Every six books we would have dinner together at a different restaurant and, once the meal was over, would each read in Greek our favourite lines from the six books just completed. In three years we got through the *Iliad* and the *Odyssey*, and then moved on to the plays and even to Apollonius Rhodius's Hellenistic imitation of Homer, *The Voyage of the Argonauts*. Every year we would try to go and see a play in Greek either at King's College, London, or at Oxford or Cambridge, or – best of all – at Bradfield School. Sacha had said to me: 'When I can no longer walk over the Downs life won't be worth living any more.' But now, as she was laid up more and more frequently with back trouble, she transferred all her enthusiasm to the Greek. It was after she had missed going to two Greek plays in a row because of illness that I think she really began to feel that life held out nothing more for her.

The Bible and Greek reading fed into her poetry. She had of course always read the Bible and had sent me 'Lot's Wife' when I was at Oxford, but in the seventies and eighties she wrote a large number of poems on biblical and classical Greek subjects. One of these, 'Choosing to Fall', was chosen by South Eastern Arts to inaugurate their imaginative Poetry Posters, collaborations

between poets and artists to produce poster-sized works that could
be hung up in schools and libraries. Tim Hyman, by then a close
friend, devised a very Blakean setting for it:

I myself had named the serpent
even before the woman came.
And now he rose beside her
coiled in a question mark
splintering the oneness
– good and evil, light and dark –
asking 'Why this not that?'
Once this and that had been the same.

So when we ate the fruit
of the one forbidden tree
we had already fallen.
We had fallen when we saw
two sides to every problem,
polarity as law
and in the art of choosing
the proof that we were free.

She had lived with the Bible for so long that she was able to make
its stories her own, whether they were in the Hebrew Scriptures
or the New Testament:

Jacob

Angels visited Abraham
before I was born,
conversed with him
foretelling the future.

I was not like Isaac
meant for greatness.
By stealth I seized it
snatching and grabbing.

My father taught me
fear of the Lord.
From my mother's kin
I took my cunning.

I saw the sky
ablaze in the East
with the heralds of God
linking heaven and earth.

The child-face of my bride
confirmed my calling:
I was the first lover,
the first father.

And from my sleep
I rose to wrestle
with him who would break
but not overcome me,

who departed at dawn
leaving me lame
and called me Israel
for the sake of my striving.

My children after me
are dreamers and schemers
steadfast and tender
lame and invincible.

In 'Martha Speaks' she is surely trying to come to terms with her relations with Chickie, and perhaps with me as well:

I am Martha
careful and troubled
about many things
but unheedful
of the good part
which is Mary's,
the one thing
that is needful.

I toil
only to forget
the harder task
of living.
Because Mary has mastered
that difficult art
I am bitter
I am unforgiving.

I fret
while she sits listening
rapt
at our guest's feet
and what
I ask
shall we drink?
What shall we eat?

I have seen
the Glory of God
when Lazarus
rose from the dead.

My faith however
is feeble
and at my table
there are many who must be fed.

'I toil/only to forget/the harder task/ of living.' That is certainly
what she sometimes felt. Felt too that 'my faith . . . / is feeble/
and at my table/ there are many who must be fed.' Yet another
part of her must have known that toiling and feeding people is
precisely what the hard task of living is, that it is only the Marys
of this world who imagine that it is otherwise. That too though
is only a partial truth, and the burden laid on the Marthas is
always to wonder if perhaps what they are doing is simply to busy
themselves so as not to face up to 'the one thing/that is needful'.

In her last years she worked on what she called 'The King
David Sonnets', no doubt feeling a kinship with the long and
complex and many-sided life of the singer and king. They were
published together in her second collection, and the last one, 'Cold
Comfort', has one of the most arresting openings of any poem I
know:

No not for me your thermal underwear
and warming-pans. For my chill bones they found
this virgin beauty Queen ruddy and round.
By then I was, worse luck, beyond repair.

It ends with a *cri de coeur*. After recalling his triumph over Goliath
and later Saul, David laments:

But now the tide has turned. Ah yes the tide
of life has turned. My blood, come rain come shine
runs cold. I cannot muster any warmth at all.

She has come a long way since her first tentative steps in transforming herself from a French to an English poet, and the voice is now distinctly hers. My favourite is 'David and Saul':

> All at his task, his cloak spread wide, disarmed
> the King squats in the cave and defecates,
> a sitting target for the one he hates.
> Unseen I trim his cloak and let him go unharmed.
> I love the man. Love that demented monarch.
> But God's displeased with him. That's why he bade
> the prophet seek me out to reign instead.
> Saul knows. His bite is fiercer than his bark.
> Ours is a duel to the death. If Saul
> is not destroyed he'll get me in the end.
> And yet against the King I cannot raise a hand.
> But God is great. And how the mighty fall,
> Saul on his spear and Jonathan my friend
> cut down. Today I rule this promised land.

Only someone deeply imbued with the ethos of the Hebrew Bible would be able to catch the mixture of resourcefulness and resignation, of down-to-earthness and idealism which gives the poem its deep resonance. How many ironies lie embedded in that 'But God is great'! Yet also, I suspect, only someone who had struggled with a language not her own and was finally its master, with a world in which she felt herself only a visitor and yet with which she had come to terms. It makes itself felt again in a poem on a classical Greek subject, 'Sphinx':

> Clever Oedipus solved
> the Theban Sphinx's riddle
> then, proud as Punch,
> strutted bipedal
> to his slain father's bridal couch.

It cost him his two eyes
and much else besides.
The Twister got him in the end.

Riddles are for asking.
They are better left unsolved.

In 1976 I won a travelling award for a collection of stories and suggested to Sacha that we go back to Egypt. I had hardly thought of the place for twenty years and I'm sure Sacha hadn't either: it belonged to the past and our future was in England. But my growing interest in my roots, my feeling that the Levantine elements in my life could not be simply shed but needed on the contrary to be recognised and understood, made me eager to go back and see what it had been like. Sacha very much wanted to go back and see Chickie, but dreaded a quarrel. She knew that they could not spend any time together without some dispute breaking out and, since she felt that if she did go this would probably be the last time they would see each other, she did not want it to end badly. Inwardly she vowed to keep calm, whatever the provocation.

We drove to Naples and left the car there, spent a week in Amalfi and then boarded a boat for Alexandria. The corridors and stairways were crammed with fridges and other electric equipment being brought home by Egyptians who had been working in Italy, and the skies remained leaden throughout the three days' crossing. We landed on 1 May. We had both completely forgotten what the Egyptian heat was like. We had of course thought it would be getting hot in May but what we encountered was barely tolerable. In the run-down taxi from Cairo station to Maadi, which kept stalling every few kilometres along the new corniche, I wound down the window to let in a bit of air and found it was like opening the door of an oven. I quickly shut it again and we baked and sweated in silence till the taxi finally deposited us at our destination.

Chickie had had to sell the house she had had built for herself in the early fifties to pay her debts and now she and Albert lived in a small cockroach-infested flat with the usual array of dogs and

cats, but also a monkey. Some of these had to be kept separated from each other as, given half a chance, they would attack and possibly kill each other; others were slowly dying of visible wounds or unknown diseases; and the whole place gave off a fetid odour of stagnant air and animal urine. We stayed close by, with John Rodenbeck of the American University and his family, who now lived in the large house that had once belonged to Mizrahi Pasha, not far from the club.

How did the return strike Sacha? I found the experience quite Proustian in its lack of relation to the memories of the place secreted inside me, but I never bothered to ask Sacha how it felt to her. Differently, I'm sure, for she had after all returned once already, in 1945, but how did this return, this encounter with her sister, differ from the other? What feelings did Egypt evoke in her? I know that in England she missed the flora but was glad not to have to endure the heat, not to have to see animals sick and beaten, above all not to have to live the indolent life the heat and culture made almost obligatory. But I know nothing else. As always between us I was eager to tell her how I felt and she would listen and discuss my response at length, but I never waited to hear how things had struck her in the first place.

It was so hot that to go out after nine in the morning required a conscious effort. I braved the heat and went into Cairo to visit the Islamic buildings I had become very interested in, while she spent most of her days with Chickie and Monica, and called in on those of her old friends from the swimming-pool days who still lived in Maadi, especially Frieda, the Austrian mother of my friend and rival, Sami el Sayed. The circle of Jewish ladies round Chickie and Albert had, of course, long since departed, dispersed to Rome, Milan, Paris, London, or further afield, to Australia, South America, Canada.

In the middle of our stay an incident no doubt typical of Chickie's life occurred. She tried to intercede in a fight between two cats by sticking her sandalled foot between them and was promptly bitten and scratched. The wounds got infected, the ankle swelled up and she was forced, against her will, to get into the car of an American friend and let herself be taken to the doctor's. He was very concerned, gave her an injection, bandaged the ankle and made her promise to lie on her back with her leg in the air till the swelling subsided. 'I can't do that,' Chickie said, 'I have to take out my dogs.' 'I'll take them out,' Sacha said. 'Will you really?' said Chickie, with a flash of the wide Rabinovitch smile the sisters shared. 'They need to be taken out at six in the morning sharp,' Chickie added. 'Mind you get there in time or I'll have to take them myself'. 'You'll do no such thing,' Sacha and Monica said in chorus. 'Chickie dear,' the American lady added, 'just think what use you'll be to your dogs if you have to have your leg amputated.'

But that is just the kind of thinking Chickie cannot or will not ever do.

The next morning Sacha got to the flat at five past six, to find that Chickie had already left with the dogs. She was furious. She came back to the Rodenbecks for breakfast and then she and I went round to Chickie's again. 'Why do you do things like that?' Sacha said to her. 'Are you trying to prove that I'm not to be trusted or what?' Chickie grew apoplectic with rage. 'Get her out of here!' she screamed at me. 'Get her out of my flat. I never want to see her again!'

I got Sacha back to the Rodenbecks, very shaken. She had given up smoking a few months previously after a particularly bad bout of bronchitis, but now she said to me: 'Give me a cigarette.' I didn't dare argue. She smoked in silence, then said: 'You'd better go and buy me a packet. I'm going to need quite a few.'

Monica, of course, mediated between the sisters, brought us news that Chickie was sorry for what she'd said, brought her mother the information that Sacha forgave her. Both felt that, with our departure imminent now, it was imperative they make up. But the quarrel had clearly affected them both deeply, perhaps made them realise once again how little any of us grows up, how deeply childhood jealousies and tensions live on in us as adults and drive our actions and reactions.

We were given a large goodbye meal by Monica and Medhat, Sacha and Chickie embraced with real emotion, and off we went, back to Alexandria, the boat, an interminable car drive through a Europe which was, that summer, almost as hot as Egypt, and back to an England turned brown and dusty. The heat we had endured over the previous two and a half months, the constant travelling, and the excitement of return had worn us both down, and Sacha developed the first of many terrible bouts of constipation. Her stomach swelled up till it was hard and round, and nothing the doctor gave her helped. In the end a nurse had to come and help her through with enemas. This, for her, was almost worse than the pain. She had a horror of people touching her and an irrational sense of shame at her own body. The indignity of what she suffered in those weeks of our return stayed with her for the rest of her life. It was, sadly, to be repeated at the very end.

That trip to Egypt was not, as it turned out, to be the last time Sacha and Chickie saw each other. Eight years later we returned, in very different circumstances. I had been invited to participate in a Writers' Workshop in Israel and proposed to Sacha that she come with me. It had always been a dream of hers to visit Palestine but, like me, she had always felt she so disliked the attitudes of the Israelis to the Arabs that it was out of the question. Like me she had been horrified at the thought, quite legitimate in early 1967, that the Arabs would overrun Israel and massacre the Jews; more clearly than me she had immediately seen what a mistake it was after the 1967 war not to have given back the conquered territories straight away. But the previous year I had been invited by the British Council to lecture in Israel and had thought this a golden opportunity: if I hated what I saw I could put on my British Council hat, deliver my lectures and return to England; if I didn't then perhaps I could establish a bridgehead and return. In the event I found that Israel was even more deeply divided than was Thatcher's Britain, and that the people I met were on the whole far more critical of their government than I would have believed possible. I made some good friends, established contacts

with one or two old students, and returned in the Autumn to stay with Aharon Appelfeld and his family. I reported to Sacha that there was much about the place and the people she would like, and the fact that by then one could fly in an hour from Tel Aviv to Cairo, and that we could therefore spend a few days with Chickie as well, clinched her decision. So, half-way through our stay in Israel we boarded a plane at midnight and were in Cairo by twenty to one in the morning.

This time we stayed in a small hotel near to the flat we had once lived in at the corner of Road 6, the one with the violent owner and his extended family. The fact that we were just passing through, that we had not made the journey specifically to be there nor were staying for any length of time made everything much easier. Albert had died since our last visit but Chickie was still living in the stinking, cockroach-infested flat with all her animals, including the monkey, Jo-Jo. Her increasing deafness made conversation with her difficult, but we sat with her at Monica's and she seemed often to be able to hear Sacha even when she couldn't hear anyone else. Both of them knew for certain now that this was the last time they would see each other. Chickie came with us in Medhat's car to the airport in the middle of the night, the two sisters hugged each other, and then we were off. An hour and a half later we were back in Israel.

Sacha's manner of walking was distinctive: her hands on her hips as she climbed a hill, or clasped behind her back, her shoulders getting more and more bent with age, her pace regular, so that the group formed and reformed around her as people stopped, slowed down or speeded up while she plodded steadily on. As the

years went by she would say to whoever was walking up a hill with her: 'I'm sorry, I can't both climb and talk.'

Even after we no longer had dogs she and I would go for a walk on the Downs round Lewes on most afternoons, and she would go by herself if I was teaching. On most week-ends we would go on longer walks with friends, from Lewes to Brighton via Rottingdean and the Undercliff Walk along the sea; from Lewes to Alfriston via Glynde and Firle; from Lewes to Eastbourne (once); from Lewes to Shoreham via the Devil's Dyke (a dull walk which for some reason was very popular in the early years at Sussex); and many many more.

One of the things I liked about Sacha was that she was always game, always ready to take up any challenge I set her, even though she must have come to see over the years that I was not the most reliable of guides. Not only was there the episode of the *camino di ferro* I have already mentioned, but once, having set out rather late to climb to the lake on the Western side of Bressanone we found ourselves, in the last stages of our descent, in the middle of a thick wood in utter darkness. We could hear the traffic down in the valley but in the wood it was impossible to see your hand, and the path we had followed without a thought ten hours earlier we could now only guess at. I was sure one of us would fall and break a leg and who knew if we would even get out of there alive? I felt my way forward, Sacha's hand in mine, frequently having to admit that I seemed to have strayed off the path and we must go back a few steps, and after what seemed like hours but turned out to be about thirty-five minutes, we came out onto one of the roads leading down into the town.

On another occasion a walk to Alfriston from Lewes turned into a nightmare as the light drizzle grew into persistent rain which drenched us completely. The final ignominy in such circumstances is feeling a little stream of water trickling down ones stomach to ones navel and knowing that ones clothes have lost all power to protect. We were quite a large group and Bernard Harrison tried to keep up our spirits by explaining that this was a mere epiphenomenon incapable of touching the essence of our being, but we were all beyond banter; we lost our way (my fault) and found ourselves on the much longer route to Seaford. Eventually we reached that dreary town and found a little fish and chip café where, once we had sat down and taken off our steaming outer layers, we learned there was no toilet. A walk like this was the last thing Sacha's lungs needed, but she never complained; I would be the one to grumble and Sacha would point out that grumbling about something you could do nothing about never helped. 'It helps me,' I would say. 'All right then, go and grumble to someone else.' That day she was in a particularly good mood though and at lunch told us about her two great-aunts who, in Alexandria, lived on different floors of the same building yet talked to each other by phone every evening. One summer, when all the windows were wide open, it was several weeks before they discovered that one of their phones was not working and that they were hearing each other not down the line but through the windows.

In Lewes on one early spring day when the clocks had just been put forward and I suddenly didn't feel like working any more I asked Sacha if she'd like a walk. I had long wanted to walk to Ditchling along the crest of the Downs and then back through the Weald via Plumpton. Unfortunately I hadn't worked out just how long it would take and we found that we were climbing back over the Downs from Plumpton as night was falling. We were both tired because it had been a punishing walk and we hadn't stopped long, but Sacha never complained or blamed me for starting out so late on so long a walk. Even the well-known and friendly terrain of the Downs became threatening when we could no longer see where to put our feet, but soon we were over the crest and the lights of Lewes appeared below. 'I'm going to sleep well tonight,' Sacha said.

Throughout our time in Lewes we got into the habit, once we no longer had the dogs, of driving up to London for concerts and – less frequently – plays. Those were the great days of the Pierrot Players, then The Fires of London, playing Maxwell-Davies's wild tongue-in-cheek expressionist masterpieces, and of the London Sinfonietta, with their complete Schoenberg and Stravinsky cycles, and when Boulez was the principal conductor of the BBC Symphony Orchestra. Sacha's tastes and mine in music as in so much else were remarkably similar: a passion for Stravinsky, a deep love of early music, the chamber music of Bach, Haydn, Mozart and Beethoven, and most of Bartok, an interest in Schoenberg and Webern (not Berg), and a hearty dislike of the entire Romantic repertory. Sacha could not stand bombast and pretentiousness in any form, whether in people or in art, and she could not stand sentimentality either. To sit through Mahler was agony for her. Where contemporary music was concerned she was always open, never dogmatic. Stockhausen she loved, and individual pieces by Berio, Birtwistle, Messiaen, Ligeti and Jonathan Harvey all moved her. Boulez she found too French, too cold, the bulk of new English works too 'pretty'. She hated what she called 'namby-pamby' music, painting and literature. She liked art that was honest, clean, physical and without self-pity. And she had no purist views about separating the art from the artist, and was always keen to go to pre-concert talks by composers, responding to their manner and gestures as much as to what they said. 'Look at how he bounded on to the platform!' she said of Stockhausen on one occasion at the Barbican. 'He may look more like a German doctor now than like the hippy he used to, but the spirit is still there!'

For the same reason she loved Steven Berkoff and, almost alone among my friends, Neil Kinnock. She remembered him, I think, even in his bitterest moment of defeat, in the 1992 General Election, as the fiery young radical from Cardiff she had first seen on TV many years before. But radicalism for its own sake didn't interest her, and while she loved Beckett she found the antics of the Living Theatre and their like both childish and embarrassing. Great classical acting too was something she responded to, whether in Paul Scofield or Ian McKellen, though she was happy to see Shakespeare done in any guise or form. 'It's like Bach or Mozart,' she would say, 'no matter how often you see or hear it, or how badly it's done, you always get a new facet and it always enriches you.'

She loved watching sport. In France before the war she and Jean had often gone to Marseilles to see the home team play, and in Egypt she had taken me to see a number of international and Cup Final matches, and to the Finals of the Egyptian Tennis Open. When we moved to London from Cheltenham we went to see the great Australian swimmers fresh from their Melbourne Olympic triumphs, and to Crystal Palace whenever there was an international athletics meeting. During the Wimbledon Championships we would cycle up from Putney during the first week, pay five shillings to get into the ground, then wander from court to court looking at the different players before picking up returns for the main courts at six o'clock and watching whatever matches were still in progress there. In Lewes we didn't have TV at first and would go round to friends' houses to watch. Tony Nuttall recalls how she once took a walk round the block because she couldn't bear to watch the final stages of a particularly tense match between someone she liked and someone she couldn't stand – was it one of the epic battles between Borg and McEnroe?

Eventually we succumbed and hired a set for the duration of Wimbledon and then, when that ceased to be possible, for the summer months. If play began at noon Sacha would be up there watching and I would have to bring her her lunch. Sometimes we had supper in front of the set as well. By the middle of the second week we would both admit we couldn't wait for it all to end and allow us to go back to our normal routines, though we were both too weak-willed not to watch. The football World and European Cups were similar occasions, though Sacha would balk at the thought of watching two matches back to back.

Apart from sport, though, she tended to avoid television. I would occasionally persuade her to watch a documentary and she was much moved by Ophuls' *The Sorrow and the Pity*, the account of the resistance and collaboration round Clermond-Ferrand, not far from La Bourboule, which caused such a stir in France by destroying the myth of wartime France as a country of resisters. But by and large she preferred to read. When I was away she would never dream of watching, or even of listening to records, though she would turn on the radio if there was a programme she was interested in.

There is a photo which sums up those years for me: a group of us sitting in the garden in Lewes. In the foreground is the shadowy form of Nimrod, our cat, the last pet we had. Then there is a circle made up of the painters Gillian Barlow and Stephen Finer, both sitting on the grass, Sacha in a deck chair, her white hair prominent, cigarette in hand, laughing and talking; Anna, also smoking, myself and Tim Hyman. The photo was taken by Gillian's boyfriend, yet another painter, Chris Couch. The roses

on the trellis are in bloom and the branch of one of the apple trees cuts into the foreground from the left, laden with fruit. The lawn is covered with daisies. In the middle is a little table with a tea-pot, milk-jug and sugar-bowl. Cups and plates lie on the grass or, in the case of Anna and myself, are precariously held. This was Sacha at her best and happiest: dispensing food and drink, out in the English summer sunshine she loved, surrounded by friends, talking, listening, laughing and smoking. It nicely balances the photo taken by Nell at the start of our sojourn in Sussex, by the sea in Rottingdean, and also forms a kind of diptych with the painting, now in my drawing-room, of precisely the same group of people except that Chris and Gillian have changed places, since he is present and she is the painter. Gillian has not succeeded in capturing Sacha though, and not surprisingly. She was very difficult to paint, though most of our painter friends had a go, partly because she was most herself when most animated and because she was very self-conscious about being looked at. Only Kitaj, because he got her to listen to music and forget he was drawing her, and because of his exceptional skill and empathy, seems to have had any success. His drawing of her in 'Sacha and Gabriel: Listening to Music' is one of his best pencil portraits, I feel, and he must think so too because he has, so far, refused to part with it.

'Are you happy?'

'Yes.'

'Are you sure?'

'Yes.'

Why did I ask her those questions? Why did I need to reassure myself that she was indeed happy? Was I really asking: Have I made you happy? Have I failed to make you happy?

Today, reading Anne Karpf's book about her experience of being the child of a holocaust survivor, I find certain uncanny resemblances to my own case, though Sacha was not, like Anne Karpf's parents, a survivor of the camps, and I was not born after those events but before them. Talking about the growth of clinical studies of the children of survivors, she says: 'The reports often detected in the second generation an extreme identification with the lives of the first. In a process labelled "transposition", survivors' children were described as living simultaneously in the present and the past, and attempting to compensate for their parents' losses.' I had never thought of myself as belonging to a group, and I still resist a lot of the healing and especially psychoanalytical jargon associated with all these reports (to be fair to her, Karpf does as well), but I see now that one aspect of the relationship Sacha and I developed over the years was conditioned by the war, by my sense of what Sacha had been through, by my sense of the sacrifices she had later made for me, and by her sense of the miracle of our survival and the need to protect me even more than a mother would normally do to compensate for what I had myself been through. So our conversations:

'Are you happy?'

'Yes.'

'Really?'

'What do you want me to answer?'

'I don't know. I want to know how you are.'

'I'm fine.'

Sometimes this would lead to talk about all that had happened since we had got to England. At other times Sacha would brush my inept questions aside and get on with her work. Sometimes she pressed my arm silently, as though to say that she understood my need to ask such questions, but that they were unanswerable. 'Riddles are for asking . . .'

All the time, of course, she was translating. It gave her great pleasure to feel that she was, as she put it, contributing to her expenses. More important, though, was the feeling of self-confidence that came with the discovery that she could do substantial intellectual work, day in day out, struggling with meanings and idioms, revising, revising again, and – which she loathed – checking the footnotes and finding the English editions of works cited in other languages. Surprisingly, after winning the Florio Prize she was not inundated with offers to translate from the Italian. In fact she was not offered another Italian translation till the eighties, when Michael Schmidt at Carcanet set in train a mammoth project to translate all the major works of the great Sicilian writer, Leonardo Sciascia, and offered her a number of his works. Instead she was offered, and accepted, *faute de mieux*, extremely boring and long-winded works by French thinkers such as Henri Levebvre and Serge Moscovici, who seemed not so much to write their books as to dictate them, so that sentences would meander on for pages at a time and as often as not end with clauses hanging in the air or the verb still to come. In the late seventies, however, Harvester Press invited me to make a selection of the essays of an author I had long admired and tried to press on English publishers, hitherto without success, Maurice Blanchot. I chose the essays with Sacha's help and wrote the introduction, while she set about the extremely difficult task of rendering Blanchot's highly personal and often arcane style into English. But the very difficulty of the enterprise was a challenge after the stylelessness of what she had previously been asked to do, and, because each essay was relatively short, she felt a sense of accomplishment each time one was completed. It was, I think, the translation she was proudest of, though she enjoyed far more working on Sciascia's tight and elliptical works and on the tough yet lightly ironic prose of the young French novelist, Catherine Axelrad, whose second novel, *La Varsovienne*, was the last book she translated, brilliantly solving the almost insuperable problem of tone it sets for all translators.

The poet and critic Lawrence Lerner, who was for many years a colleague of mine at Sussex, had meanwhile invited her to join a poetry group he and Paul Mallalieu were setting up in Brighton. The host for the evening (they met once a month) would suggest a topic on which all had to write for the next meeting. Sacha was one of the few who always produced something on the topic, and I think in fact she would have been far happier in a pre-Romantic age when poetry was considered a craft and not a means of self-expression, for she relished the challenge of different forms, the more difficult the better.

On the first evening with the group, having written a poem and being called on to read it out, she found – though she had spent the afternoon practising in front of me – that she simply couldn't get the words out, and handed the poem to Larry to read. 'No, Sacha,' Larry said, 'it's your poem, you read it. Take your time, but you've got to do it.' It was the best thing that could have happened to her. She never developed any real confidence as a reader but she did learn to read out loud without too much anguish and to read so as to bring out the meaning and not as though it was something she had never set eyes on before, which was how she read at the start. 'I owe so much to Larry,' she said to me. 'Without the stimulus of the group and his insistence that I read out loud I don't think I could have gone on writing so steadily and improving as I went, I would always have felt a fool and a failure.'

In that way she wrote many of her biblical poems, but also many others, dealing with the ordinary and the everyday in her characteristically simple, pared-down and oddly-angled style:

Expectations

An extra place
is always set
for the unexpected guest.

In the spare room
the spare bed
is regularly aired and made,

the whole house
kept spick and span
for the unexpected one.

Expectancy, alas!
made so explicit
precludes the unexpected visit.

Previous

The previous day
he walks in the garden
nods to his neighbours
reads in his room
behaves as usual
for he doesn't know
that it is the previous day.

The day after
he strolls to the shops
talks to the tradesmen
acknowledges acquaintances
behaves as usual
alas barely aware
that it is the day after.

Many of the poems deal with her inability to write or the clumsi-
ness of what she does manage to produce, or with the miracle of
poetry:

Poetry

As ladder's simple symmetry
facilitates evasion
the measured beat of poetry
permits communication.

For horizontal bars that shape
the poem on the page
translate an effort to escape
bars of the mind's cage.

Some are experiments in form, not only sestinas and villanelles,
but poems like this palindrome:

In the skull
toneless words
pebble drop
one by one,
thud and drum.
On the tongue
float and spin

senseless words
surfacing:
bubble-scum.
Patterns form,
skeins divide
cogently
in the mind:
work begun.
Work begun
in the mind,
cogently,
skeins divide,
patterns form.
Bubble-scum
surfacing,
senseless words
float and spin
on the tongue.
Thud and drum,
one by one
pebble-drop
toneless words
in the skull.

In the course of time a number of good poets passed through
the group and then left as their lives took them to other parts of
the country or they found they were too busy to attend. As always,
it was the young ones Sacha found most congenial: Stephen Plaice,
Philip Gross, Eva Salzman, Don Patterson. Then Larry got a job
in the States, many of the younger poets ceased to attend, and,
eventually, she found it no longer interested her. Shortly after
that the group was wound up, but for almost fifteen years it had
been an integral and important part of her life.

Old age has many advantages, Sacha would say. People are polite
to you in the street and in the shops; they leave their seats to you
in trains; and you can say what you like. Not that she had ever
done otherwise. But as she grew older she did often say things
other people might feel but would hesitate to utter. 'The worst
lecture I have ever heard,' she said after I had taken her to hear
a distinguished visiting speaker at the University. 'How can you
take someone seriously when they dress like that?' she said of a
colleague. And to Tim, after he had painted her portrait: 'I don't
mind your making me look hideous, I am, but what I object to is
your making me look so vile and sensuous.' 'I dread meeting him,'
she said of an acquaintance, 'he slobbers when he kisses you.'

'What I hated,' she said, 'was growing old. In my fifties and
sixties. When I felt my body ceasing to respond to what I wanted
it to do. When I watched myself growing more and more ugly
and repulsive.' 'You're not ugly and repulsive, how can you say
such a thing?' 'I am, there's no point in denying it.'

A cross between Harpo Marx and a monkey was how she saw
herself. And yet she beamed with delight when someone she had
met only once rushed up to her at the Royal Festival Hall: 'Sacha
Rabinovitch? I just wanted to say how beautiful you are.'

Total confidence and utter lack of confidence were so deeply
intertwined in her that it was impossible to use the one to eradicate

the other. I think she had confidence in her judgements, felt she had lived through and seen enough to know her own mind and not to be afraid to say it; but she lacked and had probably always lacked confidence in herself as a person and so in her physical self as well. After all, she had been abandoned by her father, her mother, her nanny and her husband, surely there must be a reason for that?

In a little poem called 'Autobiographical note' she reads her own life like that:

Father went mad and died when I was five.
His lovely widow wed again
but did not long survive.
Orphaned I was at ten.

Alone I was at ten in my small cell
outside of which all fails.
That lesson I'd learnt well.
I grew up hard as nails.

You're hard, they said, as nails and cold as ice.
They turned their backs on me
to look at someone nice.
I turned to poetry.

Like all autobiography, it is a biased view, but there is no doubt
this is how she saw herself, despite her awareness of her warmth
and kindness. And late in life she added to this an equally carica-
tured vision – but, like all caricatures, not wholly misleading – of
her physical appearance:

Selfportrait

Nothing to look at, not much to know,
– her only claim to fame her famous son
in an incredibly eventful lifetime
where more things were suffered than were done –
that sullen, sallow, dwarfish, humpbacked woman,
grey hair 'en brosse', who on fine days you see
flipflop over the downs or round the town,
a cross between a sorceress and a clown, is me.

As her fingers grew more and more arthritic she found it difficult to sew, and then even to type. At least the arthritis was an
excuse for not writing the letters she had never enjoyed writing,
and she delegated more and more of that to me. And she began
to have problems with her back. Or rather, the problems she had
occasionally experienced in the past grew more and more frequent
and prolonged. 'Sacha won't be able to come to dinner,' I would
have to ring up and say, 'she's down with her back problems
again.' When the group met for Greek on Monday evenings she
would more and more frequently let me make the coffee and
simply sit in her usual place and pour. Occasionally, if her back

was bad but we had old friends to dinner she would cook and preside at table, then ask if nobody minded if she lay on the sofa while everyone else sat. 'One thing you're unlikely to suffer from,' a doctor friend told her,'is that curse of old age, especially in women, breaking your hip-bone. You've done so much walking all your life it's unlikely ever to happen to you.' And indeed it didn't. Though once, after a particularly long and arduous walk, she fell flat on her face as we climbed the last hill and was too tired to put her arms out to protect herself, with the result that her face, when I got her to the emergency service of the local hospital, was a bleeding pulp – but she did not break a single bone. And her resistance was still remarkable. Though when I held her or saw her in her bath I shuddered at how thin and stick-like her arms and legs were – she never seemed able to get above six stone now – and though when we went to the Dolomites she took one day off walking in every two, she still coped much better than I did with ten or twelve-hour drives, insisting on taking her turn at the wheel every hour. And she was still as game as ever. Once, returning to Dieppe from the Dolomites, we were held up by an accident on the last stretch of road and just missed the 6.45 ferry we were booked on. When was the next one? we asked. Two a.m. 'Shall we find a hotel for the night?' I asked Sacha, 'and see if we can get a boat tomorrow?' 'Why don't we just wait up till 2?' she said. 'We can have a leisurely dinner, then do a bit of Greek and doze a bit and it'll be time to board.' In the event I booked us a cabin for the four-hour crossing and we were able to have a proper sleep on the boat; by herself Sacha would never have countenanced such a luxury.

One day my father surfaced again. Stella rang to say she had heard from him after all these years, that he was living in Calabria with a new wife, that he had become a faith-healer, and that he wanted to re-establish contact with me. He had sent her a number of his books and of books about him, with instructions to pass them on to me.

The books duly arrived, some published by small esoteric presses in Italy or France, some only in typescript. They were, as far as I could tell by glancing at them, an unappealing mixture of traditional Gnosticism and New Age jargon, of trite remarks about the Self in each of us which needs to be released, laced with a good deal of pseudo-science. Stella rang again to say he was inundating her with letters which showed he was quite mad: 'He says he's been very ill all his life since the war as the result of being tortured by the Gestapo to reveal your whereabouts.' 'He says he's been nominated for the Nobel Prize and that his name has been put forward to the Vatican for possible canonization.'

I had not expected Sacha to be as upset by this as she evidently was. 'I know what he wants,' she said, 'he wants an agent. He's heard of your success and he wants you to help him gain a foothold in England.' I felt I didn't want to take sides in this old quarrel, and merely wrote to him to say I didn't have time at present to read all the books he'd sent me, and sent him one of mine. He wrote back at once to say he didn't read English but was moved by my picture on the dust-jacket.

And then he rang up. It was a summer Saturday and I happened to be in. I answered the phone. 'C'est ton père,' said the voice at the other end. I mumbled something. 'On ne dit pas vous à son père,' he reproved me. But what could I do? He was a stranger. Moreover, as the conversation progressed I was amazed to discover that Sacha was right once again. 'I hear you've had a play put on at the National Theatre,' he said. 'Congratulations.' I explained that it was nothing, a platform performance and not a real production. 'I too have some plays,' he said, 'I wonder if they would be interested.' I explained that they only looked at work already in English. 'Excellent,' he said, 'you could translate them.' 'I don't think I'd have the time.' 'Oh, both our names would appear on the front of course.' 'I still think there's be a problem with time.' 'What I really need,' he said, 'is a good agent in England, my work is taking off in France and Italy and it's time it was better known in England. Perhaps you can help me.' I suggested he look in the *Writers' and Artists' Yearbook*, where the names and addresses of agents were listed, but promised to keep my eyes open. He reiterated his desire to see me in Italy and rang off.

After that I made a big effort to read what he had sent me, feeling that our relationship could only develop on the basis of frankness. I wrote a long and careful letter, pointing out that our views differed radically and that it was difficult for me to accept much of what he said. He couldn't take it. Back came a stiff letter, saying he had struggled through my book and was sorry to see it was so full of the influences of Rilke, Sartre and Jouhandeau, but that no doubt I was still young and would learn to find my voice in time. There was no point in replying.

Sacha remained shaken for some time. I don't know what she thought he could do to her or to me, and she probably didn't herself. Perhaps earlier she would have been able to deal with it more easily, but she was starting to lose her resilience. She was finding it more and more tiring driving up to London and back for concerts and plays or to have dinner with friends. Nimrod, the only pet I think we had for the entire duration of his natural life, had just died, and I suggested we try to find a small flat in London to use as a base. 'Don't be silly,' Sacha said. 'It would just be a needless expense.' She had always made do with what she had. She had never taken a taxi in her life when she could walk or there was public transport available. But I was determined to find something, and, after a long search, I did. I had decided that Putney would be the right place to look. Not that I had particularly fond memories of it, but it was reachable from Lewes in just over an hour, and within easy reach of Anna's in Chelsea and of the South Bank. I found an attic flat in a Victorian house called Vue Tamise which did indeed look out over the Thames, between Putney Bridge and the Railway Bridge. Strangely, when we had lived in Putney we had always taken our walks on the Heath and never by the river (though a friend had once taken Sacha along the towpath to Kew). I don't think I had ever set foot on the road in which our new flat was situated, though Sacha, on her way across to Putney Bridge tube station in the mornings, must have crossed it regularly as she made for the footbridge which runs alongside the railway bridge. It was the last of the many loops and returns which seemed to characterise her wandering life.

Shortly after we got the London flat Sacha suffered another bout of severe constipation, this time combined with pains in her back and legs. The doctor, after much insistence on her part, sent her to the hospital for a check. She was, as always, sure she had cancer. I sat in the crowded waiting-room, wondering how long they were going to be. Suddenly I saw her small figure scanning the rows of occupied chairs. I got up and went towards her. I didn't like the look on her face. 'Well?' I said. 'It's not cancer,' she said. She lowered her voice in embarrassment: 'It's what they call a prolapsed bowel.' 'What does that mean?' 'I could have an operation, but they don't recommend it at my age. The surgeon said it would be uncomfortable but if I could cope with it then it might be better simply to live with it.' 'And is that what you've decided to do?' 'I think so.'

But the pains in her legs wouldn't go away. The doctor was firm: 'Give up smoking and the pains will cease.' 'So I've got a choice,' she said. 'Do I go on smoking and give up walking or do I give up smoking and go on walking?'

She gave up smoking. Almost overnight the pain in her legs disappeared. Yet something had changed in her. Though I would try to coax her out on walks if the weather was good it became harder and harder to do so. And when she did come out she was much slower than she had been. She complained of getting out of breath and found even the smallest hill an effort. Walking along the river in Putney was fine, but the Downs were more or less ruled out. On fine days in London we would walk to Barnes along the river, have lunch and come back over the Common, past the old overgrown cemetery and then through Putney Common. Once or twice she even went as far as Kew, but that sort of distance, which a year or two before she would have found no trouble at all, was now a major feat for her. In Sussex we took to going to Wakehurst Place, which is open all the year round, and whose

gardens Sacha had come to love. There we could stroll for a few yards, stop and look at the plants, and stroll on. She was still as curious about everything, as interesting and funny as ever on our walks, but more and more I found myself going out on my own and now Sacha never joined us when a group of us went on an all-day walk.

She had always said that when she wouldn't be able to walk any more life would no longer be worth living, but she reacted to the setback as she always had, by channelling her enthusiasm and energy into something else – the Greek. But she felt, I think, that a decisive point had been reached in her life, that she had to start to prepare for a final separation from me and from the world.

Some of the poems she wrote at the time were simply a way of coping with her new discomforts. 'The Sleep-Trap', which was published in *The Independent* on 22 September 1993, is one such:

Not even Clarissa was less inclined
to share her lover's couch than sleep to grace
my bed tonight. Guilt grovels in the mind
whose disconnected thoughts jostle and race,
and wounds, so old that anyone would say
they'd lost the power to hurt, open and bleed.
Somewhere a clock numbers steps towards day.
I long for sleep, who will not grant my need.
Thus since I can't expect solace from her
I sample words, experiment with rhyme,
to help me through that dark tunnel of time
into the waking world's bustle and stir.
Or maybe surreptitiously I nurse
the hope that sleep will be ensnared by verse.

Others, such as 'Unwelcome Guest', dramatise and ironise the situation. There are many fine poems about mental anguish, but I know of few which deal with physical pain as this one does:

Pain, that seasoned emigré,
has come unasked to stay.

Since courtesy forbids
probings and questionings

there is no way to know
when or if he will go.

By day he's on the prowl
seeking to gain control,

then creeps with clammy feet
by night between my sheets.

There, at daggers drawn,
we toss and turn till dawn,

for he will not retreat
nor I concede defeat.

Sometimes though she creates triumphant poetry by conceding
defeat, as in 'Contretemps', which is so full of her – her wit, her
dispassionate sense of herself, her anguish:

When I went to bed
rather late that night
what did I find
but my bedside light

already switched on
and myself in bed
complete with book
specs and hoary head.

Then I thought as I stood
by the open door:

I cannot keep up
with myself any more,

and will still be wandering
on the way
when I lie at rest
in my cloak of clay.

But not all her poems of this time deal with herself and her sense of ageing and death. In 'Peonies' her friends would have been able to hear the dogmatic yet always tongue-in-cheek critic of pretension they knew so well:

Peonies
I cannot stand.
They are pompous
conceited and

silly in their
pathetic pose
as rivals to
the fragrant rose.

Devoid of grace
devoid of scent
peonies are
beneath contempt.

In 1994 I was invited to return to Oxford in the academic year 1996–7 to give a series of lectures as the George Weidenfeld Visiting Professor of Comparative Literature. I asked Sacha if she would like to spend a term in Oxford but she said she was too old to leave the comfort of her own surroundings for any length of time. You'll come to my inaugural lecture at least? I hope so, she said. At the same time she announced that her travelling days were over and that she would not be going to the Dolomites again.

Her poems at this time convey her state of mind:

The Poet at Eighty-Four

Four score years and four
are substantially more
than the three score and ten
allotted to men.

Should I call it a life?
Of anguish and strife
have I not had my fill?
Yet there's zest in me still.

Therefore happen what may
whether I go or I stay
it's thanks all the same.
I'm glad that I came.

And the same expression of her struggle to come to terms with
impending death is present in the even bleaker poem, 'The Caller':

One afternoon
at half past four
this stranger came
to my front door.

He doffed his hat
and stared at me:
'Are you the one
I want to see?'

'If you don't know
your own desire
how can I tell
whom you require?'

'I want the man
who owns this place.'
'Then here he stands
before your face.'

'Sir, I am death,
come with me, pray.'
So arm in arm
we walked away.

In the late summer of 1995 our old friend Maria Fitzgerald,
from whom we'd been estranged for some years, finally came to

see us in Putney on one of her rare visits to England. Sacha's back was bad and she lay on the sofa in the living-room, but it was a happy occasion, ending with us all meeting again in the evening at the Elizabeth Hall for a concert of Varèse, Stravinsky and Messiaen. Sacha was thrilled by the Varèse and decided not to stay for the Messiaen but to sit in the foyer and wait for us. Maria went and sat with her. Afterwards she wrote to me: 'It made me so happy to see the great care you are taking of Sacha in her old age. It must make her happy too.' I had never thought of myself as 'taking care' of her, or, really, of her as 'in her old age'. Life is full of such glimpses into our lives from other perspectives.

It had always depressed Sacha to send her poems out to magazines only to find them coming straight back to her, so I had got into the habit of gathering together her year's work, choosing the poems I preferred and sending these off without telling her. This time I decided to send them to the *Jewish Quarterly*, which had been improving steadily in quality in recent years. A few weeks later the new editor, Elena Lappin, rang to say she would very much like to take one of the poems, 'The Garden', which would appear in the Spring issue, due out in March 1996. Sacha was delighted at the news. That I should like a poem of hers, or say I liked it, though of course pleasing to her, was not much of an assurance as to its worth. I was too close to her. But that someone she didn't know, the editor of a magazine who must be inundated with poems, should actually choose one of hers gave her the sense that it had a certain objective worth. I know just what she felt, and it is probably what every writer always feels. One hopes one will grow out of it, not need the confirmation of the outside world, but of course one never does.

For her birthday, on 9 December 1995, a beautiful sunny winter's day, we invited Tony and Bet Inglis, who had been neighbours of ours all those years before in Kingston, to lunch and a little walk in Wakehurst Place. When we got there Sacha balked at the thought of the steep descent to the lake and the ascent that would necessarily follow, and suggested to Bet that the two of them sit on the grass and wait for Tony and me. We walked round the lake and up by the pinetum and as we approached I saw the two women for a moment as a stranger might see them: two white-haired ladies, one very old, one middle-aged, sitting on the grass and talking animatedly. One of them is the mother I have known all my life, I thought, and the other is my age. How strange!

Two days later Sacha sat up for a whole evening listening to all six Bartók quartets, which were being broadcast consecutively. I listened to the first three, then took a break, went upstairs and watched something on television, and came down for the last one, but Sacha was thrilled by what she had experienced. I could only marvel at her ability to concentrate. A week later we listened to an Invitation Concert from Birmingham in which a new quartet of Jonathan Harvey's was being performed, along with the first English airing of Elliot Carter's most recent quartet and one of Brian Ferneyhough's. Sacha was very enthusiastic about Jonathan's piece: 'If he can only get rid of that English softness and Romanticism he really will be a major composer.' 'You'll have to tell him how much you liked it,' I said. 'If I see him,' she said. 'I'm past writing.'

Then on 27 December Anna rang to say that her sister Monica had died in the night. She was sixty-four and had simply passed away in her sleep.

It's difficult to take in the death of someone, even someone close, when one has not seen them for over a decade and their death occurs three thousand miles away. I was shocked, but there seemed no point in postponing the three-day trip I had already planned with a friend. When I got back, however, I saw that the news had affected Sacha far more profoundly than I had at first realised. I should have cancelled my trip and stayed with her of course, but the fact is that I hadn't. As always, I was surprised at the depth of her feelings and her love. No doubt she also saw far more clearly than I, who had never lost anyone close to me except for animals and Robin, what Monica's death would mean to Chickie, who was now almost totally deaf and had for a long time been very dependent on her. In fact, we soon realised, talking to Anna, everyone had been dependent on her: her husband, the ex-basket-ball international, who could barely make himself a cup of tea; her two married daughters; and of course Chickie herself. One of the daughters had herself recently suffered a terrible tragedy when her sixteen year old son, who had been in a vegetable state since shortly after his birth, but who had, for that reason, been the focus of all her attention, finally died. In fact, it may well have been the boy's death, and the mingled relief and guilt it brought with it, which had precipitated Monica's own death.

January 1996 was a terrible month: bitterly cold, very raw, and with a perpetual mist hanging over everything. Anna had wanted to go to Egypt as soon as she heard the news, but Medhat, Monica's husband, had explained that Monica would be buried, Moslem fashion, that very day, and it would be better for Anna to come a month later to take part in the ceremony associated with the fortieth day after death. 'We must go up to London to see Anna before she goes,' Sacha said, but we kept putting it off because of my teaching commitments and the cold weather. Finally, towards the end of the month, with her departure imminent, we could put it off no longer and drove up to the Putney flat.

The flat was freezing. The ventilator in the bathroom let in a cold blast of air and nothing I could do to muffle it really helped. We put up the central heating as high as possible but Sacha couldn't seem to get warm. I had got tickets for a play and asked her if she wanted me to ring up and cancel, but she said no, she'd soon get warm. We went and had tea with Anna, but there was little to say. Anna was dumb with sorrow and there was nothing one could say or do to lessen that. We left, had a bite of supper, then walked the few yards to the theatre. The play was a big disappointment, a sub-Stoppardian farce about Freud and Dali which had received rave reviews but seemed to both of us to be straining to be funny and profound. Gloomily, we drove home through the frozen London streets.

The next morning at breakfast Sacha asked if I had slept well, then confessed that she had hardly slept at all, that she had been to the lavatory every few minutes, that she felt she had caught cold on her bladder and had even been unable to contain herself and had wetted her nightdress. 'Stay in bed today,' I said, 'and tomorrow we'll go back to Lewes and see a doctor on Monday.' 'It's nothing,' she said, 'just a chill.' She stayed in bed and I plied her with warm drinks and kept changing her hot-water bottle. By the evening she said she felt better, and that night she slept reasonably well. I packed while she dressed and we drove down to Lewes. The next morning she said she had spent another terrible night. Her stomach was hurting her and her incontinence clearly depressed her terribly.

I called the doctor and he came that afternoon, confirmed that it was a bad chill and prescribed antibiotics. But though over the next day or two the incontinence declined, her old problem of constipation set in. I called the doctor again and said Sacha was in considerable pain, which had now affected her back. He prescribed some pills to ease the constipation and told her to finish the course of antibiotics. A few days went by, with Sacha in more and more pain. Tough as she was mentally, she was a coward where physical pain was concerned, and knew it. I could hear her groaning and moaning in her room upstairs, and when I went up to see if I could help she would try to laugh it off, saying that groaning out loud actually helped to ease the pain. The doctor examined her, then said he would be sending a nurse along to give her an enema. I knew how painful and demeaning Sacha had found it when this had happened after our first trip to Egypt, but at least it had done the trick. This time though nothing happened. The doctor came back and examined her. 'It's very blocked,' he said, 'but we're getting there. You ought to make an effort to get up.' 'I can't,' Sacha said, almost crying. 'Of course you can,' he said. By now she had completed the course of antibiotics and been in bed for ten days. 'Just get up and go down for your meals,' he said. 'Or take a little walk round the house. You've got to help the pills you know.' But something seemed to have gone out of her. She made an effort one day, came down for lunch, then went straight up to bed again, and when I asked her in the evening whether she would be down again she said no, please would I bring her some broth in bed. When I brought it she was almost in tears. 'I'm sorry to be such a nuisance. I know you've got lots of work to do.' 'Don't be silly. You're not being a nuisance. But can't you just make a little effort and come down?' 'I feel so tired. Tomorrow perhaps.' 'Don't worry,' I said, 'once we've got the constipation beaten you'll start to feel better.'

The doctor prescribed a second course of antibiotics. 'Look at my tummy,' Sacha said to him. It was like a football, round and taut. And she was still occasionally wetting the bed at night, unable to get to the lavatory in time. The nurses came every day, changed the sheets, washed her, changed her nightdress, gave her enemas. 'There's progress,' the doctor said, examining her. 'Just try to walk round the house a bit every day, you need to stand up and walk about to help the laxatives along.' She held onto my arm and I walked her slowly round the house, stopping at every window to look out at the garden and the Downs, all covered by the cold unyielding mist. I tried to prolong the tour but she was anxious to get back to bed and our experiment wasn't repeated. 'We're making progress,' the doctor said, examining her. 'I'll give you some stronger laxatives. I'll get the nurse to give you a more powerful enema.'

Fortunately I had a light term and was only going to the University once a week. The rest of the time I was scurrying out to get the medicines the doctor kept prescribing and bringing the nurses what they wanted in the form of sheets, wash-basins and towels when they called every morning. Now they regularly washed Sacha in bed. She had grown dreadfully thin, her face gaunt, her arms and shoulders like sticks. Only her stomach remained round and taut as a football. The pain never left her. I had given up trying to coax her down for meals or for walks round the house, and just prayed that the combined power of the new laxatives and the enemas would finally release the dreadful blockage. 'Sacha ill,' I noted in my diary. 'Watch her slowly fading away.' But I didn't really believe it.

On Tuesday 27 January, as I was preparing to go to the University, dressing in my room below Sacha's, I heard her get up and go to the bathroom. When she came out I called up: 'How are you? All right?' 'No,' she said. 'What's the matter?' 'I just want to live to see my poem in print,' she said. 'Oh come on,' I said, 'surely you want to live to hear my Oxford lectures?' 'That may be difficult,' she said.

I went downstairs to my study to sort out my papers and pack my bag. I don't know how long I had been there when I heard a crash. I rushed upstairs and found Sacha lying on the floor at the foot of the stairs leading up to her attic room, quite still. I turned her over, calling her urgently, but she showed no sign of life. The mask had settled on her face. Her eyes were open but did not seem to see anything. 'Mum!' I said, 'Mum! Speak to me! Speak to me!' I put my mouth to hers in the foolish hope that I would somehow be able to revive her with my breath. And then she groaned and moved. I rushed to the phone and rang 999: 'I want an ambulance quickly. An old lady has fallen downstairs.' It seemed as if I had entered a new world, calling her 'an old lady', and I remember noting it at the time. She was, of course, she was eighty five. But it was as though in falling she had become just that, no longer Sacha but 'an old lady'.

I rushed back to her, dragged the duvet off my bed and covered her. I held her hand. It was very cold. But there was a pulse in her wrist and every now and again she groaned. The doorbell rang and I rushed down. One man. 'I got your call. The ambulance is on its way. Can I see the person?'

He came upstairs, knelt down by Sacha. 'What's her name?' 'Sacha.' 'Sacha,' he said, 'can you hear me Sacha?' She groaned. 'I'm going to straighten you out, Sacha,' he said. The bell went again. This time it was his mate with the ambulance and some equipment. He followed me upstairs. The two of them stood around, discussing the issue. 'No way we can get a stretcher round those stairs. Have to get a chair. OK.' He talked into his mobile phone, gave the address, explained the situation. They didn't seem to be in any hurry. They know best, I kept saying to myself, don't pester them, they know best. One of them went down and came back with a folding chair. 'Come on Sacha,' they said. She protested feebly as they tried to lift her into it. 'That's all right Sacha,' they said. I resented their familiarity. How dare they call her Sacha? They didn't know her. Why did they have to see her in this moment of weakness? And why were they so slow? Didn't they realise she needed to get to hospital as quickly as possible? And yet she was alive. She had come through this as she had come through so much. And at least at the hospital they would be able to deal with the constipation the wretched GP seemed unable to do anything about.

They got her downstairs. 'Do you want to come with us?' they asked me. I said I'd follow in the car. 'Which hospital are you taking her to? 'The Royal Sussex. Accidents and Emergency. We'll be a few minutes settling her in. Don't hurry.'

I stood by the phone, trying to gather my thoughts. I rang the university and said I wouldn't be in to teach that day. I rang the doctor, who was due to visit, and told the nurse what had happened. I rang Bet Inglis, who'd said she'd look in that day, and told her. Then, at the last minute, I thought I'd ring Jess Wood, the young painter Sacha had sat for and was so fond of, and who lived round the corner from the hospital. Jess and her partner Sheila were always in and out of the hospital, they told us, keeping tabs on their many young friends with Aids. Miraculously, Jess was in. 'I'll be at the entrance to A&E,' she said when I'd told her what had happened.

I rushed out of the house, sure the ambulance must have gone, but it was still there, all closed up. I peered into the back and saw them fitting tubes to Sacha's mouth and doing something to her wrists. I knocked on the rear door. Grudgingly, one of the men opened it. 'What's happening?' I said. 'Nothing. We're settling her in.' 'Has something happened to her?' 'No, it's routine. Just wait and follow us.'

I got into the car and waited. Sure enough, a few minutes later they set off. We went down to Falmer, turned left over the Downs, right at Woodingdean, then left again at the racecourse, into Kemp Town, then along Edward Street and right up the hill to the tall tower block of the hospital. I followed close behind them and tried to find a parking place but it was full. I went out again, down the street, found a place, hurried back. Jess was at the entrance. 'It's all right,' she said, 'they've just taken her in.' She took my arm: 'I know this place. Don't worry.'

They had taken her into a cubicle on the ground floor and a nurse was fastening various tubes to her. 'We're just checking the heart and a few other things,' she said. 'There don't seem to be any broken bones.'

The mask had disappeared and Sacha was looking at me and then at Jess. 'It's Jess,' I said. She smiled. When she liked people she adored them, and when she disliked them I'm afraid she hated them. She liked Jess. 'Hullo Sacha dear,' Jess said. 'It's a nice mess you've got yourself into, isn't it?'

'What happened?' Sacha asked.

'You fell down the stairs.'

'What time was it?'

'Just before ten.'

She lay quiet. The nurse finished her work and said they were going to wheel her out to another part of the ward to await the doctor's visit.

'When will that be?' I asked.

'When he's free.'

'You can't tell me when that might be?'

'No. I'm sorry. He has to deal with the emergencies first.'

'You'll have to wait a long time,' Jess said. 'Better be prepared for it.'

Sacha's eyes were closed. We were by ourselves with her in a small cubicle with the curtains drawn.

'I'll get you a cup of coffee,' Jess said.

'I'll come with you,' I said. I bent over the bed and said: 'We're just going to have a cup of coffee.' She didn't respond. The sedative they had given her was clearly having an effect.

We went down the corridor to a bright coffee bar with views over Kemp Town and the sea beyond. The mist kept rolling in but every now and again it would clear and a weak sun would be visible. 'You may be here a very long time,' Jess said. 'How long?' 'All day.' 'All day?' 'They're all overworked here,' she said. 'She's clearly not in any immediate danger so they'll put her at the end of the queue.' 'But there'll be more urgent cases brought in all day!' I said. 'Yes, that's why you've just got to be patient. I'll have to go at lunch, I have a pupil coming this afternoon, will you be all right?' 'Of course.' 'I'll come back afterwards.' 'Only if you feel like it. Go now, don't worry about me. You've been wonderful.' 'You're sure? I do have a bit of preparation to do.' 'Of course. Off you go. I'll come out with you and get a paper.'

So the day dragged on. Sacha would become conscious for a while and ask me urgently: 'What happened?' 'You fell down the stairs.' 'What time was it?' 'Just before ten. How are you feeling?' 'All right.'

I went out and found a nurse. 'Can you give me any information about my mother, Mrs Rabinovitch?' 'Yes. We think she had some sort of blip of the heart. She'll probably need a pacemaker. The doctor will be round to see her as soon as possible. He'll explain it all to you.' 'You can't tell me when he'll be round?' 'No, I'm sorry.' 'Thank you for the information, anyway.'

I had some lunch, looked at the sea, read the paper from end to end, sat with Sacha. It was five o'clock. 'When do you think the doctor will be round?' I asked the nurse when I finally found her. 'As soon as he can.' 'My mother's been here since ten-thirty.' 'He'll be with her as soon as he can.' 'Thank you.'

Sacha was asleep. I went out to get some air.

When I returned I made for the row of cubicles with the emergency cases waiting for the doctor, and suddenly realised I couldn't remember which one was Sacha's. I drew the curtain of one and there was Sacha lying on the bed, an anonymous old lady, I suddenly thought, just like any other. I went towards her but as I approached I suddenly realised it wasn't Sacha. It was horrible. As though old age and the fall had so destroyed her individuality that now even I couldn't recognise her any more. 'What do you want?' a voice said. 'What are you doing in here?' 'I'm sorry,' I said, 'I'm looking for Mrs Rabinovitch.' 'She's not here.' 'No, I'm sorry.'

I went down the row of curtains, peering through each one, and finally found her. I went in and held her bony hand. She opened her eyes: 'What happened?' 'You fell down the stairs. You're all right. The doctor's coming soon.' 'What time was it?' 'Just before ten.' 'I fell down the stairs?' 'That's right. You must have slipped and fallen. Then you must have knocked yourself out as you came down.' 'What time was it?' 'Just before ten.'

She relapsed into sleep.

The doctor came at last, a handsome Indian, exuding the feeling that he had all the time in the world. 'I'm very sorry I couldn't get to her before, as you can see we're rushed off our feet here. Now the situation with Mrs Rabinovitch is this. She seems to have had a temporary blackout. A sort of blip. A momentary pause of the heart. And so she fell. She hasn't broken any bones, mainly because she was unconscious as she fell and because she's very light. We're going to have to put in a pacemaker. It's not a very serious operation, we'll give you all the information about it. We're transferring her to Ward X in the main hospital. She'll probably be in here for a week or two.'

'What about the constipation?' I asked. 'That's what got everything going.' 'Yes, there's constipation there, we'll deal with that once we've got the pacemaker in, quite frankly that's less important. Now we're going to move her. You can go home and get something to eat and if you want to come and see her about eight o'clock in the new ward, that will be fine.' 'Thank you doctor, I'm grateful.'

I went home, rang Anna and told her what had happened. She had returned from Egypt and the ceremony associated with her sister's burial a fortnight before. I knew she was still in deep shock, but she was my closest relative and I needed support. I told her the story of the day, and as I spoke I felt better. Then I had something to eat and drove back into Brighton.

They had put her in a pleasant ward, a large square room with a bed in each corner and a view out over the sea. She seemed weak but fully herself again. I told her what the doctor had said, showed her the leaflet about pacemakers I had been given, and explained what they planned to do. 'Are they going to deal with the constipation?' she asked. 'Of course. I suppose you got yourself into hospital because you had lost faith in the doctor, but I wish you hadn't done it in quite such a dramatic way.' She laughed. A nurse brought round some supper but, after toying with it for a while, she left it. 'Shouldn't you try to eat something?' 'I don't feel hungry.' 'How are you feeling?' 'Weak.'

I went home greatly relieved and impressed with the NHS. What were people talking about when they described filthy conditions and inadequate provision? True they had taken a long time getting to her, but then it seemed they had taken tests straight away and realised she wasn't an emergency. And now she was in a comfortable and peaceful ward. We were very lucky.

I spent as much of the next day with her as I could. She was a little more aware than she had been, and I felt that once again she had come through. She laughed, told me about a couple of visits she had had. She said she'd slept well. Then, as I was thinking of leaving her for the night, a nurse came round and said they would be moving her in the next half hour. This was the ward to which they transferred those who had been in A&E and now she was going to be taken to an ordinary ward to await her operation. I found it a bit strange that they should move patients just before they went to sleep instead of giving them time to get used to their new surroundings, but was glad at least that I was there to bring along her things – the books and notebooks I had brought her, the flowers and cards she had started receiving.

The ward she was now moved into filled me with foreboding, though. It was exactly what I had originally expected of an NHS hospital, as though now we were getting down to reality: a vast room with ten or twelve beds, bewildered and depressed-looking patients, and a harassed-looking nursing staff. There was no view. I felt bad about leaving her there to try and go to sleep, but comforted myself with the thought that she would soon be home.

The next few days confirmed my gloom. Sacha was now in terrible pain again with her constipation. Her high hopes that the hospital would know how to deal with it were turning into a kind of depression as she found they couldn't. And nobody would tell me anything: when the operation would be taking place, what they thought about the constipation, whether or not they were pleased with her condition. Doctors and nurses, when I managed to talk to them, assured me they were aware of all the problems and were dealing with them. Finally a date for the operation was fixed. I was told it would be at two in the afternoon and to ring up at about four, when she would be back in the ward. Promptly at four I rang and was told she hadn't come down from the operating theatre yet but to phone again in half an hour. At five they told me the operation had gone off successfully but that she wasn't back yet and to phone again. 'In how long?' 'Give her an hour.' I phoned at six and was told she still wasn't back but to come along and wait for her there.

I came and waited. An old man in a dressing gown was watching television. I tried to read. Finally a nurse came in and said there'd been a hold-up at the other end and I'd better go up to the operating theatre and see her. How do I get there? I asked, but their directions were so complicated I soon lost track. Fortunately someone was going in that direction and said he'd show me. When I eventually got there a nurse at reception showed me a door and told me to go in, that the operation had been a success and she was just waiting to be taken back to the ward. I went into a large room. Sacha was in a bed at the far end. She turned towards me and burst into tears. 'Take me out of here, take me out of here! I called and called and no-one came! Oh, Gabriel, I'm in such pain and they left me here for hours. I thought I was going to die.'

I tried to calm her but she had got into such a state, was so upset and in so much pain that she wouldn't calm down. The surgeon who had operated came in. He took her hand. 'The operation went very well,' he said. 'Why did you leave me here alone like that?' Sacha said. 'I called but no-one came. No-one told me anything. I thought I was going to die.' The doctor explained that they were short of porters, that because Sacha was stuck in the post-operating room he had had to cancel his next operation. 'Why were they short of porters?' I asked. 'The hospital can't afford them,' he said. 'But wasn't cancelling an operation expensive?' 'Of course it was.' 'Wasn't it more expensive than the cost of two porters?' 'Of course it was.' 'Well then?' He raised his shoulders hopelessly.

Finally the porters arrived. They bundled Sacha into the lift and trundled her along endless corridors till we were finally back in the ward. 'At least the operation went well,' I said. 'I thought you were never going to come,' she said. 'I thought I was going to die there alone.' 'Will you be able to sleep, do you think?' 'I don't know, there are patients here who scream in the middle of the night.' 'Now you've had the operation,' I said, 'they'll be able to deal with the constipation and then you'll be able to come home.' She pressed my hand: 'I'm sorry I was such a nuisance. I didn't know what was happening. Nobody told me anything.' 'You weren't a nuisance, it's their fault.' 'I was terrified. No-one came. I screamed and screamed but no-one came.' 'It's all right. I'm here now. It's all right.' 'I'm sorry,' she said. I held her bony hand. It was ice-cold.

On my way out I told the head nurse I was furious about what had happened. 'You can file an official complaint,' she said. 'I intend to,' I said, 'but that doesn't make it any better for my mother.'

The next day the head nurse was very short with me: 'She's being very difficult.' 'What do you mean?' 'She's being very difficult with the staff.' 'What does that mean? She's an intelligent, articulate person, what's the problem?' 'She's being uncooperative.'

I sat down by Sacha's bed. 'I'm in pain,' she said. 'Why don't they do something about my tummy?' 'They will,' I said. 'Don't be impatient. What's this about being uncooperative?' 'The nurse was rude to me.' 'What did she say?' 'She shouted at me'. 'Shouted at you?' 'I'm so unhappy, Gabriel!' She burst into tears.

I waited for the doctor to come. As always he was hours late. Friends came to visit. Eventually the doctor and his entourage arrived. He checked her notes and examined her. 'We're doing well,' he said. 'When will you deal with my constipation?' 'We have to go slowly.' 'I'm in so much pain.' 'Patience,' he said, and turned away.

The days went by. Sacha said she felt that a weight had literally been lifted off her chest. 'I realise now I've felt a kind of depression weighing on me for the last two or three years. And it was purely physical all the time!'

She had told the GP countless times she thought there was something wrong with her heart, but he had pooh-poohed it.

'You've got terrible lungs and terrible arthritis, but there's nothing wrong with your heart.' I could never understand why he hadn't simply sent her to the hospital for a check-up. Then at least she could have had a pacemaker fitted without the horror of the past few days. And wasn't it clear that her reluctance to get up in the three weeks she'd been at home suffering with her bowels was due not to her laziness but to the state of her heart?

Gradually they began to get the better of the constipation. Gradually her stomach started to unswell. She was still in pain from the operation but at least the rest of her was starting to return to normal. I hoped now she might start to eat again and put on a bit of weight. She looked skeletal. There was hardly any flesh on her bones at all. 'Soon we're going to move her to the Brighton General,' the head nurse said. 'What for?' 'For general rehabilitation and physiotherapy.' 'When will that be?' 'We'll let you know.' 'Tomorrow?' 'We'll let you know.' She didn't like me and she didn't like Sacha and she wasn't going to hide it.

The next day I was at the University in the morning and decided to have a rest and some tea and then go in to see Sacha. I was just sitting down to my tea when Tony Inglis rang: 'I'm at the hospital. Sacha is in a bit of a state. They're going to move her at any moment and she wants you.' 'But they said they'd phone me.' 'They say they've tried but couldn't get you.' 'That's ridiculous, I've been here all afternoon. Never mind. I'll be right down.'

When I got there Sacha was indeed in a state. Tony was trying to calm her. He said to me quietly: 'She's a bit confused.' 'Where are they taking me?' Sacha said. 'Why didn't they call you?' 'It's all right,' I said, 'there was a misunderstanding. At least Tony was with you.' 'He's been a dear,' Sacha said, 'I don't know what I would have done without him.' I explained to her that they were taking her just up the hill to the Brighton General. 'They've finished with the operations and the medication and now you're going there for rehabilitation before coming home.' 'Why didn't you come? I was so frightened.'

Tony slipped away. The ambulance men came in. I gathered up her things and prepared to accompany them. In the ambulance she cheered up. 'Can I smoke?' she asked the men. 'If you want to blow us all up,' they said. She laughed.

The new ward was even dingier than the last, but my main feeling was one of relief. The worst was over and from now on she would be on the road to recovery.

They put her in a bed in a small room off the main ward. A woman in the bed opposite kept moaning and saying: 'Nurse, nurse, I've wet myself. Nurse, nurse, I want to go to the lavatory.' I called a nurse. 'She's not all there,' she explained to me. 'She's on a catheter, she doesn't know what she's saying.' 'Can't you explain to her?' 'She doesn't understand.' They brought Sacha some food. 'I'm vegetarian,' she said. 'Will you have a sandwich then dear?' I found the bag of food I'd brought and tried to get her to eat something, but she said she wasn't hungry, just tired. 'I'll try to sleep now,' she said. 'Nurse, nurse,' the woman opposite called out. 'Take me to the lavatory. Please nurse, I beg you, for the love of God, take me to the lavatory.' 'Is she going to go on like this all night?' I asked. 'No, she'll quieten down.' 'How is my mother going to get any sleep?' 'She'll quieten down.'

But the next day Sacha was in a state again: 'That woman never stopped calling out. I didn't get a wink of sleep. Can't you try and get me moved?' I spoke to the nurse in charge, who said he would see. I sat with Sacha and tried to calm her. The woman opposite went on mechanically: 'Doctor! Doctor! Take me to the lavatory! Nurse, I've wet myself, nurse, please, for the love of God, I've wet myself.' The nurse came back to say yes, there was a bed in the main ward. I helped bring her things, wondering what would have happened had Sacha not had me to press for her to be moved. 'When will the doctor be coming?' I asked. 'Some time this afternoon.'

When he did arrive he was noncommittal. 'We'll have to get her moving again. We'll have to give her some physiotherapy. She's much too weak to go home as she is but I hope in a week or so it'll be a different story.'

The cold mist still hung over the whole of the South Coast. I tried to do some work in the mornings, then drive down to the hospital with some lunch for Sacha, stay with her while she ate – always very little, always needing to be coaxed – and then come back in the later afternoon and sometimes again after dinner. 'Did you do your therapy today?' 'No, I had such a bad night last night I was just too tired.' The next day she was a bit more cheerful: 'I walked all the way across the room and back.' She joked with the nurses, especially the male head nurse. 'How are you Sacha?' 'As well as can be expected in a place like this.' She told me about each of the nurses in turn, what they had told her about themselves, if they were married, how many children they had. I brought her more books and the paper every day, but all she would do was the crossword puzzle, and even that she often left unfinished, which was unlike her. I bought her a small radio, but she never listened. Friends came to visit, either from London or from Sussex. As always in these situations some of the people one had expected to visit stayed away while others one hadn't thought of were the most assiduous visitors. I asked the head nurse: 'When do you expect her to come out?' I had promised to go to Princeton for a fortnight in early April and was beginning to wonder whether I should cancel my visit. 'She's not doing as well with the physio-therapy as we had hoped,' he said. 'She just refuses to budge. You must do it, I tell her, you won't get out of here unless you make an effort. I'm tired, she says. Tomorrow. Unless you do you won't be able to get home. I know. Tomorrow.'

One morning as I was having breakfast *The Jewish Quarterly* arrived in the post. I opened it. Yes, there was her poem. I couldn't believe it, little magazines never appear when they are meant to, but Elena Lappin had proved as good as her word: mid-March, she'd said, and here we were in mid-March and I had the magazine in my hands. I gave it to Sacha as soon as I got to the hospital. The old smile flashed across her face. 'Look,' she said to the head nurse. 'My poem.' He read it carefully, then handed it back to her: 'I'll have to get your autograph, Sacha.'

The Garden

When I was young I was
a landscape gardener.
I put things in perspective,
patterned my paths,
plotted the colour-scheme
of every border.
I lopped the tops of trees,
I trimmed the hedges.
My lawns were bowling-greens.
Then things got out of hand.
Nothing turned out as planned.
I let the place run wild:
growths gone to seed,
weeds high as a child
and ivy twining round
the trunks of trees
whose branches join above
against the sun.
Green shade prevails.
Nature has overrun
the garden, and I
relish my leisure.

The head nurse said he would fix me an appointment with the social worker so that we could discuss what should be done when Sacha left the hospital. The social worker was a warm, plump, intelligent Irishwoman in her forties. She asked me about Sacha, looked at her file. 'She's obviously a highly capable and intelligent woman,' she said, 'still in full possession of her faculties. The sooner she gets out of here the better. People can only catch things in hospitals and, besides, depression can set in without the patient even realising it. No, the sooner she leaves the better for her and for you. What I'll do is look into the question of nursing homes with physio facilities.' She then explained the finances to me, and I asked her to look in the Lewes area so as to make it easier for me to visit Sacha. 'What I'll also do,' she said, 'is fix an appointment for you with the consultant so that you can have a chat about her long-term future.'

I went home relieved to have had such a sensible and seemingly efficient person to deal with. The next day when I went in to see Sacha in the afternoon the head nurse told me the social worker had fixed an appointment with the consultant for the following day, Wednesday, at 9.30. I told Sacha and said I would then come in and tell her what the consultant had said. She was quite cheerful, her old smile had returned, she was sleeping a little better, and I had no doubt that I would be able to get her out within a week.

The consultant's door was open. I knocked and he ushered me in and sat me down opposite him. He came straight to the point: 'You must have noticed that things have not been going well with your mother. She hardly eats, she is reluctant to get up from her bed, and she is getting dangerously thin. What we now think happened the day she fell is that she had an actual heart attack, not, as we initially thought, just a momentary blip, and her heart has not really recovered. Unfortunately the pace-maker can only regulate the beat of the heart, it cannot actually pump. The heart is slowing down. That's why we've ceased to try and get her to walk. I don't want to sound pessimistic, but she could suddenly go. The next week will decide. She might pull round, there's always a chance of that, but she might well not.'

As he was speaking I was aware that I had both expected and not expected this. I had thought he would talk in terms of one or two years at most, but then I knew Sacha had spent her life confounding doctors' expectations. But now he mentioned it, of course I had noticed how thin she was, how unlike her it was not to open a book from one week to the next. Jess had remarked that first morning in the Accident and Emergency Unit: 'Sacha's been so frail and thin these last years she's almost a spirit already; in a way it hardly matters if she passes over completely into the spirit world or stays down here on earth.' I think she knew the end had come and was trying to prepare me. As a mystically-minded Catholic such terms came easily to her, but now the consultant had said it I understood what she had meant. I understood too why Sacha had been so surprisingly reluctant to respond to the nurses' efforts to get her to stand up, walk about. And it suddenly came to me that of course she had been suffering from her heart for a very long time, that, like Bimbo's, her heart had for several years slowly been giving up.

'Should I tell her?' I asked the consultant. 'I think you should,' he said. I was glad he had said that as I had been intending to anyway. Sacha had always wanted to know the worst, and I had always respected that. She knew that death and how one met it was the final test, and, having passed all the other tests life had set her, she was determined to pass that last one too. I would not deprive her of the chance to do so. I sat down by her bedside. Now I could see she was really nothing but skin and bone, her large mouth and ears larger than ever now there was so little flesh left on her face, her lovely hair thin on her scalp. I took her hand and told her what the consultant had said: 'So I *wasn't* being lazy!' she said, genuinely relieved that, even now, she had not refused to do what the physiotherapist wanted out of some kind of self-indulgence.

Suddenly there was nothing more to say. 'How do you feel?' I asked her. 'All right,' she said. I held her hand and she clasped mine tight, then gradually relaxed and fell asleep. I sat on, trying to come to terms with the fact that she was dying. Then I released her grip and went home. I came back in the afternoon to find Bet Inglis with her. She seemed weaker even than in the morning. I tried to get her to eat, sitting on the bed beside her and feeding her, spoon by spoon. I thought as I did so how strange it was and how inevitable that our roles of mother and child should now be reversed.

Bet had slipped away. I sat with her for a while but once again she drifted off into sleep, and I left her. When I came back in the evening she was asleep. I sat by her bedside for a while but she showed no sign of waking up and I left.

I was dreading, and had been dreading since she first went into hospital, that there would be a call in the middle of the night. But so far it had not come, and it didn't come that night either. The next morning, however, when I was at my desk, for I had determined to try and work for a couple of hours every day before going in to see her, the phone did go. It was one of the nurses: Could I come, my mother was in a very disturbed state, she kept asking for me. 'I'll be along straight away,' I said. I put down the phone and it rang again at once. It was the social worker, wanting to talk about nursing homes. I told her the time for that might well be past, wondering again at the lack of communication between the different units of the hospital.

It was just past ten when I got there. I ran to the bed, relieved to see that the curtains had not been drawn round it. Sacha hugged me and held me close. 'I'm dying,' she said. 'I just wanted to tell you how happy you've made me, how completely the happiness of the second half of my life wiped out the pain of the first part. But now I'm tired of my body and want to let go.'

She explained to me that she hadn't woken up in the usual way, only come to when she was being washed, and was terrified that she would not be able to say those last words to me. I tried to tell her what she had meant to me and how extraordinary it had been to know and love and be loved by her, but I couldn't really say it because I was crying and I was aware that we were in the midst of strangers. Even if I had managed it I don't think she would have heard: having made the effort to speak she had slipped into an uneasy sleep.

I think she let go the moment I told her what the consultant had said. Should I not have told her then? Would she have held on, her will still indomitable even though there was hardly any body left to house it? Who knows? It's hardly a real question. I had to tell her, and if she reacted as she did that was because it was what she really wanted. In the midst of my grief and confusion I was immensely proud of her, proud that she, who had, in the last few years, grown so frightened of being abandoned, should now be the one to accept and let go. Like the biblical patriarchs she had thought and written about all her life, she would at least die in the right way, old and full of years, speaking her last words in full consciousness of what she was doing. It must have been a great sadness to her not to be surrounded at this moment by grandchildren, and she must have been frightened for me, she who had shielded me from so much all through my life. But she had never been a conventional person, she did not know the meaning of social convention, and the fact that I was there and that she could tell me what she had prepared was, I am sure, as important for her as it was for me.

I sat by her bed, trying to take it in. She moaned and turned, trying to find a comfortable position, the mask of pain and otherness once more fixed on her face. She was my mother, with whom I had gone through so much, and she was an old lady dying in a public ward in a Brighton hospital. There didn't seem to be much connexion between the two.

I went home to have some lunch. When I returned Jess was there at her bedside, holding her hand. Sacha seemed at first to be asleep, but then she looked at me and smiled through her pain and confusion, then once again closed her eyes and went on moaning. Later Jess told me that she had said to her just what she had said to me in the morning: that she had been so happy for the last part of her life, that she owed me so much, that she was tired of her body and wanted to be free of it, that she had no fear of death though she had no religious belief and knew it was the end. They were the last words she ever spoke.

I rang my cousin Anna in the evening and told her Sacha was dying and she must come down the next day. When we got to the hospital they had put her on oxygen, she who had always asked me to make sure she did not end up being kept alive by means of tubes. 'It's only to help her breathe,' the nurse said. The doctor came on his rounds, looked at her notes. 'She's depressed,' he said, 'we'll give her some anti-depressants.' Who was I to believe, Sacha who said she was dying or the doctor who said she was depressed? He saw my face and said: 'You know, we wouldn't go on trying to help her if we didn't think there was some hope.' 'No,' I said, 'of course not.'

She did not die that day, but Anna and I both felt she was sinking fast. When I got home I rang Jeff Newman, an old friend and a rabbi in North London, whom I had asked to come and see Sacha at the very start of her stay in hospital and who had then said he was terribly busy in the run-up to Passover but would come immediately after. 'She's dying,' I said. 'I'll come down straight after the service tomorrow,' he said. 'I'll be there at about three.'

A recent friend, the Shakespearean scholar Margreta de Grazia, rang that evening to ask how Sacha was. I told her I thought she was dying. 'There are plenty of people around you?' she asked. 'No,' I said. 'I'm alone.' 'I can't bear to think of you alone in that

house,' she said. 'Can I come down and stay with you?' Suddenly
I realised that I did desperately need to have someone with me
and wondered at the truth of racial clichés: why did it take someone
half-Italian to respond like that, even though I had only known
her for a short time, while none of my English friends of long
standing, no less fond of Sacha and of me, I am sure, had thought
to suggest it. 'Yes,' I said, 'please do.' She said she had to see a
student at lunchtime the next day but would take a train that got
into Lewes at five-fifty.

I don't know how I got through the night, but I did. The next
morning I was at the hospital at nine. There was little change in
her condition, but the nurse said they had had to insert a catheter.
So that's how people got covered with tubes: they gradually gathered, one at a time, each inserted for a very good pragmatic reason
and all of them together making a dignified death more and more
difficult. I rubbed Sacha's hands, almost clawlike now, hoping to
make her aware of my presence, but she simply went on groaning
and turning this way and that to find a comfortable position that
kept eluding her. Bernard and Dorothy Harrison arrived and Dot,
ever thoughtful, took one look at me and said I should go off and
have coffee with Bernard while she sat with Sacha. When we
returned they stayed for a little while longer, and then I was alone
again with Sacha. The seconds ticked by. I held her hand and
thought I felt her responding to the pressure, but it was difficult
to tell for sure. She went on groaning and trying to find a more
comfortable position.

At twelve the nurses asked me if I'd wait outside while they
washed her and made her bed. They drew the curtains round the
bed and I went and sat on one of the chairs at the nurses' desk.
As I was waiting I felt a hand on my shoulder. Two good friends,
Andrew Robinson, the Anglican chaplain at the University, and
Stephen Medcalf, who had known Sacha and me since we arrived
at Sussex together in 1963. Both had brought flowers. We stood

by the nurses' table and waited, talking of this and that. A nurse emerged from behind the curtains and came up to me: 'I'm sorry to have to tell you that Sacha has just died. She died as we were washing her. You can go in and see her.'

Now that the struggles with death were over the mask had gone. Her face was calm and serene. Proust had got this right too, I thought, as I held her for the last time and kissed her. When I stood up I saw that Andrew was behind me. 'May I say a prayer?' he asked. I thought of her father saying to their Nanny: 'There is only one God, let us each worship Him in the way we want.' 'Of course,' I said. When he had done so he led me gently away.

We sat in a little room just off the ward and they brought us some tea. I blessed my good fortune in not having to endure this alone in the middle of the night. I rang Anna and told her. 'Pauvre Gabriel,' she said. I rang Jeff and his wife said she would tell him when he returned from the service and he would certainly come down all the same. Then we left the hospital. We found ourselves descending the stairs with the sweetest of the nurses. 'I'm sorry,' she said to me. 'Sacha was a wonderful person. Very funny. Very strong.' We stopped at the entrance. She produced a kleenex and wiped my eyes. I hugged her. Then Andrew drove us to his house.

In the car he explained that there was plenty of food because his wife Judy had celebrated her fiftieth birthday the previous evening, though today was the actual anniversary. And Judy, when she opened the door and learnt what had happened: 'I'm proud to share a birthday with the day of Sacha's death.'

Jeff arrived, and the two of them, the rabbi and the Anglican priest, sat me down between them and asked me what I was going to do about Sacha. 'What do you mean?' I said, but I knew what they meant. Almost more than Sacha's death I had dreaded the thought of the funeral. 'Why do people have to be tormented in this way at the worst moment of their lives?' I said. 'We're not trying to torment you,' Jeff said. 'I know,' I said. 'Just remember,' he said, 'everything is possible.' 'What do you mean everything is possible?' 'Everything is possible.' 'I know what Sacha would have wanted,' I said. 'Nothing. When our dogs died she left them with the vet to bury and she never had any time for weeping at gravesides and the rest of it. I think she felt people lived on in the memories of those who had known them and that's all. She was scathing about two distant members of our family who had spent the last decade squabbling over who should have the remaining place in the family vault in Alexandria.' 'It's interesting you should say you know what Sacha would have wanted,' Jeff said. 'But there are two people involved in this, not just one. What do *you* want?'

For the first time since I had seen the consultant and he had told me the bad news I felt myself startled and taken out of myself, out of my sorrow and confusion. I suddenly realised that what Sacha wanted, or rather her indifference in this regard, might not be what I needed, and that this was not just a matter of the difference between the living and the dead but had to do with deeper differences between Sacha and myself. I had always admired her absoluteness, her refusal ever to compromise, her lack of sentimentality and self-pity. But I had also felt unable always to live up to it. And, I now realised, it was not just a matter of being unable to meet her high standards; I was not sure I entirely agreed with those standards in the first place. 'The last time we had argued about it,' I said to Jeff, 'was actually only last month, over an essay on *King Lear* by Margreta de Grazia, who is coming to stay with me this evening.' In her essay Margreta argues that we tend to modernise *King Lear*, to read it as a proto-typical modern play which breaks free of the boundaries of the Renaissance. Lear's desire to strip himself of the trappings of office, to get down somehow to the poor bare forked animal, has too often been seen as the main thrust of the play itself. But, argues Margreta, what the play is really showing is that such a desire is a kind of folly, that we are always more than a poor bare forked animal, that the trappings of office and wealth, whether in the form of retainers or clothes, is never something that can be shed at will but is part of what makes us who we are. Sacha wouldn't have any of that. 'Rubbish,' she said. 'How can you say that?' I said, 'and you a Jew? You're speaking like a Puritan.' 'I don't care what I'm speaking like,' Sacha said, 'I think she's wrong.' 'Wrong about *King Lear* or wrong about life?' 'Both, I think; life certainly.' And indeed for Sacha, at that stage in her life, and perhaps for all her life since she had lost her parents there was a profound sense in which possessions, trappings, really only *were* trappings, ways of protecting ourselves from reality to which the sentimentalist will cling but which she could do without. The paradox is that, unlike Chickie, she really cared for objects, for clothes, furniture, crockery, and always treated them with respect, as though to offend against them was in some sense to offend against life.

I did not know if it was weakness or a different sense of reality on my part, but I felt, as I talked, that I might come to regret it if I refused to mark her death in some way. I said this to Jeff and Andrew. 'I don't think it's weakness,' Jeff said. 'Death itself is so unmarked that perhaps it is important that there be some sort of ceremony to mark it. And graves are not necessarily for weeping at but another kind of marker, a prop for memory.'

We sat in silence. 'Let's go on,' Jeff said finally. 'What do you think about the relative merits of burial and cremation?' 'I didn't think anyone was buried these days,' I said. 'I told you,' Jeff said, 'everything is possible.' We sat in silence again. 'I suppose there's something very pure about fire,' I said, 'but the cremations I've attended have given me the creeps – even more than burials.' 'I agree with you,' Jeff said. 'In Orthodox Judaism cremation is not an option, but more and more Jews are being cremated, of course. Like you though I feel there is something right about burial and wrong about cremation. And the fact that Sacha loved the Sussex

Downs and walked upon them for so many years makes me feel that she ought to be buried here in Sussex somewhere.' 'Yes,' I said, 'that seems right.' 'Wait a minute,' Jeff said. He asked Andrew where the phone was and we heard him talking in low urgent tones in the hall. He came back. 'There's a burial plot in the Hove Jewish Cemetery,' he said. 'It looks out over the sea.' I didn't even know there was a Hove Jewish Cemetery, but I quickened at the thought of its overlooking the sea, as Valéry's *Le Cimetière Marin* had been one of the few French poems Sacha cared for. 'If there has to be a burial,' I said, 'I don't want hordes of people, just those who are here now and Anna and Aleco and Jess and Margreta, who've somehow got caught up in this.' 'Fair enough,' Andrew said, 'but in that case I think you owe it to Sacha's many friends to hold a memorial service of sorts later. If you wanted we could hold it in the Quiet Room of the Meeting House, where she attended so many of our Bible and Literature Seminars.' 'Of course,' I said. 'I'd like that.'

'What do you say to this?' Jeff said. 'We have a small burial ceremony at the cemetery, with just the few people you've mentioned. Andrew and I can recite a Psalm each and I'll keep the rest of it down to a bare minimum.' 'That seems fine,' I said. It suddenly seemed appropriate that Sacha, who had no faith, who had been baptized an Anglican and felt herself to be Jewish all her life, some of whose best friends had been devout Christians and Jews, and who had known both Andrew and Jeff for a long time, should be buried in this way.

Jeff asked if he could come back to the house with me. I wondered why, but once there he said he just wanted to sit for a few minutes in silence in the room where he had so often sat with Sacha. Then I drove him to the station and put him on the train to London.

Two days later Andrew and I spent the afternoon at the Brighton Registry Office, waiting for the issue of the death certificate, and then at the undertaker's. I was irrationally pleased to see that they had put down 'old age' as the cause of death on the certificate. Somehow, I felt, it gave it – and her – more dignity. At the undertaker's I told the smart lady who received us that I didn't want to see any pall-bearers. 'I understand,' she said, 'but for insurance purposes they cannot be entirely absent. And what about the lowering of the coffin into the ground?' Once again I wondered at the absurdity of discussing such details, their total irrelevance to what had just happened. 'What do you mean?' I said. 'I think you'd better have a word with the rabbi,' she said mysteriously. I rang Jeff that evening and he explained: 'The moment of transition between above and below ground is a very important one in Judaism, and it is marked by a special prayer. However, as I told you, everything is possible. We are all imaginative people, so if you want we can imagine that moment and skip the prayer. When we arrive the body will already have been lowered and the pall-bearers will make themselves as discreet as possible. And there's just one more thing,' he said, after we had discussed the other arrangements and I had told him that Andrew and Judy wanted us to go back to their house for tea afterwards. 'I have found that it helps if, after we've chatted for a while, we can set aside forty-five minutes or so for a slightly more formal pooling of our thoughts on the occasion. Would that be all right with you?' 'Whatever you say,' I said.

The morning of the funeral Anna rang: 'I phoned the cemetery and they said no flowers. What shall I do?' 'I don't know,' I said. 'Do what you like.' So the Christians brought flowers and when I picked up Jeff at the station I asked him to explain. 'Death for the Jews is the great leveller,' he said, 'so there is only one type of coffin and there are no flowers, for if flowers were allowed the rich might wish to show off and the poor would not be able to match them. However,' he said, 'since people have brought flowers, let them throw them in the grave if they wish.'

The cold mist that had hung over the South Coast for the whole of the winter had lifted and both sun and moon were clearly visible in the bright blue sky, while the sea stretched out before us, coppery in the morning sunlight. After the ceremony Jeff said to Anna: 'I've never taken a burial service where there were flowers. They looked so beautiful as the sun caught them falling into the grave.'

Sebastian Faulks' fine book, *The Fatal Englishman*, brings out with remarkable clarity the death-wish that has infected some of the finest young English minds of the twentieth century. Though he does not dwell on the larger cultural issues raised by his three brief biographies, the reader cannot help feeling that if his story is true it is the story of men who, brought up in a Christian ethos but in a world no longer sure of Christian values, felt that the daily lives they lived were fatally at odds with their dreams and ideals, and felt, consciously or not, that only in death would they be able to enter at last into the pure realm in which they longed to exist.

For a Jew this is a terrible story. For the Jew the way to join ones admired ancestors, the way to live up to one's ideals, is to endure whatever the world throws at us and to remain ourselves. That is why the possible suicide of a Holocaust survivor like Primo Levi is tinged with so much pathos; though perfectly understandable, it becomes more than a personal tragedy. It is as if the enemy had had the final victory, as if the Nazis Levi had outwitted simply by surviving to tell his story had had the last word.

Sacha had deep suicidal impulses. She told Rosalind Belben that if she had not had a child to look after when her baby died in France in the middle of the war she would have killed herself. Later on, living for the most part happily and at peace with herself in Lewes, there were nevertheless one or two moments, especially in the wake of Robin Lee's suicide, when something came over her which terrified me and which I associated with an urge to self-destruction. She always feared, I think, that something of her father's madness had been passed on to her; and at those times she was indeed a little mad; it would not have taken much at those moments to bring her life to an end. But she didn't. The instinct for survival, the sense that carrying on, whatever the circumstances, was the right thing to do, always prevailed. She would never, I am sure, have drawn the contrast with Faulks' book herself, even if she had read it, nor would she have theorised about the nature of endurance. It is not, after all, in the nature of survivors to have theories of survival, only the instinct for it. Yet after her death a piece of evidence fell into my hands which shows that she had at least considered the matter.

One day, when I was at the Harrisons, Dot handed me a couple of typed pages. 'I was going through my papers, tidying up,' she said, 'and came across this. It's the typescript of a talk Sacha gave to a women's reading group in Kingston in the 60's, of which I happened to be the secretary.'

I took it home and read it. I must have seen it before, because Sacha would never have written it without showing it to me, but I had totally forgotten. Its subject was Bernard Malamud's novel, *The Fixer*. Its exquisite clarity and precision, the way it manages to get to the heart of Malamud's novel with the least possible fuss, makes one sad that she did not become a regular reviewer or at least an occasional critic. But then, since she seems to have picked the one work which she could discuss entirely on its own terms and yet which tells us so much about herself, perhaps it is fitting that it should be the only piece of criticism she ever wrote.

'*The Fixer*,' she begins, 'is an easy book to read but a difficult book to write about because it says just what it has to say and then stops.' 'By the time we have finished,' she goes on, 'we have so intimate a knowledge of Yakov Bok that we can't see him as either a saint or a hero. He is a human being (more human than most) for whom we feel so much respect we are incapable of feeling pity (perhaps because he himself has so little self-pity).'

After describing the plot and explaining that it is based on the famous Beiliss case she goes on: '*The Fixer*, however, is more than the retelling of a specific case of Jewish persecution. There is a mystery in Bok's uniqueness as it strikes the reader: he is both unique and very human, and also the Jewish race. Thus Mendel becomes Yakov, that is, *Jacob* or *Israel*, whose twelve sons father the twelve tribes. Like Abraham, Yakov leaves his home town to enter into history. Though some time later, in his room over the stables in the brick-yard, he writes: "I am in history, yet not in it, in a way of speaking I am far out, it passes me by. Is this good or is it something lacking in my character?", he has in fact already been caught up in it: "He had stepped into history more deeply than the others." He has already made all the little imperceptible slips that will lead to his final arrest for a crime of which he is innocent. The two years of torture and humiliation inflicted by his tormentors (who are quite aware of his innocence) stand for the two thousand years in which men, women and children have been tortured and murdered for a crime of which they were as innocent as Bok. "But some history was dangerous," Bok remarks; and "We are all in history, that's sure, but some more than others, Jews more than some." '

'This,' Sacha goes on, 'does not mean that Bok is an allegory of the Jewish race. Two years in a man's life can stand for two thousand years of mankind. Bok is the Jewish race because he is only himself, always himself. That is why the book ends before his trial. What happens to Bok after that, and the result of the trial doesn't matter. His aim was not to be acquitted but tried, and in this he has been successful against all the odds. The authorities wanted to avoid the trial; they knew that their case didn't hold water, that even if they cooked up enough evidence to condemn Bok it would be evidence that would be convincing only to those already on their side. What they hoped rather was that he would die quickly in prison, and in such a way that they would not be held responsible. Best of all they hoped he would commit some overt act of insubordination which would legitimate his immediate execution. In these circumstances Bok's survival requires an extra-ordinary control over himself, a control that he only achieves because he must. Every second that he stays alive, talking, thinking, judging his warders, is a second of triumph. Then, at the very end, his control fails him – he is only human – but he has perhaps earned the right to a stroke of good luck: the guard intervenes just as the chief inspector is about to shoot him. Is this a sign that he is, all the same, one of God's chosen people?

'Rabbi Zusya,' Sacha concludes, 'a Chassidic sage, is reputed to have said shortly before dying: "In the world to come I shall not be asked: 'Why were you not more like Moses?' but rather I shall be asked: 'Why were you not more like Zusya?'" It seems to me that the great achievement of Malamud's hero is that, through his terrible experiences, he has become a little more like Yakov Bok.'